D1475371

Coastal economies, cultural accounts

Coastal economies, cultural accounts

Human ecology and Icelandic discourse

Gísli Pálsson

Manchester University Press
Manchester and New York
Distributed exclusively in the USA and Canada by St. Martin's Press, New York

Published by Manchester University Press
Oxford Road, Manchester M13 9PL, England
and Room 400, 175 Fifth Avenue, New York, NY 10010, USA

Distributed exclusively in the USA and Canada
by St. Martin's Press, Inc., 175 Fifth Avenue, New York,
NY 10010, USA

British Library cataloguing in publication data
Pálsson, Gísli
    Coastal economies, cultural accounts: human ecology and
    1. Iceland. Fisheries
    I. Title II. Series
    338.3727094912

Library of Congress cataloging in publication data
Gísli Pálsson, 1949
    Coastal economies, cultural accounts : human ecology and Icelandic
    discourse / Gísli Pálsson.
        p. cm.—(Themes in social anthropology)
    Includes bibliographical references and index.
    ISBN 0–7190–3543–0
        1. Economic anthropology. 2. Fisheries—Iceland—Social aspects.
    3. Iceland—Economic conditions. 4. Iceland—Social conditions,
    5. Discourse analysis. 6. Ethnology—Authorship. I. Title.
    II. Series.
    GN448.2.G57 1991
    306.3—dc20   90–29067

ISBN 0 7190 3543 0 *hardback*

Printed in Great Britain
by Billings Ltd., Worcester

Contents

List of figures and tables · vi
Foreword *Tim Ingold* · vii
Acknowledgements · xi

Preface · xv

1 Social theory and human ecology: the speaker and the producer · 1
  The 'household' and the individual · 4
  Structure, agency and history · 13

2 Anthropological discussions of fishing economies · 23
  Hunters and gatherers of aquatic resources · 24
  The definition and the category of fishing · 34
  Restrictions of access to resources: closure and tenure · 44

3 Systems of production and social discourse · 54
  The relationship between representations and reality · 55
  Cultural constructs: on fish, production and gender · 61
  Concepts and social context: an hypothesis · 67

4 The domestication of nature: household production · 83
  The production system of medieval Iceland · 84
  A 'blind date' with the sea · 88
  Myth and metaphor · 93

5 From nature to society: the market economy · 103
  The social relations and techniques of expansive fishing · 105
  Hierarchical models of success · 109
  Information, competition and social honour · 122

6 The domination of nature: the modern state · 132
  Consolidated capitalism · 133
  Changing notions of fishing: the authenticity of the 'skipper effect' · 139
  Competing rationalities: science, equity and power · 145

7 Conclusions: beyond the language of nature · 156

Notes · 168
Bibliography · 173
Index · 192

List of figures and tables

Figures

1.1	The seasonal 'morphology' of Inuit identity	7
2.1	Fishing with cormorants	42
2.2	Three ways of appropriating fishing space	49
3.1	A social model of fishing economies	69
4.1	A holy man fights a mermaid	99
5.1	'Fishscape' (a painting by Erró)	111
5.2	Work on deck on a boat using gill nets	113
5.3	Binni, a famous skipper from the Vestman Islands	119
6.1	The reporting grid and fishing areas of Sandgerði boats	140
6.2	Fishworkers in a freezing plant	148
7.1	Transformations of production discourse	161

Tables

4.1	Water-beings in Icelandic mythology	97
5.1	Egalitarian and hierarchical models of fishing	117

Foreword

It is a privilege to have been asked to write a foreword to this book. I shall respond not by summarising its contents, which the author does admirably in his preface, nor by usurping the role of a reviewer to deliver a critical judgement. My aim is rather to show that although the book is ostensibly about fishing, it has a much wider significance that should commend it to all who have an interest in understanding how people relate to their environments in making a living, and how they talk about these relationships. Indeed one of the author's principal objectives is to show that an 'anthropology of fishing', whose field of inquiry is delimited by the narrowly technical aspect of the activity, cannot give us more than an impoverished view of the social lives of fishermen (and women). His argument, however, issues a more fundamental challenge, to the very foundation on which ecological anthropology and symbolic anthropology have, up to now, been constituted as largely independent enterprises.

This foundation posits human beings (uniquely among animals) as living a split-level existence, with their feet on the ground (or in the sea) of nature, and their heads in the clouds of culture. They are supposed to be doubly confined, on the one hand within the physical constraints of the environment, on the other hand within the conceptual constraints of language. Ecological anthropologists, adopting their models and procedures from animal ecology, tend to regard human beings as individual organisms (albeit culture-bearing ones), and interpret the behaviour of these organisms in terms of its consequences for their own reproduction, for the long-term viability of the populations of which they form a part, or for the stability of the entire ecosystem. Symbolic anthropologists, by contrast, envision humans suspended above reality in matrices of culturally constructed meaning, which impose an autonomous logic on their affairs. Practical interventions in the material world, then, are reduced to mere executions, the bodily realisation or manifestation of a cultural programme that its bearers, in their activities, are fated to replicate.

Human actions are, of course, symbolically significant, and they have objective consequences. The activities of the fishing skipper, as Pálsson shows, may carry a message about prestige or honour, moreover they undoubtedly have life-threatening entailments for the fish which may be caught and consumed. But there is more to any action than code and consequence. There is also, and crucially, the intention that informs it. Fishing, thus, is something that people *do*. And the source of people's intentions and purposes, Pálsson argues, lies in the domain of their *social* relations with one another. Productive activity, therefore, is essentially social activity. This means, too, that the real world in which people dwell, and which is continually coming into being through their activities, is neither a world of nature nor a world of culture, but a social world. It is as persons – intentional agents – constituted within such a world that they engage with components of the natural environment in acts of production, and with one another in acts of speech.

As social beings, humans carry on purposive projects, not only of procuring and appropriating natural resources but also of construction: they construct artefacts, such as boats and nets, that enable them to take hold of the resources; they construct strategies of procurement that may involve varying degrees of trust, co-operation and deceit; they construct regulations governing access and the exercise of property claims, and they construct models which represent – in a more or less idealised form – their own productive activities. Pálsson is centrally concerned with the processes of cultural construction by which these representational models are built. But unlike so many advocates of symbolic anthropology who share this concern, he recognises that people are the authors and not simply the inhabitants of their cultural constructions. To understand why the predominant cultural constructions or 'folk models' of a particular people in a particular period take the forms they do, we have therefore to look at the social circumstances of the constructors: as their circumstances change, so – we would expect – do the models they build. And indeed, the expectation is elegantly borne out in Pálsson's comparison of three periods in the economic history of Iceland, characterised respectively by a subsistence-based, peasant economy, a highly competitive market economy and state-based, consolidated capitalism.

This book is a pioneering attempt to link together the study of human ecological relations and cultural or discursive symbolism. It is not just another account of the ecologically adaptive significance of cultural behaviour, nor is it yet another 'ethnoecological' account of the cultural construction of the natural environment. We already have plenty of examples of both kinds of account. Their inadequacies have been amply exposed, and readers unfamiliar with the literature will find in Pálsson's review a helpful and reliable guide to the various arguments and counter-arguments. For Pálsson, the link between the ecological and the symbolic, or between production and speaking, is that both are grounded in the bedrock of the social, in the practical activities of purposive and creative human agents. His approach is one that offers a new lease of life to ecological anthropology, which in recent years seems to have become irretrievably mired in the self-replicating dilemmas of the nature–culture dichotomy.

The book is broad and ambitious in its scope, both theoretically and comparatively. But as the argument proceeds, so its focus gradually sharpens on the author's own ethnographic experience, stemming from fieldwork in his native Iceland. This, then, is an instance of 'anthropology at home', but one that mercifully eschews the hyper-reflective self-regard of so much writing in this genre, in favour of the worthy and more traditional anthropological goal of achieving scientific generalisation through comparative analysis. Yet Pálsson's perspective as a native anthropologist also enables him to turn the tables on those who claim to have a privileged, 'scientific' knowledge of human ecological relations: the scientists, in this case, are marine biologists, who have had an increasingly powerful voice in the formulation of fisheries policy. He shows that the scientists' models and projections, far from providing an objectively neutral baseline against which the veracity and appropriateness of the fishermen's own 'cognised models' may be assessed, have exactly the same status as the latter, as constructs authored by socially situated and motivated actors. The scientist and the fisherman dwell in the same social world, and if they represent it differently it is not because the latter remains trapped within his cultural conceptions whereas the former can see the reality beyond, but because their respective positions within the social world constitute them as parties with different and often conflicting interests.

It is here that Pálsson speaks to issues that are not merely academic but also of pressing practical concern. Indeed the book is as much a study in the field of environmental resource management as it is in academic anthropology. As such, it is a testimony to the contribution that anthropologists stand to make in this field. As public attention comes increasingly to focus on worldwide environmental issues, studies in ecological anthropology look set to gain renewed prominence and significance. But the new ecological anthropology cannot be one of isolated 'cultures', holding out in discrete pockets of pristine nature. It must rather start from the recognition that we are all fellow passengers on this earth, that human life involves a practical and interested engagement with other humans, with animals and plants, with land, air and sea, and that this engagement has ramifications of potentially global extent. As terrestrial mammals, we humans stake out our differences on the land; the sea, however, is a great dissolver – of time, of history, of cultural distinction. It is most fitting, therefore, that we should turn seawards to rediscover the continuities of the dwelt-in world. This is a book that points us in the right direction.

Tim Ingold

Acknowledgements

I acknowledge my intellectual debt to two fellow anthropologists who offered generous help in the course of my research and writing of this book. I am particularly grateful to Tim Ingold, Manchester University, for his detailed comments upon some of the chapters as well as his personal advice over the years. As the pages in this book testify, I have found his theoretical works immensely helpful and inspiring. I am also deeply indebted to E. Paul Durrenberger, University of Iowa, for his extensive suggestions regarding many of the arguments presented and his collaboration on some of the issues raised in the book. My discussion of the Icelandic fishing industry is heavily influenced by our joint publications. Many other anthropologists and colleagues have been of help in one capacity or another. Specifically, I would like to mention Níels Einarsson (University of Uppsala), Jón Haukur Ingimundarson (University of Arizona, Tucson), Hjörleifur Rafn Jónsson (Cornell University), Arne Kalland (Nordic Institute of Asian Studies), Sigríður Dúna Kristmundsdóttir (University of Iceland), Michael F. O'Leary (UNICEF, Nairobi), and, last but not least, Anne Brydon (McGill University), who commented extensively on language, style and argument, and Þórólfur Þórlindsson (University of Iceland), whose comments and criticisms have remained a source of challenge and inspiration. I thank them all, insisting, of course, that the responsibility for any errors made in the book must rest with me. I should like to extend my gratitude to my students at the University of Iceland, who kept me busy and provided me with an opportunity to 'test' some of my ideas, all the people who made my fieldwork possible, in particular my companions and informants in Sandgerði, Iceland, and the editors and reviewers at Manchester University Press whose comments I found most helpful. Finally, I owe one of my biggest debts to my wife Guðný Guðbjörnsdóttir for her encouragement and support.

Parts of this work have been presented elsewhere in a somewhat different form. Parts of Chapter 2 appeared in *Maritime Anthropological Studies* (1989, 2(1): 1–20) under the title 'The art of fishing'. That chapter also includes some material which appeared in 'Hunters and gatherers of the sea', published in *Hunters and gatherers: history, evolution and social change* and edited by Tim Ingold, David Riches and James Woodburn (1988). Chapters 3 and 4 contain some material presented in 'The idea of fish: land and sea in the Icelandic world-view', published in *Signifying animals: human meaning in the natural world* and edited by Roy Willis (Allen & Unwin, 1990). Chapters 5 and 6 are partly based on articles co-authored by E. Paul Durrenberger and published in *The American Ethnologist* ('Icelandic foremen and skippers', 1983, 10(3): 511-28), and *American Anthropologist* ('Systems of production and social discourse', 1990, 92: 130–41). A short version of Chapter 1 was presented, under the title of 'The language of nature', to the Nordic Anthropology Meeting in Aarhus in August 1988. Chapter 2 includes parts of a paper, 'Fast fish in troubled seas: aquatic resources and agrarian discourse', presented to the 5th International Congress of Ecology, Yokohama, in August 1990, and to the Department of Social Anthropology at the University of Oslo in October 1990. Parts of Chapter 6 appeared in a paper, 'The political ecology of Icelandic fishing', submitted to a conference on Marine Resource Utilisation in Mobile, Alabama, in May 1987. A brief version of Chapter 3 was presented to the Nordic Anthropology Meeting in Reykjavík in June 1990, under the title 'Discourse on production'.

Neither the writing of this book nor the research on which it is based would have been possible without the help of several funds and institutions. In particular, I would like to express my gratitude to the British Council which afforded me a scholarship at a critical moment in 1980, when I was a student at Manchester University preparing for fieldwork in Iceland. I also thank the Iceland-United States Educational Commission for supporting my sabbatical leave at the University of Iowa in 1987 during which I began working on this book. Further financial support was provided by the Icelandic Science Foundation and the University of Iceland. A sabbatical leave at the Department of Social Anthropology, University of Oslo, in the autumn of 1990 allowed me to make final changes to the manuscript. I thank Arne Martin Klausen for his hospitality.

The river is within us, the sea is all about us;
The sea is the land's edge also, the granite
Into which it reaches, the beaches where it tosses
Its hints of earlier and other creation:
The starfish, the horseshoe crab, the whale's backbone;
The pools where it offers to our curiosity
The more delicate algae and the sea anemone.
It tosses up our losses, the torn seine,
The shattered lobsterpot, the broken oar
And the gear of foreign dead men. The sea has many
    voices,
Many gods and many voices.

T. S. Eliot: *The dry salvages*
(*Four quartets*, Faber and Faber, London, 1968)

For Páll Óskar and Rósa Signý

Preface

This book addresses theoretical questions regarding economic production, particularly in relation to fisheries, emphasising the ways in which human-environmental interactions are represented in social discourse, among both indigenous producers and anthropologists. The first chapter explores some of the parallels between two kinds of theoretical discourse, one on production and the other on language, each of which may be characterised as a 'language of nature'. These discourses, I argue, suggest a rigid dichotomy between the individual and the superorganic (society or culture), placing production and the act of speaking outside society. The producer and the speaker are presented as autonomous individuals posited by nature; they become intermediaries rather than agents, incapable of consciously modelling their own activities. An alternative, social approach emphasises that human action, whether it be the appropriation of nature or verbal communication, is consciously motivated and necessarily embedded in human relations.

The second chapter deals with representations of fishing activities and fishing adaptations in the discourse of anthropologists. I argue that many anthropological accounts, in the past as well as the present, suggest a 'natural' model of fishing which depicts the individual producer as an asocial being, and further that such a model neither appreciates the social relations of fishing economies nor the differences between the economic activities of humans and the extractive activities of other animals. To explore social differences among fishing systems, I emphasise differences in modes of access to resources and circulation of products. The third chapter discusses anthropological analyses of production discourse, in particular representations of aquatic animals and fishing activities. I argue that it is important to distinguish between the symbolic and the real, and that folk models of production – indigenous languages of nature, if you like – do not exist of themselves but are rooted in production systems. I explore the comparative usefulness of the argument developed in Chapter 2 regarding social differences in circulation and access to resources, by looking at some of the similarities and parallels between folk accounts of different fishing societies, particularly with respect to notions of human agency and individual success.

The next three chapters apply such an approach to the analysis of different kinds of cultural models in the history of a particular discourse. Chapter 4 discusses the phase of peasant production in Iceland. In peasant society, there was a 'natural' ceiling on production. Accordingly, in the folk model the human producer was seen to be a passive recipient of value. A series of anomalous and imaginary water-beings mediated between the domains of land and sea, between human society and nature. Chapter 5 discusses the changes in the economic rationality of Icelanders that took place when the domestic economy gave way to both petty entrepreneurial fishing and large-scale capitalist production for an expanding market at the end of the nineteenth century. As labour became a commodity and the previous ceiling on production was removed, a new model was developed which redefined both the domain of the natural and earlier notions of work and productivity – a model with conceptions of nature, production and human agency very different from those of the previous one. The new model underlined the economic role and the abilities of the fishing skipper, emphasising human agency and the role of the individual in the production process. Competition for prestige, capital and labour fostered the idea that skippers' abilities to locate and catch fish determined the size of their catch. At the same time, production discourse became gender-specific. Chapter 6 deals with the third phase of Icelandic fishing, the period of 'scientific' management. With increased concentration of capital in recent years, the declining importance of labour and the integration of the industry with the state, a new cognitive succession has taken place. Sustaining institutionalised capitalism, and the social and ecological relations it entails, demands a new ceiling on production and an official, scientific rationality. This new rationality challenges the wisdom of fishermen. On the public level some important aspects of folk discourse on production are increasingly being silenced on the grounds that they are inadequate and irrelevant. In the final chapter of the book the discussion shifts from ethnographic detail to comparison, returning at the same time to some of the larger theoretical issues discussed in the first three chapters.

The 'great age of discovery' in the late fifteenth and early sixteenth centuries was very much the discovery of the sea as well as other lands. As a result of voyages by sea, different and isolated worlds were connected into a global but polarised network of power-relations. Prior to these voyages, the idea of anthropology did not exist. In a very real sense, then, anthropology, the study of humanity, is as much the child of seafaring as of colonialism. Coastal economies had an important role in some of the evolutionary schemes of the nineteenth century (Morgan, for instance, identified fishing as a mode of subsistence with particular institutions and modes of life). In modern anthropology, on the other hand, the category of fishing is much less visible. My point is not to add a new subset to anthropological taxonomy. Fishing is indeed a marginal analytical category, for fishing takes place in widely different social contexts and in combination with a range of subsistence activities. My aim is to examine some of the theoretical and ideological underpinnings of prevailing notions of fishing and to explore their implications for the study of coastal adaptations and, more generally, economic production.

A brief note on my 'discovery' of fishing and my personal relationship to the subject is in order. I was born and raised in an Icelandic fishing community, in the Vestman Islands. When I left the fishing community, entering the University of Iceland, I found the study of anthropology appealing. At that time, however, the study of fishing and coastal economies seemed rather remote subjects to me. Neither the field of 'maritime anthropology' nor the concept of 'anthropology at home' had gained the popularity they now enjoy. It was in England, during one of the 'cod wars' between Britain and Iceland, that I began to familiarise myself, as a postgraduate student in the Department of Social Anthropology at Manchester University, with the ethnography of fishing. Despite the heavy African emphasis in the department at the time, some of my teachers, in particular Paul Baxter, encouraged me to embark on the study of North Atlantic fishing. No doubt it helped that a collection of anthropological essays on modern fishing had just been published (*North Atlantic fishermen*, edited by Raoul Andersen and Cato Wadel). Some years later, I found myself doing anthropological fieldwork in a fishing community, Sandgerði – this time attempting to rediscover Iceland.

For me, the following excursion into the territory of production discourse was a voyage of discovery filled with exotic thrills and exciting events. The readers who follow the same course may not return with an identical cargo. I hope, however, that they too will find some hot spices on their way, appreciating the truth of Eliot's statement cited at the beginning. The sea *does* have many voices, 'Many gods and many voices'.

Gísli Pálsson
Reykjavík, November 1990

1 Social theory and human ecology: the speaker and the producer

The modern notion of ecology and its eighteenth-century antecedent the concept of 'economy of nature' – both derived from the Greek word *Oikos* or 'household' – emphasise connections and dependencies in the natural world. When locating an organism in a context of such relations, ecologists often refer to the concepts of habitat and niche, the former denoting the address or the home of the organism, the latter its profession or function – the place 'allotted' to it, as Linnaeus would have it. Human beings, of course, just as any other organism, have addresses and professions in the ecological sense, being part of nature. Social theorists debate, however, how to deal with them, how to incorporate the ecological domain into anthropological analyses.

At one time, academic thinking on human-environmental interactions was characterised by a rather simplistic environmental determinism which emphasised the severe limitations imposed by the environment, suggesting that the natural environment directly affected the thoughts and habits of humans. Cultural variations among nations as well as evolutionary differences between 'primitives' and 'Westerners', it was assumed, were largely explainable in terms of differences in habitat. Such a position was easily maintained as long as investigators were content with ethnocentric evolutionism and secondary information about strange lands – about 'the Other'; the diffused and fragmentary information provided by missionaries and early travellers conveniently confirmed almost any prior conception they might hold about the relations between humans and their environments. For many reasons, this position is no longer seriously entertained. For one thing, modern writing about the Other is a very different kind of enterprise from what it used to be during the heyday of Western colonialism. With the advent of cultural relativism, which questioned some of the ethnocentric assumptions of the environmentalists, and modern ethnographies and fieldwork, which provided more detailed and systematic information about human-environmental interactions, determinism became an untenable position. Most anthropologists would agree that 'whatever remains of value in the environmentalist position is not to be found in programmatic statements or rhetorical assertions, but in the application of models and hypotheses to concrete ethnographic cases' (Ellen 1982: 5). Grand generalisations in the deterministic tradition of Hippocrates and Huntington simply cannot be reconciled with the ethnographic record.

Julian Steward deserves merit for introducing an 'ecological' approach to anthropology (1955) – an approach which emphasises the *interrelations* between humans and the natural environment – at a time when many of his colleagues considered analyses of environmental relations useless or irrelevant. Steward emphasised that while the human response to the natural environment varies from one society to another, social life cannot be understood without reference to ecological relations. Given the framework proposed by Steward, an anthropological approach to fishing economies, the subject matter of this book, is concerned with exploring the ways in which people adapt to aquatic regimes – or, as McCay put it, examining 'what there is about a wet and fishy productive regime that defines the social, cultural, and economic life of fishing communities' (1978: 397). But while Steward's framework represented an important step in the development of ecological anthropology, it had a serious shortcoming in that it failed to seriously address the discursive aspects of resource-use. And so do, in fact, many recent ecological approaches to human life. Since humans are social beings – endowed with self-consciousness rooted in social relations, a 'second nature' – there is much more to *human* ecology than ecological relations. For humans, the 'state of nature' is necessarily social. In the course of our 'household' activities we construct cultural models, speaking of our 'homes' and 'functions' and investing them with meaning. To properly address the members of the human household, to account for their economic activities, then, it is not enough to refer to their habitat and niche; both their social relations and their accounts – their 'language' of nature – must be considered as well.

Human ecology should, therefore, endeavour to integrate the ecological domain on the one hand and the discursive on the other. Given such an approach, human ecology is necessarily a dialectical undertaking. Indeed, some anthropologists have defined human ecology as the study of how humans use nature and the repercussions on themselves, nature, and society (see, for instance, Bennett

1976). This book attempts to reconcile the ecological and the discursive, emphasising the cultural accounts developed by human households in aquatic regimes. The notion of the 'discursive' is to be understood in a very general sense, as 'the broadest and most comprehensive level of linguistic form, content, and use' (Sherzer 1987: 305). Discourses on fishing and fisheries embrace diverse kinds of phenomena – the words that people use in face-to-face interaction in the process of making a livelihood, the commonplace statements they exchange about their resources and their productive efforts, their 'folk' theories of nature and production, and the general paradigms within which they cast their theories about the workings of nature and human-environmental interactions. For me, discourses are not static models or reified 'traditions' detached from social life; they are historically-grounded, social practices that inform human perceptions of their world, 'practices that systematically form the objects of which they speak' (Foucault 1972: 49). I emphasise that ecological facts and realities do not speak for themselves and that ecological knowledge – the knowledge of scientists no less than that of indigenous theorists – is inevitably socially constructed. As Bird argues, in relation to modern discussions of environmental problems, 'To cite the "laws of ecology" as a basis for understanding ... is to rely on a particular set of socially constructed experiences and interpretations that have their own political and moral grounds and implications' (1987: 260–1). From this perspective, human ecology is essentially social ecology.

Before turning to the topic of fishing and coastal economies and their representations in anthropology and indigenous discourse, it is imperative that I present the general social theory I adopt, the framework on which this study is based. The remainder of this chapter explores some of the theoretical parallels between economic production and the act of speaking. My discussion of these issues is indebted to the theoretical writings of Tim Ingold (1986, 1987, 1988). Anthropologists, I argue, sometimes operate with a rigid distinction between the natural individual and the superorganic (society or culture) – a distinction which implies a 'natural' model of production as something taking place in nature, and outside society. Many students of language operate with a similar model, presenting verbal communication as a series of independent acts in a social void. In the natural model, the producer and the speaker are reduced to intermediaries who follow rules beyond their own making. The intellectual roots of these trends are traced to Durkheim, Saussure and Boas. I argue against such a model on the grounds that humans are necessarily constituted as creative social beings. As Marx argued in a famous passage in *Grundrisse*: 'Production by an isolated individual outside society . . . is as much of an absurdity as . . . is the development of language without individuals living *together* and talking to each other' (Marx 1973 [1857–8]: 84; emphasis in the original).

The 'household' and the individual

Language and nature are often perceived as analogous resource-bases, utilised through the acts of speaking and production respectively. Even though language and nature tend to be regarded as fundamentally different realms – mind and matter – they tend nevertheless to be seen as equally objective external entities, as 'things-in-themselves'. Sometimes a distinction is made between 'natural' languages like English and 'artificial' languages such as music notation and programming languages, as if only the latter were constructed by humans. The reference to the natural suggests an image of language as a 'thing' given in advance, as a predetermined order of meanings and grammatical relations, independent of speaking. Just as natural resources ensure the material provisioning of society, language is sometimes said to keep society going in the sense that it sustains the reality of its members. Human beings, Sapir argued (1929: 207), 'do not live in the objective world alone . . . , but are very much at the mercy of the particular language which has become the medium of expression for their society'. During the eighteenth century, some linguists seriously entertained the idea of language as being literally a natural organism. Franz Bobb argued, for instance, that languages must be regarded as 'organic bodies, formed in accordance with definite laws; bearing within themselves *an internal principle of life . . .*' (cited in Newmeyer 1986: 23, emphasis added).[1] Some modern theorists, notably Chomsky (1980: 39), continue to regard language as a 'mental organ'.

To apply a natural metaphor to language does not, however, necessarily suggest the image of an isolated and independent entity. Indeed, the modern concept of ecology may well be applied to emphasise the embedded nature of language, to place language in its social, 'extralinguistic' context. Haugen uses the term 'ecology of language' as a synonym for socio-linguistics, for the study of the interactions between language and society (1972: xiv), conveying an image of language very different from that of Chomsky's linguistics. For Haugen, rather than being autonomous language machines, speakers arc intimately connected with their co-resident fellows. Their utterances, therefore, are products of the household of human life. Many other scholars have applied the metaphor of the 'household' – of *Oikos* – to the study of language and language use. Thus, Bourdieu applies (1977b) the metaphor of the economy (the market economy, to be precise) to 'linguistic exchanges' and Rossi-Landi presents language as 'work and trade' (1983).

Just as nature can be used to illuminate language, so language can be called upon to illuminate nature. The discovery, for instance, by comparative linguists, of parallel changes in languages impressed thinkers like Darwin and Lyell. For them, the idea of language being guided by a uniform set of principles having developed through a series of successive stages provided a model applicable to the evolutionary process. If ancestral languages could be reconstructed on the basis of comparison of contemporary tongues it should also, they reasoned, be possible to reconstruct earlier forms in the natural world. Clearly, the metaphors have gone back and forth.

The study of language and production and their relationships to society raises fundamental theoretical questions concerning notions of the individual and the collective. In anthropology, the Durkheimian position has been highly influential. Durkheim, as is well known, was engaged in a rhetoric of professionalism, attempting to declare sociology independent of psychology. This led him to regard social facts as objective things existing 'in their own right independent of their individual manifestations' (1966: 13). A social phenomenon was a 'group condition' external to individuals: 'It is to be found in each part because it exists in the whole, rather than in the whole because it exists in the parts' (Durkheim 1966: 9). In *Suicide* he argues that the distinction between society and individual is analogous to that between life and inert matter: 'The living cell contains nothing but mineral particles, just as society contains nothing but individuals; it is obviously impossible for the phenomena characteristic of life to exist in the atoms of hydrogen, oxygen, carbon and nitrogen . . .' (Durkheim 1972: 34). Society, Durkheim suggests, is a synergic result of the interaction of individuals. Social relations are superorganic, while the individual is a material or natural entity.

The Durkheimian argument may be illustrated with reference to the work of Mauss (1979 [1906]) on the coastal economy of the Inuit. It represents one of the first and clearest applications of the Durkheimian thesis on individual and society to a particular ethnographic context. Mauss's work is not only an important one for students of coastal peoples; it is important for all those concerned with human-environmental interactions. This study, as Ellen points out, is an 'enduring paradox' (1982: 24) in the sense that the observations and analyses it contains have been interpreted in very different ways.

Mauss's analysis hinges on the simple ecological observation that the Inuit as well as the animals they hunt disperse and concentrate according to season:

In summary, summer opens up an almost unlimited area for hunting and fishing, while winter narrowly restricts this area. This alternation provides the rhythm of concentration and dispersion for the morphological organization of Eskimo society. The population congregates or scatters like the game. The movement that animates Eskimo society is synchronized with that of the surrounding life (Mauss 1979: 56).

During the summer, the Inuit are isolated and fragmented. According to Mauss, 'there is no religion' since the myths that 'fill the consciousness of the Eskimo during the winter appear to be forgotten during the summer' (p. 75). 'Life', he adds, 'is that of the layman'. During the winter, on the other hand, when the population congregates, there is a 'genuine community of ideas': 'By its existence and constant activity, the group becomes more aware of itself and assumes a more prominent place in the consciousness of individuals' (p. 76). The contrast between summer and winter, then, parallels that between individual and society. In the individual mode, during the summer, the Inuit are 'lost children, as it were' (Mauss 1979: 52), providing for themselves as individuals. The isolated hunters or fishermen keep their kill to themselves without having to consider anyone else. During the winter, on the other hand, individuals become social beings. The producers become subject to strict rules concerning the distribution of food. Food is collectively shared within a settlement rather than being limited to the individual or nuclear family.

This suggests that the Inuit are perennially split between the individual and the collective (see Figure 1.1). In winter there is a lot of society in the individual; in summer, much less. For Mauss the seasonal 'morphology' of Inuit identity is not just an ecological necessity. The change of season provides an opportunity for the Inuit to respond to a 'natural need':

> seasonal factors merely mark the most opportune occasions in the year for these two phases to occur. After the long revelries of the collective life which fill the winter, each Eskimo needs to live a more individual life; after long months of communal living filled with feasts and religious ceremonies, an Eskimo needs a profane existence (Mauss 1979: 79).

The sociology of Durkheim and cultural anthropology of Boas differ in their conceptions of the individual and the superorganic. For Durkheim, as we have seen, the individual is solely organic and everything we would call 'cultural' is therefore supra-individual. For Boas, on the other hand, the individual is a locus of culture. Boasian culture is superorganic, but it is stored in the heads of individuals. In the Boasian scheme, society is an interacting population of culture-bearing individuals and not, as for Durkheim, a

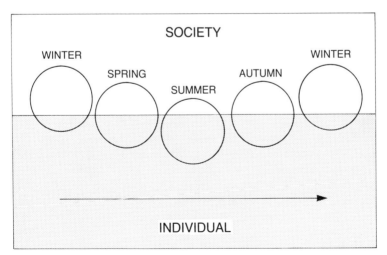

Figure 1.1 *The seasonal 'morphology' of Inuit identity* (based on Mauss 1979; the circles represent the human being passing through the seasons)

synergic or emergent entity over and above the individuals that constitute it. Despite these differences, the schemes of Boas and Durkheim have some points of resemblance. Just as the sociology of Durkheim somewhat unexpectedly leads to a natural model of production, so the cultural anthropology of Boas contains an implicit notion of a natural individual. While the historical particularism of Boas is directed *against* materialism, suggesting that the human personality is conditioned by ideas – a cultural programme stored in the memory of individuals – it nevertheless contains its own inherent materialism. Boasian possibilism considers environmental variables as limiting and modifying, but what is limiting is not the environment itself. As Hatch has shown (1973: 233), for Boas the role of the environment is 'contingent on and reducible to the nature of man's physical requirements', the *material* nature of the members of society. Economic institutions are the means by which individuals satisfy their material needs. In the monographs of the Boasians, therefore, the discussion of economic phenomena generally focuses on technique – hunting implements, fishing gear, canoes, etc. Cultural ecology and cultural materialism are not antithetical to the Boasian school, as their spokesmen often maintain (Julian Steward and Marvin Harris, respectively), but rather its 'natural offspring' (see Hatch 1973). The Boasian individual, then, remains *in* nature, just as his Durkheimian relative.

If both Durkheim and Boas portray the individual as a natural being situated outside society, it is not surprising that some anthropologists continue to operate with a private or natural model of production. Indeed, as Ingold points out (1987: Ch. 5), some anthropologists make a clear distinction between technical relations, pertaining to mode of subsistence or adaptive strategy, and social relations. Thus Cook (1973: 40) makes a distinction between the *forces* of production ('the relationships . . . that emerge from the concrete, observable technical features of any work situation') and the *social* relations of production. Given such a distinction, production must take place in nature. The appropriation of nature only becomes social when the resources extracted from nature enter relations of sharing or exchange among groups – when the Durkheimian producers associate and take off into the clouds of the superorganic, becoming social persons constructed by society. Significantly, in *The Gift* Mauss argues (1970 [1925]: 3) that there has never existed anything like a 'natural' economy since 'it is groups, and not individuals, which carry on exchange, make contracts, and are bound by obligations'. While humans are 'far removed... from a state of nature' in economic matters (Mauss 1970: 3), as producers they are natural beings.

If the Durkheimian producer is an independent natural being so is the Saussurean speaker. According to Saussure, language (*langue*) is a system of inherent relationships, best understood as an autonomous entity: 'The true and unique object of linguistics is language studied in and for itself' (Saussure 1959 [1916]: 232). Even though Saussure sometimes seems to suggest that language is a property of individuals – stored in their heads 'almost like a dictionary of which identical copies have been distributed to each individual' (p. 19) – for him language is a social phenomenon analogous to the Durkheimian superorganic. Language is 'outside the individual' for it 'exists perfectly only within a collectivity' (p. 14). The act of speaking (*parole*), on the other hand, is accidental, belonging to the individual. The individual speaker simply draws upon a 'storehouse of sound images' (p. 15), a collective inventory belonging to the speech community. Speaking, therefore, is for Saussure what production is for the Durkheimians – an activity taking place in nature. In both cases autonomous, natural individuals extract what they need from the resource-base available to them. If, for Durkheimians, production is a series of isolated events in the metabolism of nature, for Saussureans speaking is a series of individual acts in the metabolism of the symbolic.

What would Saussure, we may wonder, have made of the speech of the Inuit, had he joined Mauss in his attempt to understand seasonal variations in the Arctic? Saussure would have hardly failed to notice that on their hunting expeditions during the summer the Inuit were indeed engaged in speaking. He comments, in relation to the general problem of translation, that when we hear people speaking a strange language 'we perceive the sounds but remain outside the social fact because we do not understand them' (p. 13). But according to Mauss, the social life of the Inuit is rediscovered every winter – when people congregate in their pursuit of prey, collectively naturalising themselves in the process – only to disappear when the bands disperse again the following summer. Therefore, if there are no social facts during the summer, if the Inuit remain outsiders just as the alien observer, there can hardly be anything left for Saussure to understand. If during the summer the Inuit are autonomous, natural individuals engaged in solitary activities, unaware of any collectivity, does their speaking ever become language?

The thesis on the seasonal morphology of Inuit identity suggests the general question as to whether 'private language' is possible or not. Such a question is often posed by philosophers in relation to the world of Robinson Crusoe, the imaginary islander of Defoe – a world similar, if we are to believe Mauss, to the real world of scattered Inuit hunters and fishermen. Chomsky's answer to the question is affirmative. For him, private language is not only possible, it is essential since linguistic competence, knowledge of language, is imprinted in the structure of the human brain (see Chomsky 1986: Ch. 4). As a mental organ, language functions irrespective of context and season. This should not be surprising since his model of the self-contained individual, evident from both his theory of language and his political writings on human rights, derives from the 'private' model of Locke suggesting that humans are, by nature, free and independent. Wittgenstein argues, on the other hand, that private language is an impossibility. It is not possible, he says, 'to obey a rule "privately"' (see Kripke 1982: 89), and since language involves rule following it is only possible in the community of persons. While both Wittgenstein and Saussure employ the metaphor of the game, particularly chess, when discussing language, their approaches are in some respects very different (see Harris 1988). For Saussure, the rules of the language game are independent of non-linguistic reality. In the approach of Wittgenstein, on the other hand, the language game has no independent existence. For him, language is embedded in the larger social context of speakers and hearers, in their 'form of life'.

In using the game analogy, however, Wittgenstein emphasises that the rules of language are independent of the speaker and the hearer. The community *attributes* the property of rule-following to the activity of the individual by applying its own criteria for rule-following (Kripke 1982: 110). This is equivalent to the Saussurean notion of language as 'a sort of contract signed by the members of the community' (Saussure 1959: 14). A Wittgensteinian linguist, faced with Inuit ethnography, would therefore be inclined to ask, just as Mauss, whether the Inuit are members of a collectivity capable of deciding whether the sounds uttered are patterned and the result of rule-following, or pure noise resulting from random events. Thus while Chomsky, Wittgenstein, and Saussure may disagree on the nature of language, they all seem to apply a similar model of the individual as natural speaker. Whereas for Chomsky language is the property of *self-contained* natural individuals, for Wittgenstein, as well as Saussure, language is a matter of their *belonging* to a community, a supra-individual by-product of interaction and rule-making.

The Inuit, of course, are seldom quite alone. They interact most of the time, but less during the summer. In the spring, Mauss argues, the Inuit 'partially withdraw' from social life (1979: 79), and in the autumn the group again becomes 'more aware' of itself (p. 76). The Inuit, then, are double beings and the relative size of their individual and social components varies with the season (see Figure 1.1). The two 'jural systems' of winter and summer interact, since during the winter an Inuit 'cannot entirely let go of habits or ways of perceiving and acting to which he has become accustomed during the summer and vice versa' (p. 74). 'Without these reciprocal effects', Mauss continues (p. 75), 'the opposition between the two seasons would be even sharper and this would mean that all individualistic elements in Eskimo culture would occur during the summer and all communal elements during the winter'. In the passages just cited, Mauss is operating with two different notions of social life, both inherited from Durkheim – one quantitative, the other qualitative. On the one hand, belonging to a collectivity is a matter of degree, since people can 'partially withdraw' from it becoming less sociable. Thus economic production sometimes takes place between a pair of co-operating individuals, at other times in a large group. Social life rotates along its ecological axis; the *'amount of social structure'*, in Bloch's sense (1977: 228), varies from one season to another. On the other hand, while the social being exists by virtue of the interaction of individuals, it is *qualitatively* different from the individual being. For Mauss as well as Durkheim the dichotomy between the individual and the social is an absolute one, analogous to that between inanimate objects and living beings. There cannot be anything in between, partly individual and partly supra-individual. Either people are aware of the collectivity or they are not; they cannot be more or less aware of it. Production, therefore, either takes place in nature or society.

Similarly, there are two notions of language, given the Durkheimian paradigm. On the one hand speaking may be relatively formal or informal in style, depending on the *amount* of language, so to speak. Thus, the Saussurean model would predict that the winter speech of the Inuit would be highly bound by conventional formulae and restrictions, by propriety and etiquette, whereas summer speech would be freely idiosyncratic. If summer speech is that of the layman, to paraphrase Mauss, winter speech is that of the expert. This is equivalent to a well-known distinction by Durkheimian sociologists between 'restricted' and 'elaborated' language codes. On the other hand, for language as well as social life in general, there is no half-way house. If the identity of the Inuit oscillates between a primarily social one during the winter and a primarily natural one during the summer, one may wonder, must not speech also be subject to an endless alternation between two radically different modes – a social *langue* and an individual *parole*?

In his criticism of the notion of the isolated individual in the writings of Smith and Ricardo – the 'Robinsonades' as he called them – Marx proposes conceptions of individual and society very diffcrent from those of Boas and the Durkheimians (Marx 1973: 84). For him production by an isolated individual outside society is an 'absurdity'. It is true that the individual producer sometimes appears to be entirely independent of others; it is not rare, for instance, in hunter-gatherer society to find individuals living on their own for a long period of time. However, Marx was clearly not thinking of sociability or *physical* isolation. His epoch was that of crowds and cities, yet it produced the 'standpoint', as he put it, of the isolated individual. What he had in mind was the individual, *considered* in isolation, whether isolated or not.

The important difference between the notion of the individual for Durkheim and Marx, as Ingold shows (1986: 245), is that for Durkheim the individual is a 'ready-made' object which may or may not interact with other individuals, whereas for Marx individuals inevitably constitute themselves as social persons through mutual involvement. In the passage from *Grundrisse* previously mentioned, Marx alludes to Robinson Crusoe as a 'rare exception', a person 'cast by accident into the wilderness' and 'in whom the social forces are already dynamically present'. If we adopt the constitutive view of the person, we abandon the radical distinction between individual and society proposed by Durkheim and Saussure. Whether they be physically isolated or interacting with each other, humans are essentially social beings. In this sense, a 'private language' as something removed from social life is an impossibility. Likewise for humans, natural production, as something taking place outside society, is a contradiction in terms.

Structure, agency and history

The Durkheimian notion of the natural individual has important implications for the understanding of human action. The reduction of the social to the material, in the natural model of production, parallels that of reducing production to execution (see Ingold 1986: 253). The individual producer is regarded as an asocial being engaged in the technical act of extraction. Many attempts at defining and classifying production systems therefore emphasise technical relations and types of activity. The literature on fishing, in particular, as I argue in the next chapter, is replete with definitions in terms of technique which reduce the social reality of coastal economies to adaptive responses to the hunting of evasive aquatic prey. Production is regarded as the application of a technique, with the individual producers becoming intermediaries rather than conscious creative agents.

In their treatise on the theory of knowledge, Durkheim and Mauss (1963 [1903]) speak of 'technological classifications' (relegated to a footnote) as being independent of the social:

... man has always classified, more or less clearly the things on which he lived, according to the means he used to get them: for example, animals living in the water, or in the air or on the ground ... it is evident that these distinctions are closely linked to practical concerns, of which they merely express certain aspects (pp. 81–2).

Primitive Classification focuses on different schemes, classifications which are socially determined and whose object is 'not to facilitate action, but to advance understanding' (p. 81). This suggests that people confront reality in terms of social categories only when outside the realm of production, the moment when they discard practical activities and become philosophers. But if the premises for understanding are external to the individual and given in advance, a consciously-motivated effort on behalf of the actors to construct their world is out of the question. For, as Bloch argues (1977: 281), 'if all concepts and categories are determined by the social system a fresh look is impossible . . .'. The concept-users are the victims of knowledge, confronted with an authoritarian structure totally beyond their own making. Consequently, their thoughts do not enter the course of history, save by accident. If the producers establish a new order by their activities, it is not *their* order. The power of creativity, if it exists at all, is located elsewhere, in the realm of the superorganic.

For Boas, economics is a cultural means for satisfying given biological needs, a superorganic script imprinted in the heads of the natural producers to be performed by them for their maintenance and protection against the elements (see Hatch 1973). In such a view, production is dependent upon a cultural logic. The theory of Morgan (1928 [1877]) is based on a similar idea. Morgan claimed that the mode of life, the arts, and institutions of each period were identical upon all continents, indicating that 'the principal institutions of mankind have been developed from a few *primary germs of thought*, and that the course and manner of this development was predetermined . . .' (1928: 18, emphasis added). Morgan's almost Hegelian notion of the 'germs of thought' seems more akin to the idea of the primacy of culture than any materialist conception of the relations between base and superstructure.[2]

The programmatic aspect of the Boasian culture concept is evident in the 'new ethnography' which emerged during the 1960s. Behaviour was seen to be generated by a cognitive code, to be discovered by formal analyses of 'ethnoscience', folk knowledge and taxonomies pertaining to various semantic domains. Frake argued (1980 [1962]: 14), for instance, that ethnography should provide descriptions of behaviour which 'succinctly state what one must know in order to generate culturally acceptable acts and utterances appropriate to a given socioecological context'.[3] The metaphor of the culturally acceptable performance is typically Boasian, reducing the individual to an instrument of culture. Some anthropologists have taken the programmatic perspective quite literally. For them anthropology is an exercise in artificial intelligence, the writing (or discovery) of programmes for cultural automata. Critics have pointed out that the complexity of such a task tends to be underestimated. To Keesing, for instance, it seemed curious that artificial intelligence researchers 'were beginning to write simple "cultures" for robots with enormous difficulty while the "new ethnographers" were aspiring singlehandedly to write cultural grammars of everything the "natives" knew' (1987: 384). The writing of cultural grammar may be a methodological headache for the ethnographer – Keesing describes it as the 'hunting [of] elephants with a fly swatter' (1987: 385) – but the very idea of such an exercise should give rise to theoretical concerns as well, and for informants no less than ethnographers. While it might be argued that the theatrical metaphor endows the actors with *some* creativity – in the sense that the 'script' is interpreted in each case and, therefore, performed differently by different actors – the metaphor of the computer allows none at all. If culture is analogous to a silicon chip or a computer program, people have no say in what they do and they cannot behave differently. For those who assume that animals in general are their own makers (see Goodwin 1988), the anthropological view of the human producer as automaton must indeed be rather odd.

Just as the natural producer is an instrument of culture, for structural linguists the speaker is an instrument of language. Goody claims (1987: 261) that linguists have mostly given their attention to oral language and that written language is treated as 'a purely derivative phenomenon', but the argument can be developed that most linguists think of speaking *in terms of writing*, treating the former as a derivative of the latter and not vice versa. Roy Harris argues (1980: 18), for instance, that in the abstract analyses of the structuralists, speaking becomes 'a string of words with the sound turned off'. Just as the writer has to stick to the dictionary, so the speaker has to stick to the rules of the community. Speaking is merely the running of a programme, the obeying of rules given in advance. Even though the utterance is a point of departure for structural analysis, it does not constitute language. It merely demonstrates the systemic properties of language. But if language is an autonomous entity, whose properties are shaped by internal forces and not the activities of the speakers, linguistic creativity is nothing but the freedom to produce sentences at random. The competent speaker is a grammatical expert who has nothing to say. The pattern of the sounds produced is a synchronic event, trapped in time like the thought of the Durkheimian concept-user.

The influential model of the 'tragedy of the commons' (Hardin 1968) – which holds that in 'common-property' systems with open access, in the absence of government control, all resources must inevitably become over-exploited – illustrates the persistent tendency in Western discourse radically to separate systems and activities, the social and the individual. Hardin's thesis, McCay and Acheson point out (1987: 7), fails to recognise the social nature of production, assuming that the users of commons are autonomous, selfish individuals trying to maximise short-term gains and that the commons dilemma can only be solved through the 'technical' intervention of an external authority, the state. 'The farmers on Hardin's pasture', as McEvoy aptly puts it, 'do not seem to talk to one another' (1988: 226). Given the tendency to separate systems and activities, different political theories often have more in common than one might expect. Those who advocate 'external', governmental solutions to resource management and those who favour the free-market in fact seem to be trapped within the same kind of discourse. Despite their differences in other respects, both groups present the political and economic actor as an irresponsible and asocial being. The former emphasise a state apparatus which has nothing to do with individuals; the latter an individual who has nothing to do with society. In the first case all responsibility is removed from the actor to the state – where it eventually evaporates, given the experience of state dictatorship and military governments. In the second, individual responsibility disappears simply because it is seen as irrelevant or beside the point, not because it has been appropriated.

Just as Hardin's model of the tragedy of the commons portrays the producer as an asocial, individualistic villain, so the Saussurean model of language fails to recognise the social nature of the speaker. It is well known that the linguistic rules established by the grammarians tend to attain lives of their own, as authoritative guides analogous to the Durkheimian superorganic or the cultural programme of the Boasians. Descriptive rules tend to become prescriptive. If access to linguistic resources is 'free' for everyone, it is often argued, there arises a potential contradiction between the system and the individual. A kind of 'tragedy' of the linguistic commons occurs since the natural individuals, devoid of purpose and social relations, are unaware of the long-term consequences of their actions for the group and, ultimately, themselves. Language is therefore best left to a group of 'experts', an external superorganic authority set up against, or 'for', the individual.

Many of the assumptions of orthodox linguistics were questioned early on by Malinowski (1923), Laguna (1963 [1927]) and

Volosinov (1973 [1929]), all of whom regarded language as a mode of action rather than knowledge. Malinowski suggests that language is intimately mixed up with the activity in which the utterances are embedded:

Take for instance language spoken by a group of natives engaged in one of their fundamental pursuits in search of subsistence ... The actors in any such scene are following a purposeful activity, are all set on a definite aim ... In this, speech is the necessary means of communion; it is the one indispensable instrument for creating the ties of the moment without which unified social action is impossible (Malinowski 1923: 471-2).

Even the apparently aimless exchange of words – 'phatic communion' – is a 'binding tissue' (p. 479) creating social bonds. According to Malinowski, such a perspective should have priority in the formation of linguistic theory. In a similar manner Volosinov suggests that language is constituted by a 'stream' of utterances. Saussurean structuralism, he argues (1973: 52), reifies language as a 'stationary rainbow' arched over the stream of social life. For Volosinov, that stream of utterances *is* social life.[4]

These statements anticipate the contextualism of the ethnolinguist and the speech act theorist, both of whom attempt to provide a dynamic model of language, reintroducing speaking into the domain of linguistics. For them, the act of speaking is a social event, not an aspect of the isolated individual. However, in seeking structure in 'speech acts' – beyond the structures of the word and the sentence analysed by Saussure and Chomsky respectively – some of them merely *extend* the scope of linguistic rules. Hymes, for instance, views the 'ethnography of speaking' as entailing the description of cultural knowledge pertaining to 'ways of speaking', a project no less Boasian than that of Frake (see Hymes 1974: 90). The aim of description is to specify the cultural knowledge applied by the speaker when deciding what is an acceptable utterance in given circumstances among people occupying given social roles. The competent speaker draws upon a complex body of knowledge regarding social context, not just the rules of grammar in the narrow sense of the term. Such an approach does not reverse the Saussurean priority of rules over action; the description of the language 'game' is only more complex. Given an adequate ethnographic description of the rules, the speech community could even dispense with the act of speaking. For if the speakers could be made aware of the tacit rules discovered by the grammarians of culture, if everyone could predict the next moment in a conversation, the utterance would simply be obsolete, a useless accessory to inter-action. Just as for the structuralists the speaker is an instrument of language, for students of language informed by the Boasian culture concept the speaker is an instrument of rules.

There are similar problems with the theory of speech acts devel-oped by Austin (1962) and Searle (1969) and some others. As Rosaldo points out (1982), Searle's version of the theory is highly ethnocentric in that it projects a 'western' notion of the person as an individualistic and asocial being, emphasising speaker states and private commitments. Rosaldo's position, however, is equally ethnocentric, being based on the folk theory of the Ilongot. The Ilongots, like Searle, think of language in terms of action, but they seem to replace the individualism of Searle with a normative em-phasis on rules and interactive constraints. Rosaldo claims (1982: 213) that the Ilongot data show 'that accounts of verbal action cannot reasonably proceed without attention to the relations be-tween social order, folk ideas about the world, and styles of speaking'. While Searle speaks of the 'inner' orientation of the speaker, one of sincerity and promises, Rosaldo speaks of the 'external' rules circumscribing speech, one of directives and com-mands. In fact, both Searle and Rosaldo seem to be trapped within the Durkheimian paradigm. The Westerner and the Ilongot can easily be accommodated within the seasonal world of the Inuit described by Mauss. The individual in the approach of Searle pertains to the summer mode, being relatively independent of social facts, while that of Rosaldo's is heavily constrained by supra-individual forces and pertains to the winter mode.

Some of the problems associated with a natural model of the individual may be illustrated with a Boasian approach to the issue of property, an old topic in Western discourse. Rose (1985) ad-vances the argument that first possession or occupancy is the root of title. For her, possession involves a declaration – the declaration of *intent* to appropriate. Given such a perspective, Rose goes on (p. 79), a claim to property 'looks like a kind of speech with the audience composed of all others who might be interested in claim-ing the object in question'. This suggests the speaker must make his or her intention and claim clearly enough and in a language the audience understands. 'Possession as the basis of property owner-ship', then, Rose argues, 'seems to amount to something like yelling loudly enough to all who may be interested' (p. 81). In suggesting that people become property-holders by making their intention to appropriate and their claim to property clear to others, 'by yelling loudly enough', Rose advocates an interesting theory, a speech-act theory of property. The usefulness of such a theory, however, very much depends on the way in which it regards the property-holder and social life. When combined with a natural concept of the individual a speech-act theory of property turns out to be a reduc-tionist one – much like that of Locke which locates the root of title in the autonomous individual, the body, and its labour (see, for instance, Carter 1989). Such a theory is not really about 'doing', about purposeful acts or world-making, but rather about the obeying of rules. For Rose, a claim to title or an act of possession is a hermeneutic phenomenon, a cultural 'text' (p. 82). Speaker and audience must inhabit the same symbolic universe if they are to understand each other's claims and to interpret cultural artifacts – including declarations of intent and acts of possession – in the same way. Rose cites an eighteenth-century court-case about contesting claims to landed property, issued by an Indian tribe and the United States, as 'an example of the relativity of the "text" of possession to the interpretive community for that text' (p. 87). The Indians lost the case partly because they did not 'play the approved language game' (p. 85). The metaphor of the rules-of-the-game and the culturally-approved is a Boasian one. Given such a scheme, the appropriator is merely an instrument of culture – like a real-estate agent engaged in property transactions on behalf of a distant, anonymous client. The act of possession is simply the uttering of a claim, and no matter the loudness of the contention the speaker is nothing but an amplifier of an alien signal produced in advance. The act of possession is like a demonic voice, beyond human control. In reducing property to a consideration of symbolic systems and interpretive communities, Rose, then, removes the issue of possession from the context of social relations. In the Boasian view, to possess is to be possessed. I suggest we think of acts of possession as meaningful, social activities embedded in the relations of actors and audience, and not as the claims of natural individuals. Adopting a social model of the individual allows one to address the

question of how appropriative regimes and concepts of possessions
are constructed and how they evolve in social life – to appreciate
structural, social differences in appropriation.

The nature of the relationship between individual and society is a
key issue in debates about human nature. As we have seen, the
approaches of anthropologists draw upon three 'classical' or basic
models. There is, first, a *private* model of the self-contained rational
individual for whom group membership is optional. This is, for
example, the view of Chomsky and Locke. The second model is
dualistic. Durkheim and Mauss suggest that society is outside the
individual and that the individual is outside society. This model
differs from the first in suggesting that the context of the group is
essential for the realisation of humanity. The private model and the
dualistic one are, on the other hand, closely related in that both
regard the individual as 'natural', or posited by nature. The third
model is the *constitutive* model, often associated with Marx. This
model suggests that the notion of the individual as being independent of community is an empty abstraction (see Ingold 1986: 245).
According to this model, the human being is not, as Locke suggests,
an autonomous agent with predetermined intentions and purposes.
Neither is the individual a combination of two parts as Durkheim
and Mauss argue – one part natural, the other part social. In the
constitutive model, the very individuality and agency of human
beings derive from their involvement in social relations. According
to Marx, the individual is 'an ensemble of the social relations'
(Marx and Engels 1970: 122).

The contrast between the constraints of nature and of the mind
underlines a persistent dualism in anthropological theory. Anthropology remains trapped between two poles, materialism and idealism, 'like a prisoner pacing between the farthest walls of his cell'
(Sahlins 1976: 55). So pervasive is this Cartesian dualism that
critics of ecological determinism, whose aim is to liberate anthropology from what Sahlins (1976: 102) calls the 'prison house of
naturalism', tend simply to substitute another form of determinism,
'cultural reason' – the prison house of language, to paraphrase
Jameson (1972). Lévi-Strauss attempts to get rid of dualism, in
speaking of 'the two kinds of influence that operate on mythic
thought' (1985: 113), but rather than abandoning determinism in
general he allows for *two* different kinds. For him, a particular

mythology is the result of a rather mechanistic interaction between mind and environment. The 'cogwheels' of the mind, he argues, the structures 'dimly announced in the body itself', are 'put in gear with' technological and economic conditions (see p. 105). From this view, humans remain captives within the boundaries of their natural mind, just as they are dependent on physical nature for their maintenance and metabolic processes.

The oscillations of Inuit settlement pattern parallel those of many other hunters and gatherers, both in the North Arctic and elsewhere. Their nature and explanation are topics of frequent discussion among anthropologists and archaeologists and, indeed, there seem to be more than one reason for nomadic movements in hunting and gathering societies. Some of them are material or ecological, that is directly related to the basis of subsistence, the amount and distribution of food resources. Other reasons for movement may have little to do with ecology, for instance the competition for trade and markets and attempts to avoid external pressure and exploitation. According to Woodburn (1972), the Hadza sometimes change places just to rearrange social bonds in situations of conflict and stress. This is equivalent to what Mauss called (1979: 79) the 'natural' need of the Inuit for a 'profane existence' after long periods of collective life. At times Mauss seems to suggest that the seasonal cycle just *happens* to correlate with transformations in Inuit identity, the oscillation between the individual and collective being. The larger theoretical questions discussed in this chapter do not, however, lend themselves to simple empirical tests. While, for instance, the settlement pattern of the Inuit clearly follows a seasonal rhythm of dispersal and concentration year after year, the recognition of this fact does not commit one to a particular theoretical stance – save, perhaps, the refusal to reduce ethnographic reports to poetics and creative writing. The observations of Mauss allow for many theoretical interpretations, besides the Durkheimian reading offered by Mauss himself.

While the two forms of determinism mentioned above are antithetical, they are identical in that they reduce the individual to an instrument. The essay by Mauss on Inuit seasonal variations is not, therefore, necessarily a paradox. It may allow for a cultural as well as a structuralist or an ecological reading, but in all cases the Inuit are presented as natural beings following rules beyond their own making. For Marx, the concept of practice offered a way out of

dualism. 'It is only in a social context', he argued, 'that subjectivism
and objectivism, . . . cease to be antinomies . . . The resolution . . . is
possible *only* through practical means, only through the practical
energy of man' (cited in Schmidt 1971: 114). It is, perhaps, ironic
that while we tend to accept such a thesis in relation to the
emergence of the linguistic faculty among early humans – assuming
that the genetic capacity for speech is a result of the activities of our
ancestors and not of accidental mutations, a thesis going back to
Engels (see Faris 1975) – we are also inclined to subscribe to a
view that renders modern humans incapable of language-making.
Language (*langue*) tends to be regarded as a 'Great Tradition' in
Redfield's sense rather than as a Malinowskian 'long conversation'.
As I have argued, many anthropologists, inspired by the theoretical
distinction between the natural individual and the social or superorganic, operate with a 'natural' model of human action as something taking place in nature, outside society. Such a model is
anthropologically inadequate in that it both reduces the producer
to an instrument and conflates fundamental social differences
amongst production systems.

2 Anthropological discussions of fishing economies

Mauss's work on the coastal Inuit, repeatedly referred to in the previous chapter, has become an anthropological classic. Some of the pioneers of fieldwork and modern ethnography, including Firth (see, for example, Firth 1946, 1965), have also described fishing adaptations in great detail. Furthermore, in recent years, with extended fisheries jurisdiction and tight resource management, anthropologising on fishermen has become quite an industry. Often, however, the anthropological attitute has been that as far as theory and model building is concerned fishing 'doesn't count'. There is a tendency to see fishing activities either as a last resort, a compensation for the deficiency of the terrestrial environment (Osborn 1977), or as mere fun (see Wright 1985: 87). For a long time anthropologists have operated with broad categories of adaptations in order to gain the cross-cultural knowledge deemed necessary for dealing with problems of social evolution. Classificatory labels derived from nineteenth-century evolutionism are still with us, given that people frequently speak of 'hunter-gatherers', 'agricultural societies', 'pastoralism' and so on. While fishing occupies a significant position in some early evolutionary schemes, particularly that of Morgan (1928 [1877]), generally the category of fishing is a curious taxonomic misfit. Given the somewhat obsessive demand for typologies of adaptations in anthropological discussion, the relative absence of 'fishing' from the scene is rather surprising.

In this chapter I discuss the place of fishing activities and coastal economies in anthropological discourse. Focusing on the boundary between land and water may be helpful for drawing contrasts between economic or social systems which are organised in *similar* ways – for instance, for comparing hunter-gatherers of terrestrial and aquatic resources. On the other hand, there is no point in establishing a unitary category of fishing, for in so doing we would have to ignore the social relations in which production is necessarily to be found. I argue that anthropology tends to operate with a 'natural' model of fishing which depicts the individual producer as an autonomous isolate, engaged in the technical act of catching fish.

I emphasise an alternative approach to fisheries which distinguishes between social differences in circulation of products and access to resources.

Hunters and gatherers of aquatic resources

One of the best known evolutionary schemes of the nineteenth century is Morgan's (1928). For him the advent of fishing was of great evolutionary importance. He suggested that the experience of humans had run in 'nearly uniform channels' and that there were three major successive stages or 'ethnical periods' – savagery, barbarism, and civilisation – each representing 'a distinct culture' and a 'particular mode of life' (pp. 8–9). According to Morgan, it was during the period of savagery, the earliest period in his scheme of human history, that fishing had a particular role to play. The acquisition of fishing and the knowledge of the use of fire marked the important transition to the Middle Stage of Savagery, during which humans left their original habitat and spread over different parts of the earth's surface. Fish, Morgan suggested, were the 'first kind of artificial food' (p. 21). Having acquired the knowledge of the use of fire for cooking, humans became 'independent of climate and locality', since fish were 'universal in distribution, unlimited in supply, and the only kind of food at all times available'. The interval of time from the introduction of fishing to the emergence of hunting represented a large part of the period of savagery. Fishing represented an important step in the history of humans, the beginning of a 'new career' (Morgan 1928: 20), *prior* to the hunting of terrestrial animals.

Morgan had little to say about the earliest stages in his scheme and he did not cite many ethnographic examples. Africa, he said (p. 16), was 'an ethnical chaos of savagery and barbarism', while Australia and Polynesia were in savagery 'pure and simple'. He claimed that there were no surviving examples in his day representing the Lower Stage of Savagery, the period of gathering representing the origins of the human race and of articulate speech, but nevertheless he felt confident in claiming (p. 20) that 'neither an art, nor an institution' was developed during this stage. Indeed, the whole reasoning on which Morgan based his ethnical periods does not show much respect for empirical detail. On the one hand, he claimed that the division into ethnical periods directed investigation to tribes which 'afford the best exemplification of each status, with the view of making each both standard and illustrative' (p. 16). This would render it possible to treat a particular society 'according to its condition of relative advancement' (p. 13). But on the other hand timing really did not matter. 'It does not affect the main result', Morgan wrote (1928: 13), 'that different tribes ... on the same continent ... are in different conditions at the same time, since for our purpose the *condition* of each is the material fact, the *time* being immaterial'. Just how the condition of relative advancement was determined was never made clear. Morgan's theory of evolution rested on a rank order of essential types rather than the reconstruction of chronological sequences.

Engels (1942 [1884]) greeted Morgan's theories with enthusiasm, since he asserted that during the first stage of evolution, social life was undifferentiated and the notion of private property non-existent. He began his book *The Origin of the Family, Private Property and the State* with a dedication to Morgan as 'the first man who with expert knowledge has attempted to introduce a definite order into the history of primitive man' (p. 19). Morgan's writings were particularly useful since some of them were based on comparatively detailed and original fieldwork. In *The Origin* Engels adopted a scheme very similar to Morgan's, restating his ideas about the stage of Savagery and the role of fishing during its Middle Stage. In *The German Ideology* he had, however, along with Marx, identified the stages in the history of humans and their progression somewhat differently. Hunting and fishing represented the first substage of the 'undeveloped' stage of production, identified by tribal ownership and the elementary or natural division of labour imposed by the family (see Marx 1964: 122).

According to some of the important evolutionary theories of the nineteenth century, then, primitive fishing represented a separate and early stage in the history of humans. Such an idea was underlined in many contemporary accounts of particular groups of people largely dependent on fishing. In his *Journal*, Darwin provides a lengthy description of the fishermen of Tierra del Fuego. Having met a group of Fuegians, Darwin noted that these 'poor wretches were stunted in their growth ... [and] their skins filthy and greasy ... Viewing such men, one can hardly make oneself believe they are fellow-creatures and inhabitants of the same world' (1871: 234). As Meehan points out (1982: 5), Darwin's observa-

tions on Tierra del Fuego were sometimes used to illuminate archaeological information on shell-middens discovered in Denmark,
the so-called 'kitchen-middens'. Lubbock reproduced Darwin's
description, adding that it gave 'a vivid and probably correct idea
of what might have been seen on the Danish shores long ago'
(1913 [1869]: 242). Tylor came to a similar conclusion, describing
how 'shell-heaps . . . are found here and there all round the coasts
of the world . . . for instance on the coast of Denmark, where
archaeologists search them for relics of rude Europeans, who, in the
Stoneage, had a life somewhat like that of Tierra del Fuego' (1916
[1875]: 207).

   In a study of the Emeryville shell-mounds in California, Uhle
expressed opinions similar to those Darwin had expressed for the
Fuegians. The collecting of shells, he said, 'in itself indicates a low
form of human existence' (1907: 31). Such opinions clearly had
a life of their own. Whereas Lubbock used ethnographic bits to
illuminate the records of the past, Uhle was quite prepared to
leap in the other direction, from the archaeological record to the
ethnographic present:

In all parts of the world, even today, people may be seen on the shore
at low water gathering for food the shells uncovered by the retreating
tide; . . . these people always belong to the lower classes of society, and
lead in this manner a primitive as well as a simple life (Uhle 1907: 31).

   The evolutionary scheme proposed by Morgan has probably few
adherents nowadays, even though some twentieth-century scholars,
notably Childe (1944, 1951), continued to discuss the stages of
social evolution in similar terms. Morgan's scheme, however, fore-
shadows in some respects some fairly recent ideas, including those
of Sauer (1962) regarding the sea-shore as a 'primitive home of
man'. Sauer rejects the popular 'man the hunter' hypothesis of
human origins. He suggests, like Tanner (1981), that primate
behaviour fails to indicate that aggressive males were the founders
of human society. Humanity began, Sauer says (1962: 308), with
the maternal family, 'not out of a roving promiscuous troop
dominated by the strongest, most virile, and most aggressive male'.
But while Tanner refers to a 'woman the gatherer' hypothesis to
explain human origins, Sauer reinvents Morgan's idea of fishing
being a new career:

The hypothesis ... is that the path of our evolution turned aside from the common primate course by going to the sea. No other setting is as attractive for the beginnings of humanity. The sea, in particular the tidal shore, presented the best opportunity to eat, settle, increase, and learn ... It gave the congenial ecological niche in which animal ethology could become human culture (Sauer 1962: 309).

A similar hypothesis of 'aquatic man' (perhaps more fantastic) was proposed by Hardy (1960), in a speech delivered to the British Sub-Aqua Club. He suggested that human ancestors, some proto-humans in the tropics, were forced because of the competition of 'life in the trees', to feed on the sea-shores where they learned to swim and physically adapt to aquatic life:

The graceful shape of Man – or Woman! – is most striking when compared with the clumsy form of the ape. All the curves of the human body have the beauty of a well-designed boat. Man indeed is streamlined (Hardy 1960: 643).

We tend to laugh at Hardy's theory of 'aquatic man', but some distinguished archaeologists took it quite seriously at the time, while disagreeing with some of its aspects.[1] Dart argued (1960) that human exploitation of aquatic resources was more recent than Hardy suggested, and much more significant. According to him, early humans were mighty hunters, 'confirmed killers' (see Binford 1983: 36). The adaptation to aquatic regimes, he suggested, did not alter the physiology of humans, rather it was significant because it sparked a 'mental' discovery which led to civilisation. Humans learned to swim by capturing their breath and blowing it into some kind of float. Such knowledge in turn was the source of articulate speech:

Man's first intellectual *tour de force* was equating the power of the spirit within him with that in the float and with that of the air or wind about him, and expressing that concept by specific breaths or words ... (This) intellectual achievement ... transformed the isolated hordes of hunters into those communities of fishermen and boatsmen that launched mankind on the sea of civilization (Dart 1960: 1670).

Unfortunately, speech does not preserve well in the archaeological record, but if Dart is right about the late origin of civilisation, human physiology must have then developed totally independent of culture and the neurological capacity for language must have been 'vacant' for tens of thousands of years among silent, at least speechless, hordes of hunters, who finally got into deep waters and started to speak. That is a rather fishy theory of language and human evolution.

Indeed, such 'man the fisher' or sub-aqua club theories contradict the archaeological records. Rather than being particular or specialised stages, as Morgan and many others suggested, fishing, hunting and gathering often occur together. Also, fishing seems to be a much more recent occupation than Sauer and Hardy suggest. There is no indication that fishing preceded hunting and that human physiology was adapted to aquatic life. The oldest remains to indicate an economy in which fishing was of considerable importance, shells and fishbones from Haua Fteah in Libya and Klasies-river in South Africa, have been dated at 50 to 80 thousand years old (Yesner 1980). The evidence indicates that marine subsistence had progressively intensified by the end of the Pleistocene, from about 20,000 BP onwards, and that there was an 'explosion' in the use of shell fish during the Holocene in many parts of the world (Bailey 1983: 560).

The archaeological interpretation of the 'facts' concerning the recency of human exploitation of aquatic resources is, however, contradictory. Some scholars suggest that, from the point of view of early humans, aquatic environments must have been an inadequate source of food, and therefore the negative evidence must be taken for granted (Schalk 1979: 57). Washburn and Lancaster (1968: 294) conclude that, whatever the nutritional value of aquatic resources, water must have posed a danger to early humans: 'it is likely that the basic problem in utilisation of resources from sea or river was that man cannot swim naturally but to do so must learn a difficult skill . . . For early man, water was a barrier and a danger, not a resource'. Given such barriers, some scholars suggest that it is surprising that marine resources were exploited at all even at this 'early' date; see, for example, Osborn's article (1977: 158), significantly entitled 'Strandloopers, mermaids, and other fairy tales'. Others suggest that coastal zones must have been quite attractive, providing a worthwhile challenge, and that people may have exploited them long before the Holocene without leaving us modern groundlings any evidence. Shells are not particularly perishable and some shell-remains are in fact older than the earliest evidence for human exploitation (Cohen 1977: 94), but it is still quite possible that earlier coastal adaptations were submerged by rising sea levels (see, for example, Perlman 1980).

Many archaeological debates have centred around the formation of sites and the meaning of existing deposits, for instance the debate about Dart's theory of early man as a bloodthirsty killer.[2] The modern debate about the recency or antiquity of coastal adaptations is somewhat peculiar in that the issue is not existing sites but rather the *absence* of any sites at all. Bailey concludes (1983: 561) that while there is some evidence for the latter view mentioned which emphasises the importance of rising sea levels, the evidence available at present suggests only that *some* marine exploitation took place during the earlier period and that it was not of comparable intensity to later Holocene exploitation levels. While the archaeological evidence indicates that, contrary to Morgan's claim, fishing was not a new career predating the hunting of terrestrial animals, none the less among hunter-gatherers fishing may have played quite an important role.

An influential model of hunter-gatherers emphasises their unity as nomadic food collectors (Lee and DeVore 1968). It has been customary, as Childe remarked years ago (1965: 71), to contrast settled life with the nomadic existence of the 'homeless hunter'. It has long been known to both archaeology and ethnography that some hunting and gathering societies, in particular the fishing societies of the north-west coast of North America, do not fit into the classic image of the simple society of mobile hunter-gatherers (see Murdock 1969), but deviations from the classic model of hunter-gatherers have usually been taken as exceptions. It has rarely been suggested that there is a *general* relationship, among hunter-gatherers, between reliance on aquatic resources and social organisation. Recently several authors have seriously considered such a possibility. Thus Renouf (1984) develops a model of coastal hunter-fishers in northern environmental zones, in order to explain characteristics resembling food-producing societies and differing from stereotypic hunter-gatherers. Compared with the latter societies, she argues, northern coastal hunter-fishers live in larger groups and in more permanent settlements. Yesner (1980) distinguishes maritime adaptations generally as a subset of hunting and gathering, capable of supporting complex social organisation and permanent settlements. What exactly is the evidence from the 'ethnographic present'?

Illustrative comparison is often employed by anthropologists. While such an approach is important for raising interesting issues and for clarifying key concepts, for instance concerning mobility and sedentism, it has serious limitations. Those who rely on illustrative comparison sometimes assume they are testing hypotheses or discovering correlations where none exist (Barnard 1983: 199). By definition, the illustrative sample is unsystematically selected. Larger and more carefully selected samples provide an opportunity to examine a number of questions derived from isolated cases and to test statistically hypotheses which would otherwise remain sheer speculation. The use of cross-cultural data-bases, however, is not devoid of problems. First, there are problems relating to ethnographic significance. Just as the archaeological record has to be considered in terms of both context and the processes which produced it, similar interpretations are ideally required if quantitative information is to be made meaningful. Also, there is a problem of sampling, the so-called 'Galton's problem'. We can never be sure that the cases in our sample are genuinely independent or distinct cases to allow for a meaningful cross-cultural comparison. As Wolf has put it, 'we are back in a world of sociocultural billiard balls, coursing on a global billiard table' (1982: 17).

A simple way to operationalise nomadism in hunter-gatherer societies, perhaps the most straightforward, is to define it in terms of continuous interval variables. This is Kelly's approach (1983). He employs Binford's influential distinction (1980) between foragers who 'map onto' resources and have a high residential mobility and collectors who are less nomadic and employ a logistical strategy, supplying themselves with specific resources through specially-organised task groups. It may be argued, however, that some population movements in hunter-gatherer societies resist the simple dichotomous distinction of Binford and Kelly between foraging and collecting (Eder 1984); Everybody is on the move all of the time, apparently simultaneously employing 'logistical' and 'residential' strategies. Kelly (1983) defines residential mobility as the number of residential moves per year, and logistical mobility as the distance covered on travels to and from a residential camp on foraging trips. His analysis, based on a sample of thirty-six hunter-gatherer societies selected from a variety of environmental biomes, demonstrates a series of relationships between mobility strategies and the structure of the environment, resource accessibility and monitoring characteristics. Kelly, however, is not concerned with the exploitation of marine resources and much evidence indicates that mobility strategies *are* related to reliance on aquatic resources (Perlman 1980; Testart 1982). Indeed, Kelly notes himself (see p. 289) that some of the expected relationships between mobility strategies and environmental properties, given the approach of Binford (1980), only hold true as long as one controls for reliance on aquatic resources and that a division between terrestrial and marine resources 'may prove to be heuristically useful' (p. 279). Reanalysis of Kelly's data for residential mobility shows that there is no relationship between reliance on gathering and number of residential moves per year (Pálsson 1988a). In the case of hunting, on the other hand, the Pearson correlation is strong and positive (0.50) and in the case of fishing there is a fairly strong negative correlation (−0.40). The more reliant on fishing, the fewer residential moves there are per year. Just to mention the extremes in Kelly's sample, the Aleut make only one move per year and receive 60 per cent of their diet from fishing, while the Ona make 60 moves and receive 20 per cent of their diet from fishing.

Nomadism, it is often argued, involves different kinds of population movements. Some groups seem to be fully nomadic, moving without any reference to a fixed place. Thus, several groups of south-east Asian sea-nomads or 'sea gypsies' as they are sometimes called – including the Mawken (the Selungs), the Orang Tambus, and the Sekah – live in boats and migrate continually from one location to another, fishing and gathering in nomadic fashion (see Sopher 1965). Murdock remarks in relation to the Mawken that they 'have no land settlements but ... wander at will' (1969: 144). Secondly, there is movement between one fixed point and several peripheral locations each of which is reused irregularly. An example is provided by the Tlingit who are tied down to a central place but follow annual runs of fish for weeks and even months at a time. As Krause observes, for the Tlingit the canoe is a 'second home, ... in it they carry all their household possessions, as well as the gear for fishing and hunting' (1956: 120). A third case involves movement between a centre and several peripheral locations each of which is reused regularly. This applies to some seasonal changes of residence in the Salmon Area of the north-west coast of North America: 'nothing could be more stable than the repetition, year after year, of the same shifts of residence from winter village to a round of summer fishing camps, invariably at the same sites, and in the same sequence' (Hewes 1948: 241). Murdock's (1967) operationalisation of 'settlement pattern' in the *Ethnographic Atlas* assumes these kinds of nomadic movement to be not only qualitatively different but also differing in degree of movement.[3]

Computations show that for the the 220 hunter-gatherer societies recorded in the *Atlas* there is a relationship between mode of subsistence and settlement pattern (see Pálsson 1988a). The more important is fishing, the more compact and permanent the settlement. The fishing societies with compact and relatively permanent settlements are Aleut, Alsea, Bellacoola, Chinook, Chugach, Coos, Eyak, Haida, Hupa, Karok, Kwakiutl, Paraujano, Quileute, Siuslaw, Sivokakmei, Tanaina, Tillamook, and Wiyot. The opposite picture emerges in the case of hunting and gathering of terrestrial resources; the relationship between it and permanence of settlement is significant and negative. Binford (1980) seems to assume that settlement pattern is a response to 'effective temperature' (ET) or the length of the growing season and the distribution of resources. And several scholars have made use of his argument that there is a latitudinal gradient in the occurrence of logistical strategies and permanence of settlement (see Schalk 1979; Cohen 1985). One might argue, however, that the relationship between terrestrial ecology and settlement pattern is a spurious one, and that settlement pattern is responsive rather to the nature of the resources exploited, i.e. the extent to which they are terrestrial or aquatic (see, for example, Perlman 1980: 293).

Using the information of the *Atlas* one can further examine the relationship between settlement pattern, fishing, and ecological conditions. If one controls for terrestrial ecology, holding it constant, the relationship between degree of fishing and permanence of settlement remains fairly strong. This indicates that settlement pattern is responsive to a reliance on aquatic resources and that one must qualify Binford's interpretation that permanence of settlement is a function of distance from the Equator. Reanalysis of Kelly's data (1983) shows similar results (Pálsson 1988a). Settlement pattern is not the only measure of social complexity which correlates with the importance of fishing. There is also a positive correlation with group size and degree of local hierarchy or social stratification. The more reliant on fishing a group of hunter-gatherers is, the larger and more stratified the group. The fishing societies with the largest communities (100–399) are those of the Aleut, Haisla, Lummi, Makah, Shuswap, Tareumiut, Tenino, and Tlingit. In the case of hunters and gatherers of terrestrial resources, on the other hand, there is either no correlation with group size and degree of stratification or a negative one. One has to conclude that fishing societies differ significantly from other hunter-gatherer societies in that they exhibit a greater social complexity.

One may speculate – on the basis of such relationships amongst reliance on aquatic resources, permanence of settlement and social complexity – on the possible role of aquatic resources for prehistoric social development. Childe (1965: 71) has argued that the contrast between mobility and sedentism is 'quite fictitious' and that sedentism itself does not mark a neolithic transition. He emphasises the distinction between food-collection and food-production; the collector, he says (p. 66), 'remained content to take what he could get', while the neolithic revolution gave the producer 'control over his own food supply'. Given such a distinction, the kind of evolutionary change usually referred to as the neolithic revolution did not occur among settled fishing peoples. Such an assumption is made explicit by Steward: 'no one doubts that hunting and gathering preceded farming and herding and that the last two were preconditions of "civilization" . . .' (1955: 28). Others suggest that the abundance of resources in coastal zones may have provided an opportunity for the development of complex civilisations. Murdock argues, for instance, that 'it is by no means improbable that fishing may have played a very important cultural-historical role in mediating the transition to early agriculture' (1969: 144). Godelier makes a similar point (1986: 116). This is what Binford terms the 'Garden of Eden' principle. He rejects such a model of agricultural origins on the grounds that it leads to the view that some people must have been more intelligent than others: 'why else would they have grasped so early the Great Truth of the Least Effort Principle, while others ignored its self-evident advantages?' (Binford 1983: 202).

There is some evidence for a transformation of hunter-gatherer social relations in coastal regimes although many of the important issues involved are far from settled (see, for example, Marquardt 1986 and 1988 on the Calusa in Florida). In sixteenth-century Cuba, one may note, turtles were caught with the aid of sucker-fish and kept alive, presumably as property, in underwater reed corrals

(Weddle 1985: 28). But just as on its own an abundant supply of coal does not explain an industrial revolution, the abundance itself of aquatic resources does not account for a transformation in social relations. To account for the transformation of the hunter-gatherer way of life different models are needed (see Hitchcock 1982). Among the models proposed are those which emphasise changes in the social demands of production in response to intergroup competition or the need to establish and maintain alliances (Lourandos 1988; Bender 1978), and those which draw attention to the relationship between coastal and interior zones (Yesner 1987). Rather than seeing aquatic resources themselves as determinants of complexity one should regard coastal niches as just one possible avenue for intensification.

The issues involved in the debate on the development of complex society and the importance of aquatic resources are not simply empirical. There is a conceptual issue at stake as well. Complex and sedentary societies should not simply be seen to be quantitatively different from simple and mobile hunter-gatherers. Presenting evolutionary change in terms of a continuum from mobility to sedentism conflates the different meanings of 'settling down'; it may refer both to an irreversible transformation and a reversible process (see Eder 1984). But the question remains, how and why does the quantum leap take place as either land or animals become appropriated through property relations? Somehow, the study of variability among foragers and its social and ecological correlates in the ethnographic present must be relevant for the understanding of diachronic social processes, of evolutionary change. Interesting as these issues may be, they are beyond my main concern. I briefly return, however, to some of the issues involved later on, in my discussion of social differences among fishing systems.

The definition and the category of fishing

So far we have taken the category of fishing as given. But what does it contain? In medieval Europe it was customary to distinguish between three kinds of technique on the basis of the medium in which the prey moves – i.e. fishing, fowling and hunting. Walton, for instance, makes much of such a distinction in his book *The Compleat Angler* [1653]. It begins with a chapter entitled 'A Conference betwixt an Angler, a Falconer, and a Hunter, each commending his Recreation'. In everyday language, the notion of fishing still has similar connotations, usually being broadly defined as the 'attempt to catch fish by any means or for any purpose' (*Webster's Dictionary*). An even broader notion of fishing is implied in Hornell's cross-cultural survey *Fishing in Many Waters* (1950). Not only does he describe the different ways of fishing among humans, but he also provides a whole chapter on 'Animals trained to fish and fishes that angle for their living'. Some animals (including otters, cormorants, and sucker-fish) can be forced into the fishing service of humans, while others (including sea birds, 'feathered fishers', and angler-fish) fish for themselves, independent of humans (Hornell 1950: 33). Apparently, for Hornell, fishing is anything catching anything that is under water.

An interesting early paper which deliberately addressed the problem of definition is that of Hewes (1948). He claims that the distinctiveness of fishing activities has two aspects. First, objects behave in a particular manner while in an aquatic substance, due to special conditions of buoyancy, turbulence, solubility and refraction of light. Second, hunters and their prey occupy different media. For land-dwelling animals like humans, aquatic environments are 'a realm which can be exploited as if the exploiters moved in a universe with an additional dimension. The horizontal surface of water bodies, through which or from the edges of which a fisherman inserts his catching devices, has no counterpart in the terrestrial environment' (Hewes 1948: 238). This 'reality' of the distinction between land hunting and gathering on the one hand and fishing on the other, according to Hewes (p. 239), suggests a definition of fishing based upon the habitat of its object. Accordingly, he proposes (pp. 239–40) an 'ecological' definition of fishing as 'that category of human activity which is connected with the capture or gathering, of animals (or plants) which regularly dwell in the water'.

Such concepts of fishing, as a particular kind of hunting which happens to yield fish, are one element of a widely-accepted anthropological scheme for classifying types of technique: gathering, collecting, hunting (including trapping), husbandry (including fish farming), and plant cultivation. Ellen suggests (1982: 128–9) these categories have some degree of cross-cultural objectivity, 'being recognised indigenously as distinct types'. The argument has been developed that fishing is 'best considered as a kind of hunting activity' and that such a notion is implied in many languages (Leap 1977: 252). Leap examines fishing-related terminologies in thirty-three languages and concludes that, from the point of view of indigenous speakers, fishing and hunting are similar strategies, 'differing only with respect to the commodity which serves as the focus of the subsistence effort' (pp. 256–7). It is necessary, how-ever, to qualify Leap's generalisations. The classification of aquatic organisms, including 'fish', varies from one society to another. Also, indigenous terminologies do not necessarily distinguish be-tween hunting and other subsistence activities, including trapping, collecting and gathering. For instance, the coast Salish, who har-pooned salmon and netted seals and ducks, used a broad term which translates as 'sea-food producer' (Suttles 1968: 63). Another example is the Icelandic term *veiðar* which can be applied to fishing, the gathering of shellfish, and the trapping and hunting of terrestrial animals. A further example is provided by the Gidjingali of Australia who use the same term to describe both male and female 'hunting prowess', the skills needed in the pursuit of shellfish as well as more mobile species (Meehan 1982: 119).

Much like medieval European hunters often distinguished be-tween fishing, fowling and hunting, modern anthropology tends to operate with three concepts of foraging – fishing, gathering and hunting. Both schemes are exemplars of what Dumézil called (1958) the 'ideologie tri-partite' of Western culture, the tendency to postulate three categories on the basis of pairs of binary opposi-tions. Thus the distinction between three modes of foraging is usually based on two oppositions relating to the species exploited (mobile:stationary) and their habitat (terrestrial:aquatic). Such a classification was used by Murdock (1967: 154) in the construction of the *Ethnographic Atlas*. When coding societies according to their economic basis, the relative importance of different modes of subsistence in each case, Murdock used the following categories: (1) 'gathering of wild plants and small land fauna', (2) 'hunting, including trapping and fowling', and (3) 'fishing, including shell-fishing and the pursuit of large aquatic animals'. Such a broad definition of fishing incorporates different kinds of activities, from the capturing of mobile prey to the gathering of passive objects, on the basis of their common link to water. Thus Hewes states that the distinction between 'capturing' and 'gathering' should not be emphasised since 'clams may elude the gatherer by burrowing, while highly mobile small fishes are usually acquired by some scooping process with an effort as unlike "capture" as shaking fruit from a tree' (1948: 240). The participants of the Man the Hunter symposium argued (see Lee 1968: 41) to the contrary that the pursuit of large aquatic animals was more properly classified as hunting and that shellfishing should be classified as gathering.

Ingold argues (1987: 79) that such categories are fraught with ambiguity, even as categories signifying types of activity, and that there can be no reasoned comparison until anthropologists reach agreement on what they mean. The contrast between gathering and hunting, he points out, is usually based on the distinction between collection and pursuit as fundamentally different methods of procurement, whereas the contrast between fishing and hunting is based on biological classification, i.e. the kinds of species obtained. A strict adherence to behavioural or technical criteria would not, he suggests, eliminate the problems of orthodox classifications of food-getting activities. For one thing, in such a scheme the category of fishing would have no place at all, for fish-yielding activities would be included under different categories – gathering, hunting and entrapment (Ingold 1987: 81). Sopher remarks, one may note, in relation to the sea-nomads of south-east Asia who use the 'simple' methods of harpooning and diving in shallow water, that 'it would certainly be preferable . . . to refer to these people as "sea hunters and gatherers" rather than "fishermen" (Sopher 1965: 218). Ingold suggests a characterisation of hunting and gathering which is independent of both technical and biological criteria. For him, the essence of human hunting and gathering, as opposed to animal predation and foraging respectively, lies in the prior intention that motivates the producer and not in some overt behavioural characteristics associated with a particular type of technology or a particular organism, mobile or stationary.

From this perspective, both fishing (in the sense of capturing fish) and the procurement of shellfish may be 'hunting', because both activities involve expectation, excitement and a purposeful search for sites (Ingold 1987: 92–3; Meehan 1982: 119; Plath and Hill 1987), and not simply (as Hewes argues 1948: 240) on the grounds that shellfish may be no less evasive than fish. Thus, Plath and Hill suggest (1987: 153) that abalone diving in Japan, a women's occupation, 'deserves to be classed with hunting rather than lumped with other forms of marine collecting' on the grounds that even though the quarry may be sedentary 'it can be taken only by aggressive search and seizure'. An expert diver, they argue (p. 155), 'has to be something of an adrenalin freak'.

Some recent models of fishing go far beyond the narrow context of techniques and food-getting activities in their attempts to embrace its social aspects. However, in some respects they do resemble the ecological and technical models of fishing activities previously discussed. A few examples from the literature will help to illustrate this. Acheson (1981) emphasises that fishing takes place in a relatively uncertain environment in a physical and social sense. He suggests that for this reason 'fishing poses some very unusual constraints and problems' (p. 277). People who adapt to earning a living by exploiting marine resources seem to manage their lives in similar ways and develop similar social institutions which reduce competition and uncertainty and spread the risks of production. Crew organisation is often flexible and based on voluntary ties but not on structural principles or kinship obligations, to ensure co-operation and the right combination of skills. In sum, Acheson suggests fishing societies have a range of characteristics in common due to the fact that their members have to adapt to corresponding environments and cope with identical problems. A similar approach is that of Norr and Norr (1978). Having surveyed the literature on fishing communities, both pre-industrial and modern, they conclude (pp. 163–4) that several 'technical and environmental constraints' distinguish fishing from other modes of subsistence. Even though differences in terms of such constraints are associated with differences in work organisation, the constraints common to *all* fishing encourage a particular organisation, including teamwork and equality among workers (p. 169). A further example is Breton's analysis (1973) of changes in fishing communities in Eastern Canada. Breton argues that different ways of organising work groups must be seen 'basically' as 'adaptive strategies' for the exploitation of a given resource (p. 412) and that despite their variability, fishing communities in general are characterised by relatively 'fluid' social units (p. 393). One aspect of this flexibility is the predominance of dyadic contractual ties between autonomous individuals.

These approaches are reminiscent of Steward's method of cultural ecology. Steward defines his concept of 'cultural core' as the 'constellation of features which are most closely related to subsistence activities and economic arrangements', including 'such social, political, and religious patterns as are empirically determined to be closely connected with these arrangements' (1955: 37). In his view, social life is mechanistically adapted to the material world. One of the best-known exemplars of Steward's approach is his analysis of the band in hunter-gatherer societies. For Steward, the ecological basis of bands arose from the nature of the animals people hunted. In the approaches of Acheson, Breton, and Norr and Norr, the constraints of uncertainty and resultant organisational responses are equivalent to material context in Steward's approach. And fishing crews are somehow equivalent to the band. The social organisation of coastal communities is seen to be primarily an adaptive response to the hunting of evasive aquatic prey, a response analogous to Steward's 'cultural core'. In his comparison of work groups (which, significantly, cites Steward's work) Breton argues, for instance (1973: 412), that 'it is at the level of the factors of production . . . that each type of group achieves greater specificity. Although their formation is influenced by socio-demographic factors, such as residence patterns and community size, they depend primarily upon particular ecological and technical requirements'.

Archaeological accounts of fishing also tend to emphasise technical requirements. Torrence (1983), for instance, contrasts hunting and fishing largely in terms of technology. She points out, following Oswalt (1973), that tools used for the capture of aquatic animals tend to be particularly complex because the medium in which the animals move demands complicated retrieval strategies. The fish must not only be speared but also they must be successfully brought ashore. The emphasis on technology is not surprising, given that archaeologists are concerned primarily with material evidence. Childe comments, in his evaluation of archaeological classification of stages of technological development (Thomesen's 'Ages'), that 'a classification based on the property relations within which tools were used might be more significant', adding that 'however sound this may be in theory, one trouble is that the archaeological record is, to put it mildly, vague as to the social organization of preliterate communities' (1944: 23).

Many models of fishing, then, emphasise material and technical constraints. Why such 'natural' models have gained the popularity evident from the literature on fishing remains open to question. One reason relates to the fascination of the leisured classes of

Europe during earlier centuries with the individualistic pursuit of mobile aquatic (and terrestrial) prey. For them, fishing was a non-subsistence activity, with a distinct recreational value or quality of its own. Walton's *Angler*, which for long time held a position in book sales similar to that of the Bible or of Shakespeare (see Jonquil 1988: 68), provides a good illustration. Walton comments on his own work that although 'it is known I can be *serious* at seasonable times ... the whole Discourse is ... a picture of my own disposition, especially in such days and times as I have *laid aside business, and gone a-fishing*' (n.d.: 6, emphasis added). For Walton, catching fish was an artistic experiment. He describes angling employing the metaphors of mathematics and poetry: it is 'so like Mathematicks, that it can never be fully learnt' (p. 7), and 'somewhat like poetry' for 'he that hopes to be a good angler, must not only bring an inquiring, searching, observing wit, but he must bring a large measure of hope and patience, and a love and propencity to the art itself' (p. 27).

The English Game Laws from 1671 defined hunting as the privilege of substantial landowners (see McCay 1987: 197). Inland fishing was also transformed into a privilege of the upper classes. For Walton and many of his contemporaries, hunting and fishing were, above all, manly activities for 'princes and noble persons'. Walton describes hunting as 'a game' which 'trains up the younger nobility to the use of manly exercises in their riper age ... How doth it preserve health, and increase strength and activity?' (n.d.: 20). It is easy to see how the Western explorer who usually placed himself at the top of the evolutionary ladder could none the less identify with even the most 'savage' fisherman as a fellow *homo ludens*. Fishing was a game, a test of sportsmanship. Tylor remarked (1916: 214) that 'on the whole it is remarkable how little modern fishermen have moved from the methods of the rudest and oldest men'. These cultural values of Western society are reflected in early theories of human evolution. As Tanner points out (1981: 23–4), the concept of 'man the hunter' pervades most earlier speculations about the life of the first hominids. Nineteenth-century theorists and observers often showed explicit admiration of the individualistic pursuit of mobile aquatic prey. Lubbock states (1913: 539–40), for instance, that 'having few weapons, ... savages acquire a skill which seems almost marvellous'. Some Patagonian tribes, we are told, live chiefly on fish 'which they catch *either* by *diving*, or striking them with their darts', South Sea Islanders dive after fish which 'takes refuge under the coral rock; thither the diver pursues him and brings him up with a finger in each eye'. They are 'even more than a match for the shark, which they attack fearlessly with a knife' – and so on.

The natural models of fishing are not without their faults and critics. Alexander points out (1982: 259) that while there are real empirical differences between fishing and other modes of subsistence (agriculture), the use of such differences establishes a framework which gives misplaced importance to marine ecology. 'Almost unwittingly', he says, 'ecological functionalism has become the major mode of explanation'. Indeed, the notion of adaptation – to the 'nature of the game', as Steward put it – used by many writers on fishing is similar to that employed by the founders of ecological functionalism. Several authors have pointed out that there has been a tendency, 'something of a *tour de force*' (McCay 1981: 2), to look for parallels between trawling, 'industrial hunting' (Andersen and Wadel 1972), and small-scale fishing. Faris remarks (1977: 235) that a taxonomy which regards such widely different organisational forms as worthy of comparison on the grounds of their common link to water makes as much sense as 'a biological classification which lumps together whales, fish, and submarines and separates them from bats, birds and airplanes'. From this perspective, the category of fishing is a clumsy taxonomic lumpfish.

Not only does the materialist emphasis conceal differences between fishing societies, it also ignores differences between the fishing activities of humans and those of other species. Ingold argues (1986: 252–3) that in Steward's discussion (1955) of the band, social organisation reduces to a behavioural pattern, an instrumental apparatus pertaining to ecological or material relations and not the social relations of production, and that such an approach makes no distinction between the sociality of animals and the purposive activity of socially-constituted human beings. The same may be said of many accounts of 'co-adventure' in fishing. Thus, the comparative work of Hornell (1950) deliberately correlates the fishing activities of humans and animals. Hornell describes the purposeful action of pelicans which follow a familiar plan when they drive schools of fish into shallow water. Such 'co-operative' fishing, he says, is 'carried out *in much the same way*' as the fish-drives of Indian villagers (p. 29, emphasis added).

Figure 2.1 *Fishing with cormorants* (from Hornell 1950)

In Japan, we are told, humans sometimes fish with the aid of cormorants (see Figure 2.1). A group of cormorants, which have a ring of metal around the lower part of their necks, spread out in their search for fish and when one is caught it is swallowed. If the fish is small it passes the ring and becomes the 'perquisite of the bird', but if too large to pass it remains in the gullet pouch. Every now and then the 'master' lifts the bird from the water and lets it disgorge the contents of the pouch.

While there is no mention of the social relations of humans in Hornell's account, the cormorants are said to be 'exceedingly jealous of their rank and of the privileges belonging to seniority' (1950: 32). But even though both birds and humans interact with each other in the process of extracting fish, and in both cases some may be more equal than others, it would be wrong to assume that both groups are doing 'the same', as Hornell implies. Just as the spider does not 'hunt' when it captures insects (see Ingold 1987: 95) – in the sense that, unlike humans, it captures its prey without any consciousness of self and time – the cormorant does not fish. Hornell's account of fishing as the application of a technique may be somewhat extreme, but many attempts at defining and classifying production systems similarly emphasise technical relations and types of activity.

One way to understand similarities and differences among fishing systems, to emphasise the *social* context of production, is to distinguish between societies in terms of mode of circulation – the motivation of the producers and the destination of the products. There are two modes of circulation in the sense that production may be primarily for exchange or primarily for use. In the former case where production is motivated by the accumulation of profit and capital, in market economies, production targets are indefinite. What matters, from the point of view of the producer, are abstract exchange values, not concrete goods or use values. In the other case, the 'domestic mode of production' (Sahlins 1972), production is motivated by the subsistence needs of the domestic unit. The household unit is not a self-sufficient one, but given the emphasis on use values and livelihood, production is set low and resources consequently under-used. Summing up the evidence in relation to hunter-gatherers, Barnard and Woodburn argue that the theory has stood up well to ethnographic research, emphasising that it is not *wants* that are set low but production targets (1988: 12). The theory of the domestic mode of production was developed earlier in relation to peasant economies. Chayanov's theory predicts that there is a 'natural' limit to peasant production in that the intensity of labour is proportional to the total needs of the household, including the ratio of consumers to workers, taxes, and debts.

Many economic anthropologists have made use of Chayanov's theory (see, for example, Durrenberger 1984a).

Restrictions of access to resources: closure and tenure

Another way to compare fishing systems is to distinguish between modes of access to resources. This distinction merits some discussion because of the important conceptual and practical issues involved. For some time it was generally assumed that, since fishermen are usually unable to control the resource-base they exploit, the seas have everywhere and always been open to all. Pastner suggested, for instance, that 'among fishermen cross-culturally there is ... a characteristic policy of viewing the sea as a collective resource' (1980: 17). Norr and Norr even declared that 'there are no reports of fishermen asserting rights to specific fishing areas' (1978: 166). Recently a number of anthropological studies have shown beyond doubt the falsity of such statements, pointing out that in many fishing societies people have developed indigenous means of regulating access to fishing grounds (see, for instance, Durrenberger and Pálsson 1987b; McCay and Acheson 1987; Berkes 1989; Cordell 1989; Pinkerton 1989). In some cases, local groups of users successfully control the reproduction of renewable resources without external intervention, effectively 'co-managing' local resources (Jentoft 1989). In Asia and the Pacific, the ownership of fishing territories has a very long history and such coastal regimes have been well documented (see, for example, Ruddle and Akimichi 1984; Ruddle and Johannes 1985).

It would be wrong, however, to view ethnographic reports about restrictive access to aquatic resources and fishing space as entirely new phenomena. Early reports on Californian Indians, for instance, contain numerous references to the appropriation of fishing places. Waterman's work is particularly outspoken in this respect. Waterman argues that among the Yurok fishing places represent 'private holdings', 'a primitive form of real estate' (1920: 218). Ownership of fishing places was inherited (often through females) and contracted in marriage negotiations. As a result, the property holdings of an individual or a single family were often scattered over a large area. Private fishing places, typically pools where a dip-net could be used for catching salmon, 'were owned by individuals. They could be sold, bartered, and bequeathed like any other property, and they changed hands quite frequently. Their value depended on the number of fish they supplied...' (Waterman 1920: 219). In practice, Waterman argues, the rules of ownership of fishing places were highly complex. Some places were jointly owned by several individuals, others were owned by one man 'for salmon' and by another 'for eel', and still others were appropriated by squatting on them if the 'original' owner had been forgotten. Kroeber makes similar remarks for the Patwin. Some fishing places, he argues, are 'privately owned', 'used only with consent, part of the catch being given the owner' (Kroeber 1932: 277).[4] While such ethnographic reports were neither unique at the time nor restricted to river fishing or North American Indians, they remained largely forgotten. In Murdock's *Ethnographic Atlas* (1967), one may note, there is some information on 'property rights' in relation to land and rules for inheritance, but no information at all is provided on restrictions of access to aquatic resources.

Anthropologists, then, have demonstrated beyond doubt that access to fishing territories is often restricted. There remains, however, a conceptual disagreement as to how to account for property rights, how to define the concept of property, and how to interpret restrictions of access. In *Moby Dick* (Chapter 88), Herman Melville discusses the problem of deciding when wild animals in a state of nature, 'loose fish' as he called them, become somebody's property or 'fast fish'. Did a whale become fast fish as soon as a whaler invested his labour in the chase or, later on, at the moment of capture? For Melville and his fellow whalers the problem of deciding what constitutes property was often a pressing one: 'after a weary and perilous chase and capture of a whale, the body may get loose from the ship by reason of a violent storm; and drifting far away to leeward, be retaken by a second whaler, who in a calm, snugly tows it alongside, without risk of life or line' (1962: 422). In drawing the contrast between the 'weary' chase of the first whaler and the 'snugly' capture of the second, Melville seems to opt for a labour-theory of property, much like the one of Locke, which suggests that one becomes an owner of a thing by mixing one's labour with it. Melville's problem has often been discussed in real life with reference to the famous court-case of *Pierson v. Post* which attracted the attention of New York judges in 1805, a case that continues to intrigue students of property institutions and human-environmental relations (see, for instance, Rose 1985; McEvoy

1988). This case involves a contest between two fox hunters. One hunter had chased and flushed his prey when another hunter entered the scene, shot the animal, and carried it away. The majority of the court agreed with the second hunter. The fox, they reasoned, remained in a 'state of nature' (*ferae naturae*) until someone took possession of it by performing a clear act, by capturing the fox or killing it. By extension, the court abandoned the theories of Melville and Locke. A fish stops being 'loose' and becomes 'fast' at the moment of capture, not before. Such a definition of property was not only clear-cut and time-saving for judges; it also encouraged hunters to compete against each other, thereby making hunting more efficient.[5] Rose points out (1985: 75) that while an examination of the ways in which title to wild animals is acquired may seem a silly, academic question, the analogy of the wild animal continues to show up when courts have to make decisions on a non-statutory basis about 'fugitive' resources that are being appropriated for the first time. Oyster planting in New Jersey is one example. In this case American courts had to decide whether planting oysters in natural spots where oysters grew naturally entailed private property or not. The court decided in 1808 that oysters in unnatural beds were 'tame' and therefore subject to property claims, while oysters planted in natural beds were 'wild', an 'abandonment' comparable to capturing a deer in a forest and setting it free again, making it fair game for anyone (see McCay 1984: 25).

The issue of ownership of aquatic resources, of course, continues to have important practical implications. It is also an issue which touches upon larger theoretical discussions of the relationship between the individual and the collective. A labour-theory of property may well hold cross-culturally in that, generally, people seem to assume that 'whatever I, as an individual, obtain from nature or make by myself using my own labour is residually recognized as in some sense my property' (Barnard and Woodburn 1988: 23). Possessions, however, take many forms and, moreover, they should not be seen to reside in the autonomous individual. Adopting a social or constitutive view of the individual, allows one to locate the issue of property – to search for the roots of title and possession – in the community of persons. As Ingold argues (1987: 227), 'the chain of property can neither begin with individuals nor end in the resources they procure; rather it must end where it began, in the community of nurture from which spring the producers and in which the food is consumed'. Given a constitutive model of the producer, the act of possession derives its power – its 'illocutionary force', as speech-act theorists would have it – not from an 'external', superorganic script, nor from the natural powers of the self-contained individual, but from the momentum of social life itself.

One of the conceptual issues raised in the growing anthropological literature on appropriative regimes, often referred to by the label of 'territoriality', involves the distinction between the spatial and the social. Some anthropologists subscribe to what may be called a *proxemic* approach in that they tend to talk about appropriative regimes in terms of a spatial continuum. (The term 'proxemic' is borrowed from Hall who used it to refer to the ways in which humans structure and use space in face-to-face interaction (Watson 1970).) While followers of the proxemic model in the human sciences are unlikely to agree with biologists who claim that the general function of territorial behaviour in the animal kingdom is 'to gain property rights' (see Jolly 1972: 140), the proxemic approach in the comparative study of humans emphasises, much like that of biologists, that restrictions of access differ in degree rather than kind, and, furthermore, that their application and development in different societies and historical contexts are explicable in terms of a single analytical model of territoriality. Hall suggests that somewhere along the proxemic continuum there is private territory, a broad category including, beside landed property, a beggar's beat and a man's 'favourite chair' (Watson 1970: 35). For Sack, a geographer who uses the term 'territoriality' in a general sense for spatial strategies developed in order to influence people and resources, the task of the theory of territoriality is 'to disclose the possible effects of territoriality at levels that are both general enough to encompass its many forms, and yet specific enough to shed light on its particular instances' (Sack 1986: 216). Levine (1984) presents three different types of 'ownership' or controlled access in New Zealand – each of which is a response to a particular degree of 'social distance' or 'community connectedness' – as lying on a punctuated continuum. As long as the people defending territorial claims speak of 'ownership' they must be regarded as 'owners': 'To deny the significance of . . . ownership because it is not recognized by the state', he says, 'seems ethnocentric' (p. 97). Cashdan (1983) and some others have argued that the characteristics and manner of territorial control in different societies are similar, differing mainly with respect to ecological factors that determine the cost-benefit ratio for various forms of defence – in particular, the density of distribution of a resource and its predictability. Smith (1988) develops a similar analysis. While he distinguishes between several ways of managing territorial access, he emphasises that different land-tenure systems in hunter-gatherer societies should be seen as a continuum and that 'the labelling of types and enumeration of their characteristics is heuristic rather than typological in intent' (p. 246). Acheson discusses restrictions of access to fishing space in similar terms, suggesting that different appropriative regimes are best regarded as responses to uncertainties, particularly ecological ones (1989: 375). No doubt, knowledge of the species fished (mobile versus stationary), technology (the gear used), and environmental features (bottom characteristics), to some extent allows one to account for differences in territorial control (see, for instance, Levieil and Orlove 1990 on Peruvian fishing).

While knowledge of ecology and fishing techniques is important for the understanding of different forms of managing access to fishing space, one should not ignore the social space in which they occur. Different ways of managing access – for instance, the informal exclusion of outsiders by means of secrecy, the division of total allowable catch into quotas, and the formal, communal ownership of local territories – should not be regarded as functionally equivalent proxemic devices. To subsume every form of restriction of access under the label of 'territoriality' is simplistic ethnography. Equally, to refer to them with the Western label of 'ownership' seems ethnocentric. Applying spatial or proxemic criteria alone, we may distinguish between systems with 'open access', with no limitations of access of any kind, and systems with restricted access. Adopting a *social* approach to the issue of territorial access, considering the social system of the producers, allows one to make a further important distinction – namely, between 'tenure' and 'closure' (see Figure 2.2). Relations of tenure, property relations, are means of disproportionately appropriating resources within given boundaries. While closure also involves erecting and maintaining spatial boundaries and excluding outsiders, and sometimes with success, it does not, in contrast to tenure, involve social appropriation of the resources themselves. The distinction between closure and tenure, then, underlines the fact that while territorial access may be 'closed' or restricted, the resources need not at the same time be appropriated as property. On Ponam Island in Papua New Guinea, for instance, 'ownership' of fishing territories or uncaught fish 'in no way denotes rank of any sort, . . . what is reserved . . . is the right to catch the species, not the right to eat it or to enjoy first fruits' (Carrier and Carrier 1989: 104). Closure occurs in a variety of contexts: skippers may occupy the same fishing location for extended periods, as I argue later on in relation to Icelandic fishing, by misleading their competitors or by threatening them to destroy their gear. Local groups of fishermen using different kinds of fishing gear may agree upon privileges of access merely to prevent conflicts and the intermingling and loss of gear. And sacred grounds may be demarcated for religious purposes, for the purpose of identification, or for preventing over-exploitation. What I am referring to as 'closure', is often referred to as 'territoriality' in the literature on hunter-gatherers.[6] I prefer to speak of 'closure' when speaking of humans, simply because of the general biological and ethological connotations of the concept of 'territoriality'.

Given the distinction between 'open access' and 'closure', the appropriation of fishing space is only a matter of *degree*. Some territorial claims may be strong while others are weak. The contrast with 'tenure', on the other hand, is a matter not of degree but of *kind*. What counts is the character of the social relations involved,

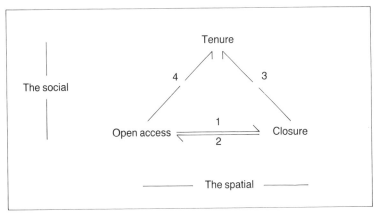

Figure 2.2   *Three ways of appropriating fishing space*

the presence or absence of relations of property. Resources are either ownable or non-ownable. I am not suggesting that this is the only distinction of relevance for the discussion of the ways in which people appropriate fishing space. Indeed, a refinement of concepts denoting property and spatial access would be a worthwhile task for a human ecology of fisheries. I should also emphasise – and this follows from the argument about the social nature of the individual presented above – that the act of closure is every bit as social as a property claim. I am merely emphasising the importance of paying attention to social differences among appropriative regimes, differences which have often been ignored in the literature. It is essential to recognise such differences if one wants to understand evolutionary change.

Indeed, an important anthropological problem is to understand the adaptive and evolutionary significance of systems of appropriation – of their construction, logic and historical transformation. It may be helpful to refer again to the triangle of Figure 2.2, this time paying particular attention to the arrows indicating a change from one mode of access to another. Open access is characteristic of hunter-gatherers. Among the Batek of the rain forest of Malaysia, where most food resources are relatively abundant, resources are regarded as non-ownable, and no attempts are made to restrict access to them. The Batek 'are not territorial in any of the usual senses of the term' (Endicott and Endicott 1986: 140). No doubt, as pointed out above, the change from open access to closure, represented by arrow number 1 in the figure, is related to ecological variables. Ecology, however, does not fully account for variability in closure. The Endicotts conclude that the models of systems ecology do not provide adequate explanations for the absence of territoriality among the Batek, emphasising that territoriality 'is not merely a relationship between people and their resources, but also one between people and other people' (p. 158).

Closure is not necessarily a permanent state of affairs for it can easily be reversed. Arrow number 2 represents groups that reverse back to open access. Some production may take place in open territories while some resources are subject to territorial constraints. As a group places less emphasis on the latter, for whatever reasons, it becomes less territorial. Arrow number 3 represents the transition from closure to tenure. It may be argued that such a change is more likely among sedentary groups than among more mobile ones. As

I argued above, hunters and gatherers of aquatic resources are typically of the former category. Generally, the change from closure to tenure is not a reversible one; once territories are defined as property they tend to remain so. The evolution of tenure is not a matter of a gradual change, but a quantum leap, a transformation in social relations.

In state societies, access to fishing territories is often restricted by informal 'territorial' means, by 'closure'. In the lobster fishery of Maine in the United States, described by Acheson (1988) and Bowles and Bowles (1989), to have access to fishing space means to belong to a harbour 'gang', to respect its rules and to identify with its members. Access to fishing areas is negotiated among informal groups of fishermen. Similarly among crabbers and shrimpers in the Gulf of Mexico, a communal, territorial system of 'self regulation' has developed (Overbey 1989). How such informal rights are translated into formal property institutions remains a puzzle to anthropologists, no less than resource managers and indigenous producers in different parts of the world. Sometimes such a transition takes place within a framework of ethnic conflict whereby indigenous claims are translated into formal rights recognised by the state; see, for example, Davis (1989) on the Yolngu of Australia and Levine on the Maori of New Zealand (1989). Levine shows how, in the midst of an ethnic revival, the Maori managed to gain formal recognition of their traditional fishing rights, after a fierce cultural and legal battle. Native demands for the acknowledgement of cultural rights to resources were 'successfully translated into . . . material claims' (Levine 1989: 31). Libecap (1989) has developed a micro-oriented approach for understanding the bargaining and lobby efforts involved in such cases – the 'contracting' for property rights. The transition from open access to tenure, indicated by arrow number 4, may be exemplified with recent developments in many Western fisheries. During the last years fishing grounds have been appropriated by national authorities which divide the total allowable catch for a season among producers, often the owners of boats. The Icelandic fishery is one example.

The differences among fishing economies emphasised above – in terms of modes of circulation of products and access to resources – insufficiently represent the variety of production systems there is. On the other hand, they help to illustrate the fundamental point that fisheries are embedded in social life. As we will see in later

chapters, such distinctions are helpful analytical tools if one wants
to account for differences in cultural models and cognitive change –
to account for indigenous theories of the 'art' of catching fish.

With European exploration and the discoveries of new worlds
from the fifteenth century onwards, an ever-increasing body of
information regarding the different forms of human society was
accumulated. Bewildered by the perplexity of available data and the
problems they posed for their ethnocentric world-views, Europeans
established typologies for classifying different societies and making
sense of their variability. Somehow the new worlds had to be assimilated. Nineteenth-century evolutionism deliberately addressed
the problem, and so does, by definition, modern anthropology. The
early anthropologists, however, did not only turn to the study
of the 'tribal' stage to assimilate the exotic but also in order to
demolish the familiar. In domesticating the primitive in their discourse, the founders of anthropology constructed a classic image
of the original condition of humanity, a condition fundamentally
different from that of their own society. The general image of the
primitive among early evolutionists accommodated many ideologies
and rhetorical purposes. The 'illusion' of the primitive, as Kuper
remarks, was 'good to think' (1988: 9). Fishing was an important
category, along with other 'arts of subsistence', in many of the
evolutionary schemes of the nineteenth century. With the advent of
fieldwork and modern anthropology, on the other hand, descriptive
accounts tended to replace evolutionary speculations, crude environmentalism was replaced by possibilism, and 'fishing' became
much less visible than before – often being subsumed under the
label 'hunting and gathering'. As I have shown, however, the social
organisation of hunter-gatherers of aquatic resources is significantly
different from that of hunter-gatherers of terrestrial resources.

In Western, agrarian society, fisheries have for long been considered inexhaustible. If they were inexhaustible, there was no need
to claim exclusive rights to aquatic resources or fishing territories
and, as a result, fishing space was generally defined as an open,
undivided territory. Colonial expansion during the sixteenth and
seventeenth centuries further reinforced the legal definition of the
seas as a free territory. Such a definition, formulated by Hugo de
Grotius in 1608 in the well-known and highly influential treatise of
the 'freedom of the seas', became accepted in international law

to further the expansion of European capitalism. Open-access, common property in European fishing, then, is a social institution with a history of its own. While the rationale may have differed from one area to another (American law originally favoured a common-property definition to avoid the kind of suffering that the common man in medieval Europe had experienced as a result of the enclosure of terrestrial commons, the 'tragedy of the commoners' (McCay 1987)), generally, open access was taken for granted in Western law. If open access was regarded as a natural state of affairs in Western fisheries, it is not surprising that many scholars have been 'blinded by a Western conception of the sea' when dealing with fisheries in other parts of the world (Kalland 1990: 188). Sometimes anthropologists and early travellers failed to notice customary restrictions of access to fishing territories simply because ordinarily they associated institutions of property with the land (Cordell 1989: 9).

As we have seen, many approaches to fisheries, both of the present and the past, suggest a 'natural' model of fishing, emphasising material context and ecological relations. Such an approach has important implications for the anthropological understanding of coastal economies and fishing activities. In focusing on extraction and removing 'fishing' from the context of social relations, anthropologists have often failed to recognise the importance of the relations of men and women and the significant economic role of women in fishing economies. The issue of gender, then, tends to be suppressed or distorted due to the application of the 'natural' model. The issue of territorial access, discussed above, is another example. If one follows the 'natural' model of fishing, assuming that fishermen are merely operating on nature, the 'wild', one is likely to assume, as Mauss seemed to do, that resource-use, by definition, cannot be subject to social constraints, the 'tame'. The different kinds of social restrictions that *are* employed with respect to fishing territories tend to be presented as equivalent proxemic devices. An alternative anthropological approach to fisheries is needed which appreciates the social differences between fishing systems.

3 Systems of production and social discourse

In this chapter I discuss production discourse in fishing societies – the ways in which people represent fishing and fisheries to themselves and to others. Some representations, it is often argued, have a primarily utilitarian purpose in the sense that they provide guidance in terms of how to act – for instance, the cognitive maps that fishermen use to find their way on the seascape and to revisit good fishing locations. Such representations are 'recipes for action' (Hunn 1982: 844) or 'models *for*' (Geertz 1973: 93). Other representations are largely constructed for making experience apprehensible – for example, folk accounts of fish, their natures, and relations with humans. In this case, representations seem to transcend the practical sphere as models *of* reality (in Geertz's sense), having 'zero value' (Lévi-Strauss 1963: 159) in that they only give meaning to the society in which they are found. To some extent, however, 'models of' are also 'models for'. They are ways of making the world not only statements of fact or interpretations. And this applies to both folk models and scientific theories. People *invent* their worlds, involving each other in particular kinds of acts which reinforce or transform the worlds of their predecessors. Representations of nature and production, then, are constructed in the course of speech and praxis. Despite their varied purposes and dimensions, different kinds of representations are intimately connected in the flux of social life. Otherwise social discourse would be chaotic and meaningless.

Anthropologists must inevitably address the question of how to make sense of indigenous discourse. How do the products of discourse – the cultural models of the world-makers – relate to social reality? I suggest that a cognitive analysis which conflates the real and the reflective, by assuming that ethnographic realities are no less mind-dependent than symbolic expressions and that everything is symbolic, leaves nothing to understand or explain. I argue that folk accounts of the natural world and human-environmental interaction are based on a fundamentally social logic, emphasising that cognitive representations should not be regarded as given and static but as something created and changed in the course of practical activity. I explore this argument in greater detail in the following chapters with illustrations from Icelandic fishing. Here I briefly examine the comparative literature on representations of fishing activities. I suggest that an anthropological analysis of the initiation and reproduction of models of fishing in social discourse requires understanding of fishing systems.

The relationship between representations and reality

A character in one of the novels of the Icelandic writer Halldór Laxness comments that the difference between a novelist and a historian is that 'the former tells lies deliberately and for the fun of it; the historian tells lies in his simplicity and imagines he is telling the truth' (Laxness 1968: 108). Some of the advocates of 'post-modern' anthropology similarly suggest that ethnographic realities are essentially *manufactured*, for aesthetic or therapeutic purposes (see, for instance, Tyler 1986) – replacing Laxness's historian with the ethnographer. In doing so, they question the reality of the ethnographic. The making of ethnographies, as the saying goes, is 'creative' writing.

No doubt the predicament of the novelist and the ethnographer have something in common. To do ethnography is to familiarise oneself with local action and discourse, to participate in the social life of a particular place, and to report the experience, usually in writing. The way one does the reporting depends on a host of personal and contextual factors, some of which also pertain to the writing of a novel. The discourse of the anthropological mono-graph, therefore, much like that of the novel, is located within a specific historical context. And since the discourse between in-formant and ethnographer is a dialogue carried out in a specific context of power relations, not simply the stating and recording of 'objective' facts, ethnographic 'truth' is far more elusive than strict empiricists like to think. For some anthropologists – notably Geertz (1973), for whom culture is a 'text', offering different kinds of interpretations – the historicity of anthropological understanding justifies the juxtaposition of fiction and ethnography. However, as Spencer points out (1989: 149), the advocates of 'interpretive' anthropology rarely leave much room for interpretation for their readers. In filling the dual role of the maker and the analyst of ethnographic texts, the practitioner of this technique tends to adopt a style of ethnographic writing which eliminates alternative under-standings of the ethnographer's material (a style Spencer calls 'ethnographic naturalism') – in other words, legislating on inter-pretation rather than questioning ethnographic truth. Interpretative liberalism turns out to be an authoritarian ethnography. Contrary to the claims of some of the post-modernists, it is one thing to recognise the limits of objectivism and naïve realism and quite another to abandon the real altogether. Fiction may be better to read than anthropological monographs, but what distinguishes the most incompetent ethnographer from the best of novelists is that the former strives to provide an authentic account of a particular reality, a finite world, while the latter is free to attempt to create independent worlds of fiction. To abandon the real is to abandon anthropology.

Given such a position, students of folk models inevitably face the 'problem of reference', or how to relate cognitive representations to the world external to them. The nature of the connection between the symbolic and the real – the link between 'heaven and earth', to borrow a popular metaphor – is an age-old topic in Western discourse. Plato's dialogue the *Cratylus* discusses the problem in terms of the relation between names and things. Cratylus offers a natural theory of names, arguing that 'everything has a right name of its own, which comes by nature', and that 'there is a kind of inherent correctness in names, which is the same for all men, both Greeks and barbarians' (citation in Harris 1988: 9). Cratylus' opponent Hermogenes disagrees, asserting that names are entirely arbitrary, being a matter of convention and habit. Plato's dialogue has some parallels in anthropological theory. In some respects the naturalism of Cratylus anticipates the Lévi-Straussian thesis (1972) of the ideal knower. According to his structuralism, the properties of the environment are 'naturally' encoded by the human mind. Perception and cognition are seen to be determined by the structure of the brain itself or some mechanistic reading of the external world. No doubt some natural discontinuities – the spectrum of colours and life-forms, for example – are in fact more salient than others for the human mind, since, after all, the human brain and the sense organs are the products of an evolutionary selection process. Humans, just as other animals, are therefore likely to be particu-larly sensitive to some pre-existing structures in the environment presumably essential for survival. From such a perspective, the problem of reference dissolves.

Other anthropologists would argue, following Hermogenes, that knowledge of nature is not a given skill, a property of autonomous individuals, but rather a matter of social convention. While a general theory of human cognition may account for cognitive universals, the manner in which humans organise their world, it cannot account for the many ways of interacting with nature in different societies at different points in time nor the problem of cognitive variability. The cultural meaning attached to natural discontinuities varies from one case to another, since meaning is constructed in social life within a context of action and discourse. The category of nature itself, it is often pointed out, is a social one. As Marx argued (1961: 169), '*nature* ... taken abstractly, for itself – nature fixed in isolation from man – is *nothing* for man'. Nature has many discourses, languages and dialects, but each of them has a social logic or 'grammar'. To illuminate the issue of cultural and temporal variability in representations we need to focus on social relations.

Sociological functionalism offers one way of addressing the problem of reference. For Durkheim (1965), collective representations are 'objective' facts, generated by society. Evans-Pritchard proposes a slightly different sociological analysis of representations – in terms of their 'relation to other beliefs, as part of a system of thought' (1965: 111) – arguing that Durkheim elicits social facts from 'crowd psychology' (p. 68). But the 'relational analysis' suggested by Evans-Pritchard fails to specify an analytical starting point which could possibly replace the crowd psychology he takes to be implicit in Durkheim's thesis. Durkheim and Evans-Pritchard rightly insist that social phenomena are interrelated, but in doing so they abandon the possibility of making causal statements about them. Both are careful not to associate their sociologism with the kind of 'vulgar' materialism which postulates a deterministic relationship between mind and matter. Durkheim argues (1965: 423–4), for instance, that collective consciousness is 'something more than a mere epiphenomenon of its morphological basis'. For Evans-Pritchard any attempt to introduce developmental priority into the analysis of cognitive systems is unsound, even if the necessary information for such an understanding is available. 'I hold', he says, 'that it is not sound scientific method to seek for origins, especially when they cannot be found' (1965: 111).

Cultural determinism is no less circular in reasoning than the functionalism of Durkheim and Evans-Pritchard, for it too accounts for one anthropological explanandum in terms of another. For Sahlins (1976: 57), culture is 'an order that enjoys by its own properties as a symbolic system, a fundamental autonomy'. According to Holy, 'social phenomena . . . are *constituted by meaning* in the sense that they do not exist independently of the cultural meanings which people use to account for them and hence constitute them' (1987: 5–6, emphasis added). French superstructuralists – including Althusser and Baudrillard – carry this tradition to its extreme, deliberately inverting the base-superstructure model. Humans are seen to submit themselves as servants to the forces of language and culture. In such a metaphysical idealism, not only the category of nature is invested with meaning; nature itself is regarded as a cultural construct. Vulgar economic and ecological determinism has similar defects, strange as it may sound. In seeking to unfold the causal connection between ecology and representation, Marvin Harris (1980), for instance, presents cultural institutions as infrastructural steering mechanisms independent of the projects of the people who make them, alienating people from their mental constructs. In such an approach, the rationality of bounded and balanced ecosystems – with their energy flows, cybernetics and negative feedbacks – is regarded as an autonomous reality with a logic independent of social relations.

The economy, it is often argued, occupies different positions in different societies. If this is the case, 'economic' categories of explanation are anthropologically inadequate; they may be useful for understanding some societies but they are less adequate when applied to others. In his recent critique of economic explanations, Godelier goes even further. For him, the shifting place of the economy in the real world is not the only problem. He argues that a general translation problem is involved, pointing out that the terms 'infrastructure' (or economic base) and 'superstructure' fail to capture the meaning of *Grundlage* and *Überbau*, the terms used by Marx. Such translations, he argues (1986: 7), often suggest a model of society as a stratified structure with unequal layers (as a 'cake'), reducing superstructure to 'an impoverished reality'. Godelier, however, fails to clarify the issue of reference. For him, the mental 'can under no circumstances be simply reduced to reflections in thought of material relations originating outside it, prior to and independent of it' (pp. 10–11). Accordingly, he suggests: 'the *Überbau* is a construction, an edifice which rises up on foundations, *Grundlage*; and it is a house we live in, not the foundations' (1986: 6–7). I would argue, employing a similar metaphor, that *Grundlage* (not the *Überbau*) is the household itself – social life or the human *Oikos* – while *Überbau* encompasses representations of it in social discourse – in short, what it means to live in the household and be part of it. Godelier seems to abandon the analytical priority of the social, asserting that 'every social relation exists both in thought and outside it' (1986: 11). Unexpectedly, his marxism agrees with some of the principles of interpretive anthropology.

The three kinds of logic already mentioned – circular sociology, cultural determinism, and vulgar materialism – do not exhaust the possibilities of anthropological explanation. To humanise the architectural view expressed by Godelier, we need to redefine the household of human life with social beings – the members of the household – in mind, rather than the dwellings. This demands that we return to the social or constitutive model of the producer, to the concept of mode of production 'in the full sense' (Thompson 1977: 264). Such a model does not require that we abandon the distinction between the symbolic and the real. On the contrary, as Ingold argues, we reaffirm it:

... culture alone is symbolic in that it represents conduct, furnishing a set of ideal 'meanings' to which conduct may be referred. Social life, to the contrary, is the intentional presentation of that which is represented in culture. Constituting consciousness rather than models in consciousness, social relations ... *are* the reality (Ingold 1986: 336–7).

In such a scheme, the Marxian concept of *Grundlage* is rendered as 'social relations' while *Überbau* becomes 'culture'. Given such an anthropological perspective, models of nature are not to be regarded as 'free' or independent phenomena, but as embedded artifacts firmly rooted in production systems.

Contemporary folk models are the result of an historical process and not simply the works of the present. They are mediated by a long process extending into the distant past. But while the past cannot be ignored, there are many ways to act upon it in the present. How, then, are symbolic expressions generated and changed over time? Anthropological theory has rarely dealt with such a question. In general, anthropologists have emphasised a synchronic and static analysis of symbolic systems. For the Durkheimians symbolic innovation is an impossibility, since in their scheme concepts and classifications are necessarily trapped in time, given the Saussurean distinction between the synchronic and the diachronic. The social or superorganic leads its own life independent of the individual; *langue* is immune to *parole*. Consequently, the activities of individuals have no history. The suppression of time similarly prevails among those who advocate the Boasian scheme of the superorganic, the programmatic culture concept. If culture is regarded as an authoritative design for living, a programme which generates behaviour, cultural change cannot possibly be the result of human action. In the approach of Sahlins, for instance, culture is seen to be reproduced by one generation after another independent of context. The cognitive system of the Moalans in Fiji 'seems to develop an immunity to changing circumstances' (Sahlins 1976: 41). The oppositions of land and sea, male and female, Sahlins argues (pp. 42–3), survive a 'variety of historical attacks'.

Similarly, in the structuralism of Lévi-Strauss, myth is a relatively static phenomenon. The temporal and social is reduced to the spatial and ecological, for change only occurs when myths are taken from one kind of environment to another (see Lévi-Strauss 1985). Change, then, is rendered as a cognitive mutation induced by an external force. In this sense, structuralist analysis is analogous to the application of the periodic table of the elements in the laboratory of the chemist; the 'reactions' have no subjects. In such a scheme there is no designer, only designs. To facilitate understanding of how representations are constructed in the course of social life a different approach is needed. Recently, there have been several attempts to accommodate history and agency in social theory (see Giddens 1979; Ortner 1984; Ingold 1986). The view adopted here is that representations are generated in the context of social practices. In the course of social life, utterances and activities are interwoven. Some utterances are reproductions of utterances made some time before and some may even be reiterated time and time again. Others, however, contain the seed of a new kind of discourse, a new model or paradigm. Such shifts in natural language, as Foucault points out in his 'genealogy' of knowledge (1980), are rooted in relations of power; some utterances are suppressed, but others attain the status of an established 'episteme' in the 'regime of truth'.

Cultural constructs: on fish, production and gender

I now return to the cultural representation of fish and fishing activities. In many societies, fish are bred as animal pets. In China goldfish have been domesticated for centuries, and no Chinese home, it seems, is complete without aquariums or pond fish (Tuan 1984: 95). Fish are kept for the pleasure of the pet-keepers, much like dogs and other terrestrial animals. The representations of aquatic species, however, are likely to be different from those of terrestrial ones, for the simple reason that normally fish and humans inhabit different media. Hewes points out that this difference has important implications for the human producer. Since fish are relatively incapable of coping with the producer, their chances of using evasive tactics are very small:

Compared to the relation between the hunter and the hunted animal on land, where the sense organs of both are on a nearly equal basis, *the fisherman holds all the trumps against the fish* (1948: 238, emphasis added).

The difference in medium, however, has contradictory implications and some observers have emphasised the *dis*advantages to the fisherman. If humans are invisible to the fish so are fish to humans. Accordingly, Morrill argues (1967: 407) that folk knowledge of marine organisms is bound to be relatively restricted:

Except for life in very shallow and clear waters, virtually nothing can be known about the inhabitants of the sea except what they look like when (and if) they are caught.

In this sense, fishing is very much the hunting of an invisible prey. The properties of aquatic environments demand that the producers are actively engaged in constructing what goes on underwater on the basis of present and previous catches. The mental operations involved are often similar to those used in long-distance navigation. In both cases, the 'destination' is hidden and, as a result, the coding system or the model for orientation is projected into the air; knowledge of celestial movement and bird life is used to account for and act within or upon the environment (see, for example, Gladwin

1970). The producers build up a model of the ecological relationships that affect their operations, by relating observations of 'events
in the air' and information about catches in the past. Having built a
model, they can then apply it and make inferences about 'events in
the sea'. Much like the archaeologists' pursuit of the past, fishing
entails fundamental problems of inference from a limited set of
facts, in order to transcend the given information.

In many societies, fish are classified according to an elaborate
taxonomy, depending on their shape and usefulness to humans.
Often, however, the category of fish is rather ambiguous. Among
medieval Icelanders, the word 'fish' (fiskur) was often applied
to water-beings in general (sæbúar, literally 'sea-dwellers'). The
Icelandic Sagas provide numerous references to 'whales, seals and
other fish'. The ambiguity of the category of 'fish' (fiskur) continues
into the present, since sometimes 'fish' refers only to cod.[1] Brown
argues (1984: 15) that 'fish' represents one of the largest and most
diverse categories found in most environments and that fish terms
are at times extended to all creatures inhabiting aquatic environments, including turtles, frogs, crocodiles, crustacea and fish-shaped
mammals. In some languages, however, there is no term for fish;
fish are included in a heterogeneous category along with snakes,
worms, lizards and other elongated creatures. In some instances fish
are not eaten since they are considered to be snakes (see Brown
1984: 32).

Fish often serve as mediums for metaphorical expression. An
indication of a preoccupation with fish symbols is provided by
ancient rock art – for instance in Arnhem Land, Australia, where
fish were a powerful symbol signifying life and fertility (Tacon
1989). Not only are fish a convenient medium for metaphorical
expression in that, along with other vertebrates, they leave traces of
their lives long after they are dead, in their fossilised bones. Fish
have an additional physiological property in terms of both shape
and colour (summarised by the concept of 'rainbowness') which
has great symbolic potential, particularly for visual expression.
From the point of view of the Aboriginal people fish were 'good to
paint' (Tacon 1989: 245).

In some cases fish are used as a medium for talking about social
relations. In Shakespeare's Pericles, one of the characters comments,
'I marvel how the fishes live in the sea' to which another responds:
'Why, as men do a-land – The great ones eat up the little ones'.

Ethnographically, the metaphorical role of fish has been documented by, for instance, Anderson (1969), Cove (1978), Knipe (1984), and Firth (1981). Firth argues (p. 220) that among the Tikopia, fish have been an 'outstanding' metaphor: on some occasions fish are described as pets, as being dependent on humans. Humans are said to be superior to fish in their strength and skills. Fish are exposed to a one-way ritual communication, and sometimes caught by the fisherman's devices. On other occasions, however, the Tikopians reverse the relations between fish and humans. Fish are said to be superior agents; they are aggressive, free, evasive, and able to manipulate humans. Firth suggests that the Tikopia treatment of fish may be represented as a series of asymmetrical but balanced relations.

The ethnographic examples just cited contradict some anthropological statements about totemism. Lévi-Strauss suggests in a well-known passage that some life-forms are better than others for metaphorical language, and that birds are particularly suitable:

Birds . . . can be permitted to resemble men for the very reason that they are so different . . . they form a community which is independent of our own but, precisely because of this independence, appears to us like another society, homologous to that in which we live; birds love freedom; they build themselves homes in which they live a family life and nurture their young; they often engage in social relations with other members of their species; and they communicate with them by acoustic means recalling articulated language (1972: 204).

According to Lévi-Strauss, then, humans tend to think of the bird world as separate but parallel to human society and, therefore, as a particularly convenient metaphor. Later, Lévi-Strauss seems to have taken the view that the choice of species for symbolic expression is entirely arbitrary, arguing that each culture decides on some distinctive features of the environment and that 'none can predict which these are or to what end they will be put' (1985: 103). Some anthropologists have argued, however, following the earlier suggestion of Lévi-Strauss regarding the metaphorical role of birds, that fish are rarely used as metaphors of human society. Kleivan argues that while fish are separated from humans by the element in which they move – even further removed than birds, since they are cold-blooded, live in the water, have fins instead of legs and multiply by spawn – they have few points of resemblance with human beings: 'they do not build homes in which they live a family life and nurture their young, and they do not communicate by acoustic means similar to articulated language' (1984: 887).

Surprisingly, Kleivan follows her generalisations with an analysis of an Inuit myth which metaphorically represents a human family as a fish world. Kleivan's statement does not, however, only contradict the ethnographic record. It is also contrary to much ethological evidence. Darwin observed long ago that 'fishes . . . make various noises, some of which are described as being musical' (1952: 444) and that some groups of fishermen even catch fish by imitating the sounds they make. Darwin also pointed out that 'certain fishes . . . make nests, and some of them take care of their young when hatched' (p. 443). Among Malay fishermen, one may note, the 'hearing' of fish is an acknowledged and important expertise (Firth 1946: 199). On the other hand, ethological evidence need not necessarily concern us as the evidence is in any case beyond the awareness or recognition of many fishermen. In Icelandic, one may note, a person who remains quiet is said to be 'silent as fish' (*pögull sem fiskur*).

Many folk models of fishing economies are gender specific, treating women's labour as not only different but also somehow secondary to that of men. In nineteenth-century Cornwall, for instance, only the work of men at sea was regarded as 'productive'; women's labour ashore in relation to the processing of the catch was presented as auxiliary and unproductive (Cove 1978). The male:female boundary coincided with that of the aquatic:terrestrial and the productive:unproductive. In some cases native classifications of food-getting activities also exhibit a male bias. Among the Niuans of Polynesia, for instance, smaller fish procured by women are said to be merely 'picked up' like shellfish, while the pursuit of big fish is regarded as 'proper' hunting (Kirch and Dye 1979: 65). Similarly, the Miskito Indians of Nicaragua make a distinction between the procuring of 'flesh' (small game and shellfish) and the hunting of 'meat' (sea turtles), the latter activity being restricted to men (Nietschmann 1972: 55). The procurement of small game and shellfish does not entail much prestige, there is no formality associated with the division of the catch, and the food is consumed by the immediate family of the producer. The hunting of turtles, in contrast, is a highly prestigious activity, and the kill is carefully divided among kinsfolk of the hunter. Chipewyan culture is known for its extreme 'devaluation' of women and their contributions. Chipewyans emphasise that males (the sole possessors of *inkoze* and hunters of game) are predators, while women (the processors of food) are scavengers, dependent on men: 'the roles of male and female, in a public sense, place the former in the position of highly valued, active hunter and the latter as low-valued, passive, continuously working drudge. This view is built into the symbolic system and continuously reinforced' (Sharp 1981: 235). Sharp adds that in practice the situation is often quite different from the model and that the 'public' distinction between food production and food processing does not hold at the 'private' level. Both men and women can, in fact often do, survive on their own for weeks or months at a time (Sharp 1981: 237). In such circumstances both men and women must produce and process food.

The devaluation of women's work is not restricted to folk accounts. Karen Endicott argues that the extent of the pursuit of small mobile animals by women has been obscured by a systematic observers' bias (see Ingold 1987: 87). Such pursuit has been regarded as mere 'gathering' or 'collecting' if performed by women, but as 'hunting' or 'fishing' if performed by men. As I have argued, Western society tends to project a 'manly' image on to fishing. The collection of molluscs in particular has often been dismissed as insignificant by Western observers. The explorer would not recognise those people, mainly women, who were engaged in the mundane collection of relatively stationary shellfish. Morgan (1928 [1877]) does not mention shellfishing at all in his influential account of 'ethnical periods'; it cannot belong to the earliest period in his scheme of human history ('Savagery') which was restricted to the collection of fruits and nuts. Meehan points out that shellfish have a 'fairly consistently bad press' (1982: 8), citing Linnaeus' opinion of cold and slippery animals as 'a horrible, naked and gruesome rabble', and the Biblical taboo of *Leviticus*: 'And all that have not fins and scales in the seas, and in the rivers, of all that move in the waters, and of any living thing which is in the waters, they shall be an abomination unto you: . . . ye shall not eat their flesh'. Meehan speculates whether such taboos might reflect deeper psychological factors, pointing out that shellfish are sometimes eaten raw (which some people find disturbing) and that some species of shellfish are recognised as symbolic of the female genitalia, by both collectors and taxonomists (e.g. *Modiolus vagina*). No wonder, she concludes, judgements of the people who eat such food become clouded. Being mostly male, Western explorers had difficulty in getting information on women's contributions to subsistence. And no doubt some of them were interested only in what the males were doing; women were simply not the focus of their enquiry. Lubbock (1913 [1869]: 441), for instance, makes a clear conceptual distinction between 'the natives' and 'their wives' in his account of the Australians in his *Prehistoric Times*: 'the natives (are not) able to kill whales for themselves, but when one is washed ashore it is a real godsend to them . . . They rub themselves all over with blubber, and anoint their favourite wives in the same way'. Such a bias is not simply a relic from the distant past. Marilyn Porter notes that anthropologists who have worked in Newfoundland fishing communities have hardly talked to women (see Thompson 1985: 25). Chapman shows (1987) that women's fishing has generally been overlooked in subsistence studies in Oceania. In their review of the anthropological literature on fishing economies Nadel-Klein and Davis imply (1988: 18) that women's roles and involvement have generally been ignored.

In fishing communities generally, it has sometimes been suggested, 'one could reasonably expect a sharp division of labour along sexual lines' (Faris, cited in Andersen and Wadel 1972: 141) in that men do the fishing while women are responsible for the processing of the catch. Even though in modern fishing economies the division of labour is often along gender lines, a rigid sexual division of labour should not be regarded as 'natural' or inevitable. In many cases women's participation in fishing is no less important than that of men. Thompson (1985), Chapman (1987), and Nadel-Klein and Davis (1988) cite many relevant ethnographic examples. According to Murdock's (1967) *Ethnographic Atlas*, one may note, women's role in fishing is greater or equal to that of men among the Ainu, Andaman Islanders, Alacaluf, Chippewa, Ellice, Kaska, Mimika, Tareumiut, Tokelau, and Yahgan – in 10 of the 102 fishing societies represented in the *Atlas*.

One important difference among folk models of fishing regards the notion of agency. In some models, the producers are presented as inactive recipients in a system largely beyond their control, as vehicles for the transport of value and energy. Such models employ a *passive* notion of human labour. Other models present the producers as creative agents with an instrumentality of their own, employing a *generative* notion of labour. Production models also differ in the extent to which they accredit particular individuals with a greater amount of productivity than others. Some models pay little or no attention to a comparison of individual contributions. In other models some producers are said to have a far greater production-value than others.

Concepts and social context: an hypothesis

How could we account for the fact that relations with aquatic species are constructed in different ways in different societies? Some anthropologists have extended the Marxian approach to production systems, usually restricted to human relations, to the analysis of relations with animals: to 'human-animal relations of production' (Tapper 1988: 52). Among hunter-gatherers, Tapper argues, relations with animals are often construed as ones of co-operation. In other production systems, he goes on, people think of their relations with animals in different terms; pastoralists, for instance, employ the metaphor of the feudal contract, settled farmers speak of draft animals as 'slaves', and urbanites think of factory animals as mere sources of surplus and profit. Such a 'political-economy' approach to the animate world, emphasising the nature of human-animal relations, might explain some differences in modelling, those of fish-farming and sea-ranching, for instance. On the other hand, it can hardly explain variability in models among those engaged in the pursuit of 'wild', undomesticated fish.

Some anthropologists have attempted to account for indigenous models of fishing in terms of ecological and technical constraints. Brandt implies, for instance, that the competitiveness and individualism of Korean fishing is a reflection of the nature of the resources exploited. He argues that due to differences in 'cycles and patterns of activity' (1971: 65), fishing and farming are spoken of in quite different terms: 'In contrast to farming, fishing is regarded as highly speculative, and investment, profit, and losses are often spoken of in terms similar to those used for gambling' (p. 62). Stiles attempts (1972: 48) to explain a very different model of fishing in a Newfoundland fishing community – involving the desire to maximise uniformity within the local fleet – in similar terms, referring to the 'nature of the exploitative pattern'. Further examples are provided in the ethnography of Shetland fishing. Goodlad suggests

(1972) that the role of expertise is related to the kind of technology employed. During the period of the peasant economy, Shetlanders fished for herring with drift nets, a 'passive' technology. The fishermen placed the nets and hoped to catch fish, and no one was personally held responsible for success or failure. Later on the Shetlanders began to use the 'active' ring net, hunting herring schools and surrounding them with the net. Goodlad implies that the ring net made more 'competitive demands' (p. 69) than the earlier drift net and, as a result, the skipper was made responsible for the success of fishing operations. Byron (1986: 119–25) likewise attributes changes in notions of fishing success in the Shetlands to changes in boat design, fishing techniques, and the physical arrangement of crewmen during fishing.

No doubt, ecological and technical factors are relevant for understanding differences in the organisation of fishing. For one thing, the nature of the species exploited (mobile or stationary) limits the range of potential fishing gear. And the gear used, in turn, affects interactive patterns among fishermen, as Barth pointed out (1966) in his famous account of Norwegian herring crews. One would also expect organisational differences to be somehow related to differences in models of fishing. For instance, one would assume that, other things being equal, fishermen who fish individually, using handlines, would construct theories of fishing activities different from those of trawlermen who co-operate in teams, using more complex gear. Generally, however, the explanatory value of ecological and technical factors is fairly limited – given our present concern, the different ways in which people speak about fishing activities. Hypotheses that emphasise the organisation of fishing simply do not seem to be confirmed by the comparative evidence (see Pálsson and Durrenberger 1983). Models of production often undergo significant changes *despite* the fact that people are exploiting the same fishing stocks as before, even under the same ecological conditions – the Shetlands case just mentioned being an illustration. Also, some groups of fishermen using passive gear *do* invoke personal explanations of differential success – the lobster fishermen of Maine, to mention one example (Acheson 1988). Furthermore, models of fishing are not only informed by what happens on fishing boats. As I argued earlier, no fisherman – no crew or a fleet, for that matter – is an island unrelated to the world ashore, the community to which fishermen belong. The reasons why people invoke different kinds of explanations of fishing in different contexts cannot, therefore, be purely ecological or technical. More likely, the temporal and cultural variability in models evident from the ethnography reflect differences in human relations.

In Chapter 2 I distinguish between different modes of circulation (production for use versus production for exchange) and different modes of access to resources (systems where fishing territories are non-ownable versus ones where areas of the sea are subject to relations of property). Combining the modes of circulation and access, enables us to distinguish four kinds of fishing societies, represented by categories 1 to 4 in Figure 3.1. The modes pertaining to circulation and access are not unrelated. Both are embedded in social relations, and change in one mode may be accompanied by a change in the other. In some cases, for instance, traditional licensing systems have broken down with the development of a market economy – 'when resources are converted to cash rather than gathered for village consumption' (Haines and Johannes, cited in Pernetta and Hill 1983: 189). In some other cases, however, the development of the market economy seems to have had the opposite result for access (see Kalland 1988: 169). Clearly, there is no intrinsic relationship between mode of circulation and mode of access. Whatever the connection between them, the particular combination of circulation and access in each case is likely to influence the construction of folk theories of production.

Now I explore the comparative potential of this model with reference to the ethnography of fishing. The first production system

		MODE OF CIRCULATION	
		For use	For exchange
ACCESS	Non-ownership	1	3
TO *RESOURCES*	Ownership	2	4

Figure 3.1 *A social model of fishing economies*

in the model, the one where resources are non-ownable and where production is focused on use values, may be represented by hunter-gatherer societies. This is not to say that these societies are necessarily a unified category. One may, for instance, distinguish between systems with delayed and immediate return (Woodburn 1980), intensive storage and no storage at all (Testart 1982). As I argued in Chapter 2, some hunter-gathering societies are more hierarchical than others, depending on the kind of resource-base used – whether it is aquatic or terrestrial. For present purposes, however, such differences may legitimately be ignored. Given the ceiling on production and the emphasis on use values in hunter-gatherer societies, differences among individual producers are unlikely to be emphasised. Lee provides an interesting account (1984) of attitudes towards hunting success among the Dobe !Kung in the Kalahari. Here, the news of a successful kill are typically met with indifference, even hostility. While men are encouraged to hunt, the successful hunter is expected to be modest and to understate the size of his kill. There may be short-term differences in hunting success, but they tend to be levelled out by joking, insults and gossip. A local healer explains the reasons in the following manner:

When a . . . man kills much meat, he comes to think of himself as a chief or big man, and he thinks of the rest of us as his servants or inferiors. We can't accept this. We refuse one who boasts, for someday his pride will make him kill somebody. So we always speak of his meat as worthless. In this way we cool his heart and make him gentle (see Lee 1984: 49).

Hunter-gatherer society, then, is characterised by an egalitarian ethos – sharing and generalised reciprocity. Lee defines this ethos as 'primitive communism': 'a useful way of looking at primitive communism is to visualize a ceiling of accumulation of goods above which nobody can rise, with the corollary that there is also a floor below which one cannot sink' (Lee 1988: 267).

If each producer *expects* to succeed and differences among producers are suppressed, as is typically the case among hunter-gatherers, one can reasonably expect to find passive notions of human labour. Examples of such modelling abound in the literature on the societies being discussed. The animals are said to be offered to humans. Humans, animals and spirits are said to engage in a complex series of transactions. In the model of the Mistassini Cree, for instance, wild animal species are seen to bend to the will of a spiritual agent, their 'animal master' – much like domesticated dogs do to that of their owner, the hunter (Tanner 1979: 139). The hunting and killing of animals, consequently, does not simply involve the application of human skills and energy *upon* the animate world, but rather a dialogue or exchange which is often patterned after human relationships. Hunting activities are regarded as love affairs where hunters are 'seduced' by their prey. Similarly, in Chipewyan society hunters must enter into relationships with game animals in order to have any success (Sharp 1988: 185). Prey animals may refuse to be killed and to make the animal consent to its death, the hunter must possess a particular magical power, *inkoze*. Only if properly applied, will the animal offer itself to the hunter.

The first kind of production system not only includes hunters and gatherers but also some peasant societies. In this case, the concept of private ownership is applied to some resource-bases, in particular the soil and domesticated animals, while the sea remains non-ownable. Traditional small-scale fishing in Cape Verde is one example (see Pálsson 1990b). Fishermen use small wooden boats, all of which have outboard motors. Each boat has an individual style that is associated with the household to which it belongs. The boat is usually painted in two or more bright colours. Not only are boats numbered to comply with official safety regulations, they also have a name. Some boats are named after a Catholic saint, others are named after a local person (often a woman), and still others have idiosyncratic non-human names. To the peasant fisherman the boat is a personal instrument for the satisfaction of household needs. But while the folk model emphasises the 'individuality' of boats and other personal belongings, differences among fishermen in terms of their ability to fish are rarely discussed. Crews – a foreman (*mestre*), who is in charge during fishing operations, and 2–3 ordinary fishermen – are stable groupings of relatives, friends and neighbours. In most respects the foreman is seen to be equal to his crewmen, and his role does not signify great respect. The foreman decides when to go fishing and which places to visit, but during fishing operations the crew may freely discuss the alternatives open to them. There are 'good' and 'bad' foremen; however, the main criterion is the extent to which the foreman is a good colleague who cares about his crew and his equipment. On any day, catches vary from one boat to another, but according to the folk theory of fishing the catch is mostly a matter of luck (*sorte*) and chance. Luck is an unexplained and transitory phenomenon. The lucky ones only *happen* to be at the right place at the right moment and the next day others will have luck. As one fisherman put it, 'luck travels from one boat to another'. Fishermen assume that while some of them are more lucky than others during any day, week, or month, in the long run such individual differences are bound to disappear. In many respects foremen claim to be guided by unexpected insights (*instincto*), hunches (*imaginação*) and unexplained rules of thumb (*superstição*). While a foreman should be knowledgeable about such issues – indeed anything which has to do with weather, fish migrations, and fishing technique (*teknika pesca*) – such knowledge is assumed to be evenly distributed among foremen. Villagers do not show the slightest interest in a comparison of foremen in terms of their ability to fish. The foreman is only interested in the catches of other boats in so far as they may provide useful information on the relative productivity of fishing locations on the following day. When asked to rank their colleagues in terms of their abilities, foremen sometimes asserted that a distinction between 'good' and 'bad' foremen was absurd. To raise the issue of differential success seemed to violate local rules, the ethos of egalitarianism.

Many other groups of peasant fishermen ignore or understate individual differences. Jorion shows (1984) that in traditional fishing in France there is a ceiling on production targets. He also points out that a series of 'equality-inducing' factors discouraged comparison and competition among producers (1976: 3). In such cases decisions as to the location of gear are likely to be made only after the discussion of alternatives among *all* crew members. Among some fishermen in Newfoundland, decision making is similarly characterised by 'considerable involvement of crew members, regardless of age or relation to the owner' (Stiles 1972: 41). While in this case the leader of fishing operations is usually the owner of the boat, Stiles emphasises (p. 39) that owners tend to 'underplay their authority, trying to under-communicate as much as possible their putative right to make strategic decisions'. In some cases, for instance among Baluch fishermen in Pakistan, the minimisation of differences among boats may represent an attempt on behalf of fishermen to keep a good catch for themselves, to *evade* rules of sharing. When a boat returns with an exceptional catch stored below decks those on board are likely to put off onlookers enquiring about their catch with all sorts of disclaimers: 'Who me? Oh, I didn't catch anything much . . .' (Pastner 1978: 164). While such behaviour is an attempt to 'disguise good fortune from kinsmen who might then place demands on the lucky fisherman for gifts of fish . . .' (p. 164), it underlines at the same time the importance of the ethos of generosity and co-operation among kinsmen.

In the second kind of production system in the model, production is geared for subsistence, as before, but in this case the resource-base *is* defined as property. Faris argues that due to the nature of the resource-base they exploit, peasant fishermen 'lack the same possibilities that peasant agriculturalists have' (1977: 246). He implies that since fishing involves no fixed investments in the primary resource-base, since peasant fishermen cannot invest labour in promoting the growth and reproduction of living resources prior to their extraction, potential entrepreneurs are faced with 'a somewhat unique' investment problem. But while in Western societies the sea has for long been regarded as an open territory, in other societies the ownership of fishing territories has a long history (see Chapter 2). In Micronesia, several forms of tenure apply in relation to reef and lagoon fishing. Sudo describes Micronesian sea tenure, where the right to fish is privately owned by particular extended families, as 'systems of social relationships between persons or groups of persons' (1984: 205). In Sri Lanka, where access to fishing grounds is divided between local lineages by a system of rotation, fishing grounds are similarly regarded as property. Alexander describes this form of tenure applying the concept of the 'estate' (1977). In Meybrat in Indonesia some fishing grounds are collective, belonging to villages, but the most productive areas are 'private property' (see Miedema 1986). Ownership of fishing grounds is inherited through the male as well as the female line.

Once access to the resource-base is divided, differences in success and influence can be translated into a permanent power-base. In such production systems, the leaders of fishing operations tend to fill an ascribed position – more like chiefs than big men, to use Sahlins's distinction (1972). In Micronesia, those who lead fishing operations and practise magical rites in fishing sometimes occupy a formal status as 'Chiefs of Fishing', a status which is 'assigned to particular estates' (Sudo 1984: 225). Their authority and contribution to the production process reside more in their office than their person. In systems of this kind, production models still tend to assign a passive role to human labour. Both land and sea tend to occupy a central place in folk models as domains of fertility and value, while human labour tends to be treated as a secondary factor. In this case, however, unlike that of the hunter-gatherer previously mentioned, fishermen are unlikely to be concerned with the mutual bond or contract between the individual and his or her prey. Success is not so much regarded as a personality attribute as a political and economic fact. Excessive and unusual differences in wealth and success may nevertheless provoke envy and conflict. Among the Nunu of Equatorial Africa, where fish ponds were personal property and economic activity was regarded as a zero-sum exchange, differential success was met by accusations of witchcraft: 'if one fisherman had good luck and another using similar methods had bad luck, it was assumed that the one was stealing fish from the other' by means of a magical spirit (Harms 1987: 126–7).[2] People obtained charms for their economic protection, for minimising the power of the rich. Often, however, people find it unnecessary to account for any personal differences there may be in effort and success. In Sri Lanka, for instance, the fishing expert is simply the oldest man around, 'for this is the least physically demanding task and the fishermen place little emphasis on differences in skill' (Alexander 1977: 238). In Meybrat, people deliberately avoid comparison between individuals by fishing in groups; a person who is successful at the same time as others are less fortunate 'runs the risk of being suspected of having used... black magic' (Miedema 1986: 16).

While in this system individual differences in catches tend to be ignored or assumed, being simply a fact of life, production discourse tends to emphasise social distinctions, justifying the privileged access of particular groups to the resource base in 'ideological' terms. In Meybrat, ownership of fishing territories is justified with reference to myths which explain how the 'first inhabitant' of the area learned to fish and divided the fishing grounds among his fellows. However, to have any luck at all, the producers have to meet certain conditions collectively – in particular maintain relationships with the dead, for fish have to be 'made willing to be caught through the ancestors' (Miedema 1986: 18).

The third category pertains to market economies with open access to fishing territories. In this case, unlike those previously mentioned, there is no ceiling on production targets. Labour is a commodity, accredited with a particular force or 'power'.[3] Skippers fight each other, competing for necessary facilities, equipment and crew men. Norwegian folk accounts suggest, for instance, that 'herring fishing is war' (Barnes 1954: 41). Such a competition suggests an exponential utility curve; the utility of the next unit of fish always has exponentially higher utility than the last. Where this is the case, differences in fishing ability have to be explained. Models of production not only emphasise the generative power of human labour, differential success is conceived in personal, psychological terms. Some evidence indicates that such an explanation would apply to the models of Shetland fishermen previously mentioned. Both Goodlad (1972) and Byron (1986) discuss the decline of the domestic economy, changes in the seasonal allocation of labour, the increased emphasis on fishing income, and the specialisation of roles associated with market economies. In the market economy, labour became a commodity. A new element of competition emerged. As Goodlad observes, there was 'competition for places on the vessels with the better record' (1972: 70).

Shetlanders developed what I later call 'hierarchical' model (see Chapter 5), a model which both applies a generative notion of labour and a notion of individual success. In the hierarchical model, skippers are usually credited or blamed for the size of their catch relative to that of others. Among fishermen on the east coast of Scotland, for instance, honours for successful fishing are bestowed upon the skipper alone: 'his skills as a fisherman . . . and an amount of good luck that is also regarded more or less as a personal quality, are held responsible for a skipper's success or failure' (Baks and Postel-Coster 1977: 29). The Norwegian herring skipper occupies a similar position:

While a competent crew and high quality equipment are considered as important for successful fishing as the leadership of the skipper . . . substantial variation in catch in relation to other purse seiners is likely to be attributed . . . to the latter. Indeed, fishermen often rank purse seiners according to who holds the position of skipper . . . (Wadel 1972: 107).

In the western state of Oregon, where catches declined as a result of more boats fishing the same stocks, many fishermen emphasised that this 'affected each fisherman differently because of . . . different degrees of fishing success' (Smith 1974: 375–6). The most successful skippers (the 'highliners'), it was argued, continued to be successful while others experienced reduction in income.

In the towns of Cape Verde, a production system has developed which is very different from the peasant fishing I referred to above. In the towns most of the artisanal fleet is owned by absentee investors. The fact that boats are primarily a means for profit for non-fishermen is reflected in local attitudes towards boats. Most of the boats are painted in a dull, grey colour and all boats are more or less the same. For boat owners, fishing is a way of ensuring continuous returns. Some owners even have two crews working shifts on the same boat, to maximise profits. Here, foremen are sometimes said to be 'elected' (*eleito*). In order to secure a 'good' foreman, boat owners sometimes offer part of the boat's share to the foreman. In such a situation foremen are bound to compete for reputation and prestige. Local informants suggest that some crew-men prefer to join those foremen who are fishing better than their colleagues, and that 'good' foremen tend to have more stable crews than others. Fishermen sometimes express the view that some foremen have more energy (*forca*) and determination (*vontade*) than others. I did not hear statements of this kind in the fishing villages. Changes in the organisation of fishing in Cape Verdean towns, then, seem to have been followed by changes in folk theories of production.

The kinds of personal capabilities mentioned as the causes of exceptional fishing success vary from one society to another. Shetland fishermen emphasise the skipper's 'nose' or 'his ability to make correct guesses about where to find fish' (Byron 1980: 228); Malay fishermen speak of a particular 'flair', especially the 'hearing of fish' (Firth 1946: 99); and Californian industrial tuna fishermen stress the importance of having 'good eyes' (Orbach 1978: 82). In some cases the notion of personal catching-power seems to include a measure of effort, that is the time and energy spent in fishing; Hilborn and Ledbetter base their statistical analysis of Canadian trawling (1985) on such a notion, but it is not clear whether it is an ethnographically valid one for the fishermen in question. In other cases, in lobster fishing in Maine, for instance, the chief quality of a 'good' skipper is held to be independent of the frequency of its application. For the lobstermen, the distinction between abilities and effort is just as important as the distinction made by many educators between the 'cleverness' of a student and how often he or she puts it to work, i.e. the difference between intelligence quotient and diligence. 'Hard work' may bring economic success, but it is not one of the qualities which characterise a 'good' fisherman; indeed, those who work especially hard are said to be 'compensating for lack of skill' (Acheson 1988: 56).

As the emphasis within production discourse changes from the passive to the active, from the medium to the agent, it sometimes becomes 'gendered', establishing a particularly heavy stress on the male/female boundary. Women tend to be presented as unproductive, less active than men. Cole (1988) provides an interesting description of such a conceptual change in a Portuguese fishing village. Early in this century, during the period of the Portuguese maritime household economy, women participated in a number of activities which gave them autonomy and authority. Women were defined as productive workers (*trabalhadeiras*). Later, however, with increased wage employment and consumption of manufactured goods, women lost their economic independence. The woman's role was redefined as that of consumer and housewife (*dona de casa*). A comparable redefinition of women's roles has been observed for many fishing communities in other parts of the world (see Nadel-Klein and Davis 1988).

The fourth category in the model represents market economies where the resource-base is subject to rules of ownership. Many fisheries have seen spectacular developments during the last years, in response to the 'tragedy of the commons' – developments which have led to what may be referred to as 'consolidated capitalism'. Fishing territories are appropriated by regional or national authorities which divide the total allowable catch for a season among producers, often the owners of boats. Production is being subject to an intricate, institutionalised apparatus which limits the scope for free competition between boat-owning fishermen-entrepreneurs. Many kinds of quota systems and licensing schemes are being introduced in different parts of the world in an attempt to put a ceiling on production.

This kind of production system fosters a notion of homeostatic fisheries. At the same time, folk discourse is likely to pay less attention than before to individual differences in catching-power and to emphasise instead the role of capital and equipment in the production process. While the implications of scientific management for production discourse have rarely been explored by anthropologists, some recent studies indicate potential conflicts and changes in folk models of success. Miller and van Maanen suggest (1979), for instance, that the prevailing ethos of fishermen in Massachusetts in the east coast state of the United States – summarised in the slogan 'boats don't fish, people do!' – negates the rationality of the quota system instituted by the authorities. Under the quota system, access is no longer free. For each skipper, the annual catch is decided upon in advance. The utility of catches, therefore, only increases exponentially up to a certain point. As competition between skippers declines, a new model of fishing is likely to emerge.

The privatisation of fishing grounds is not restricted to modern market economies. During the Tokugawa period in Japan (from 1603 to 1868), one may note, fishing territories were owned by feudal rulers. The right to fish was given to particular coastal communities in return for tax payments and corvee labour. This system was a highly complex one, 'a patchwork of criss-crossing rights that had developed through prescription and mutual agreement' (Kalland 1988: 174). Not only were exclusive rights of access given to communities, in some cases affluent net owners were able to gain privileged access within the fishing territory of the village: 'These rights', Kalland observes, 'could be . . . sold, mortgaged or inherited' (p. 179). In this case, however, there is no ceiling on production. Kalland argues that the fishing success of the crew is 'largely the result' of the skills of the skipper (1988: 161).

A distinction can be made between fisheries where personal differences are important for success and where they are not. As Sahlins remarks, 'for certain forms of production, notably hunting and fishing, the likelihood of differential success is known to common sense and experience' (1972: 73–4). But, as we have seen, some models of fishing suggest that differential success is due to personality differences among leaders of fishing operations while other models do not. Thus, there are four logical possibilities: first, there are societies where there is neither a measurable difference among fishermen nor a model claiming that catching abilities vary from one person to another. Secondly, there are societies where there is both a measurable difference among fishermen and a model to that effect. Acheson suggests that his statistical study (1977) of lobstering in Maine, probably the first attempt to establish statistically the causes of differential fishing success, forced him 'to take seriously the fishermen's statements about the importance of skills ...' (p. 115). The evidence shows, he argues, that the place-ment of traps is one of the important factors explaining differential success (Acheson 1988: 147).[4] Thirdly, there are societies where there is a personal difference in catching-power but no model. Finally, there are societies where there is no such difference but nevertheless a model emphasising differential success. In the first two cases the models are authentic, agreeing with reality. In the latter two they do not, either understating differences among producers (in the third case) or overstating them (in the fourth case). Clearly, representations relate to reality in different ways. There is no simple or direct relationship.

Some anthropologists have been willing to entertain the idea that differences among producers are under-communicated in folk accounts; there are numerous examples of such cases in the literature on hunter-gatherers. The other end of the scale, however, the overstating of differences, has received little attention. As I argued earlier, ethnographers often seem to be impressed by the skills of their informants. In his study of a fishing community in Brazil, Kottak argues that an 'objective evaluation' of differential success would 'closely approximate the successful captain's model' which assumes that some captains are better than others (1966: 215–16). Wadel similarly agrees with the Norwegian skipper: 'The high "productive-value" or expertise allotted to the leaders would ... seem to be a function of their actual contribution to the productive effort' (1972: 107). As Acheson points out (1981: 290), 'the vast majority of anthropologists are convinced that ... differential suc-cess is primarily due to marked differences in fishing skill'. Given the ethnographic emphasis on differential fishing skills, it is not surprising that fishing tends to be presented as a highly individual-istic act, independent of social context. Thorlindsson is tempted to compare his empirical results relating to differential success in Icelandic herring fishing to those of international chess, 'where individual performance is beyond any doubt based on skill' (1988: 206). Such a comparison, he argues, puts correlations into context and facilitates 'a more adequate interpretation'. Recall, however, that in using the analogy of chess in relation to human speech, Saussure emphasised that *parole* is an individual act, suggesting a natural model of the speaker as a person who holds no account to the reality of the socio-linguistic community (see Chapter 1). When applied to fishing, such an analogy similarly suggests a natural model of the skipper as a person operating outside society – removing his actions from his relations with crewmen, other skippers, and the wider community to which he belongs. Comparing fishing to an individualistic game like chess draws upon a culturally-specific view. The claim that differences in fishing success are 'most commonly attributed to fishing skill or the expertise of those in charge, both by social scientists and the people at large' (Thorlindsson 1988: 199) is not substantiated by the ethnography. Thorlindsson (1988) and Acheson (1981) cite plenty of evidence for the emphasis on personal skills and differential success, but both of them discard the extensive ethnography which suggests the opposite.

Among the problems raised in the study of folk models is the extent to which they can be regarded as authentic or genuine representations. The indigenous producers referred to in this chapter may not regard the account of discourse on agency and gender that I have provided as convincing. Bird-David suggests that anthropological models of reciprocity and sharing in food-gathering economies, phrased in terms of modern economic and ecological ideas, are 'unlikely to be acceptable to food-gathering people themselves' (1990: 189). She suggests a revision of earlier models, drawing attention to 'a particular type of economy that has not previously been recognized' (p. 189). But some anthropologists go much further. Gudeman writes that economic anthropologists 'deny the capacity' of their subjects to model their own behaviour in that they 'arrogate themselves a privileged right to model' their economies (1986: 38). Similarly, Holy and Stuchlik argue (1981: 10) that for a social scientist a false or naive folk model is a 'contradiction in terms, because it means legislating on social life and not studying it'. Such an argument echoes that of Cratylus', mentioned above, about the inherent correctness of names. For some anthropologists, the subjects of ethnographic enquiry are above all 'rational' beings who always find the right solutions to their problems. This notion is reflected in the primitivist fallacy of ecological functionalism which assumes that 'simple' societies are always in harmony with their environment. Given such an assumption, the producers always develop sound analyses of ecology and environmental problems, unable to make mistakes. To some extent, perhaps, this view was necessary to redress the balance, to contest the earlier and equally simplistic view of Tylorian intellectualists, for whom 'primitives' were badly informed and seriously misguided in their efforts to understand the world. But just as some ethnographies are more trustworthy than others, some elements of natural discourse are more authentic than others. Lakoff points out (1972: 650) that 'in the gap between the way the universe is and the way people conceive of the universe, there is much philosophy'. There is much anthropology too. Folk models and anthropological models need not agree.

There is no need, then, to assume that informants are always right in their claims; that would be equivalent to the 'all-embracing logical charity' criticised by Gellner (1970: 36). The falsity of a folk model can itself be an object of study. Nor should one assume that people's conceptions are inevitably mystifications of reality, to be decoded by intellectually-privileged observers. The important thing, as Asad points out (1979: 619), is to pose the question of how different kinds of discourse are initiated and reproduced as authoritative systems. The important question regarding the folk model is not whether it agrees with 'reality' but the extent to which it encourages people to act in accordance with the rationality of their social system. Natural discourse serves many purposes besides making true or false statements; people *do* things with words.

As we have seen, production discourse takes many forms. But while every model of human-environmental interaction is the product of a particular historical context, there are different kinds of context and discourse. Comparative anthropology looks for parallels or similarities between different models, attempting to contextualise them. Production discourse, I have argued, must be understood in terms of social life and history. Representations are not developed at random nor do discourses exist by themselves. In the following three chapters I will further examine the usefulness of the approach presented above with reference to the ethnography of a particular fishing society – the three phases of Icelandic fishing represented by peasant production, the expansive market economy, and the consolidated economy of the modern state.

The agreement between ethnography and the hypothesis of the relationships between kinds of fishing economies and production discourse should not be exaggerated. Nor should the sketchy explorative account presented above be regarded as a thorough literature review. After all, to do anthropology is to make statements about probable consequences of human actions – not rigid, categorical rules. And while some scholarly schemes are more illuminating than others, any scheme necessarily conflates some differences. It seems necessary, however, to assume a fundamental distinction between the finite and the real on the one hand and the symbolic and the reflective on the other, a distinction which is explicitly rejected in some schools of thought. If we were to subscribe to the opposite view, assuming that 'there is no "aboriginal" reality against which one can compare a possible world' (Bruner 1986: 46) and that 'mental constructs . . . are as real as anything they stand for' (Caws 1974: 1), the animals we call fish would be as symbolic as the various symbols associated with fish.

4 The domestication of nature: household production

I now shift the discussion from social theory to ethnography, applying the perspective outlined above to models of nature and production found in the discourses of Icelanders. This chapter describes how the models of medieval Icelanders (from the time of settlement in the ninth century to the late nineteenth century), particularly those relating to fishing, reflect the constraints and opportunities of household production. When talking about the 'medieval' period, I am referring loosely to the period of peasant production, to provide a contrast to the period of the market economy which in Iceland emerged at the end of the nineteenth century. I am not arguing that the Icelandic economy remained unchanged during the entire period discussed but rather that the character of the production system remained similar and, therefore, also discourse about the sea and the appropriation of coastal resources. The usefulness of the term 'medieval' is debated among historians. Le Goff (1988: 10) offers an extended definition of the Middle Ages in terms of 'a set of slowly evolving structures' which endured from the third century to the middle of the nineteenth century, pointing out (p. 9) that while 'the past will resist any attempt to impose a periodization upon it . . . certain ways of dividing it up are more illuminating than others'. What follows is a necessarily brief treatment of what are complex historical issues pertaining to the production system and social relations of medieval Icelanders, the complete understanding of which would require a much more detailed analysis than is possible here. In Chapters 5 and 6 I discuss successive changes in the production system of Icelanders and their representations of water-beings and fishing activities.

The cultural models of medieval Icelanders can be discerned in early Icelandic literature, the sagas (most of which were written in the thirteenth century), and published accounts of oral traditions of the eighteenth and nineteenth centuries. The sagas do not provide the kinds of analyses we count as proper ethnography, but their authors may be regarded as anthropological informants, bridging the temporal gap between their reality and ours, between the past and present. Through the years saga scholars have debated on whether the sagas are fiction (book-prose) or the authentic representation of an oral tradition (free-prose). The tendency nowadays is to regard the sagas as essentially written compositions but still based on a lively oral tradition. Such a general view, however, allows for a number of different approaches. Just as anthropologists approach their field-notes with differing questions, so saga scholars bring differing perspectives to their texts. Our fieldwork in medieval Iceland is not without problems; at times our informants have been deliberately lying, we only know some of the names, many accounts have been thoroughly edited and revised by those who copied them, and some are forever lost. But despite the limitations of the sagas as ethnographic documents, they are a rich source of information. Even if events do not occur as written – given the storyteller's licence to elaborate – none the less the assumptions of how the social context ought to work (how it is represented) is reflective of the writer's own reality. Recently, several anthropologists have turned to the study of the sagas, asking questions about medieval society and culture, questions which are informed by anthropological theory and comparative studies of contemporary societies (see, for example, Durrenberger 1989; Hastrup 1985a). Anthropologists, then, are trying to construct the ethnography of medieval Iceland – to make sense of the field-notes.

The production system of medieval Iceland

Iceland was colonised by chieftains from Norway and the British Isles between AD 870 and 930. The early settlers established a stratified society, a 'commonwealth', with divisions among slaves, landless freemen, and freeborn landholders. By the year 1000 there was increasing pressure on land (McGovern *et al.* 1988). Access to resources was increasingly determined by the political manoeuvres and battles of competing chieftains (*goðar*). While the chieftain occupied a formal position and there was a fixed number of political units or *goðorð*, the bond between a chieftain and followers (*þingmenn*) was personal and temporary. Chieftains had to create alliances and recruit followers by feasts and luxury goods. From the twelfth century onwards – especially during the so-called Sturlung Period (from about 1220 to 1262, named after one of the most dominant families) – the most powerful chieftains in the country sought to consolidate their power by appropriating property on a large scale. Due to internal conflicts and expansive policy of the Norwegian state, the commonwealth finally came to an end. After fierce battles among themselves the chieftains agreed in 1262 to cede their authorities to the king of Norway. In the year 1380, both Iceland and Norway became Danish possessions.

During the early Commonwealth Period, the rule of reciprocity prevailed and the gift was an important mode of exchange; but according to the sagas, *abuse* of the rule of reciprocity was a major concern. Divination was one way of discovering free-loaders. In one saga (*þorvaldar þáttur víðförla*) a woman named þórdís 'The Diviner' accuses a man of earning his money 'with force and power', collecting it 'by greed in debt and rent beyond fairness'.[1] With the tax law enacted in 1096, the so-called Tithe Law, owner-ship of churches became an important source of wealth and power. At the same time, there was a reserve of landless, free labourers and, as a result, slavery disappeared. On one occasion, in 1208, a group of more than 300 unemployed people, many of whom were strong and healthy, followed a travelling bishop in the hope of some sustenance. Early on, then, there was much inequality within Iceland – among landowners, tenants and landless labourers. In the fifteenth century, small fishing villages formed where foreign fishermen, mainly English and German, had established permanent bases of operation. These new centres were attractive to labourers from the countryside but contrary to the interests of the landowners, who soon managed to impose a ban on foreigners fishing from Icelandic harbours.

In 1783, new legislation required every landless person to form an annual contract with a landowner. By co-operating with the Danish rulers, landowners were able to gain increased control over the landless. The legally-enforced, labour-service contract (*vistar-band*) institutionalised patron-client relationships. The labour force was guaranteed by law. During the eighteenth and nineteenth centuries the Icelandic political elite represented the interests of the wealthier landowners in trade with the Danes, rather than those of fishermen. When the terms of trade were negotiated, the elite supported higher prices for agricultural products, and lower prices for fish in which they had less interests. As a result, the price of fish remained comparatively low.

During much of the medieval period surpluses were syphoned off through colonial relations. Timber and handlines were imported as well as other necessities, such as grain, and these could only be obtained by selling household products to colonial merchants. Colonial influence on the Icelandic economy was particularly strong from 1602 to 1787 when Danish merchants monopolised foreign trade with Icelanders. Under this system, the producers were compelled to sell their products to one particular merchant who determined the terms of trade. The right to trade with Icelanders was sold to the highest bidder at auctions in Copenhagen. The Danish capital was partly built on the profits from Icelandic trade.

In the peasant economy, then, there was always some kind of ceiling on production. Fishing was a seasonal activity practised in conjunction with other tasks, particularly animal husbandry. Peasant fishermen had neither the motivation nor the technology to explore distant fishing grounds. Handlines, operated by one man only, were the typical fishing gear. Further access to foreign markets was limited because of Iceland's status as a colony. People could have invested in boats, but capital accumulation was negligible due to colonial relations and restricted markets for fish. In addition, the periodic worsening of the climate reduced the size of livestock holdings and limited opportunities for making fishing trips, leading to chronic scarcities of food and periods of starvation. The average peasant was unable to accumulate capital. Fishing effort was limited by a series of ecological, social and technical factors.

In the old Icelandic law books (*Grágás*, compiled in the twelfth century, is the oldest one) no simple clauses were applied to the resources of the sea. Rights of access depended upon a range of factors – the occupation of coastal areas, the type of resources exploited and the method of extraction. The early laws seem to have been developed gradually when particular conflicts demanded some sort of solution and, as a result, clear-cut definitions are often missing. The resources of the beach belonged to the owner of the land. The landowner was also given privileged use-rights in relation to resources of so-called 'net areas' (*netlög*), defined in terms of the depth at which a net of 20 meshes could be located. Beyond that, the rule of capture applied. If a prey was caught further out and brought ashore by boat it belonged to the hunter. Particular areas, both on land and sea, were defined as commons (*almenningar*). In general, at sea the commons began at the point where a flattened cod could no longer be seen from land, this being the criterion used to define the 'fishing limits' (*fiskhelgi*). For early Icelanders, collective rights did not imply ownership of unharvested resources. The resource became a property only when it had been found, as in the case of dead whales, or, in the case of hunting, when the animal had been caught. The legal clauses concerning the commons seem to have applied only to the collective 'right' (*ítök*) to use particular resources. A look at the etymology of Icelandic concepts of property relations suggests that the Icelandic verb *eiga* (to 'own' or 'have') was applied in the old law not to direct ownership, but only to limited usufruct rights. Such rights are similar to the Kachins' rights to 'make use of and enjoy for the time being' (Leach 1964: 141). Collective rights to use particular terrestrial resources sometimes applied to the exploitation of areas permanently occupied by other people. But while most of the seas were conceived of as not ownable, in early Icelandic history access to the sea was often controlled by ownership of sites in the bays where boats could land. Landing a row-boat on the coast was risky, especially during the winter season, and access to the ocean therefore depended upon the availability of good landing sites. Access to the fishing grounds was largely controlled by inhibiting others from gaining access to landing sites.

Subsistence production on the Icelandic coast always included the exploitation of marine resources. The subsistence value of a boat was considered to be equal to the value of a cow. Some early documentary sources describe fishing in detail. The archaeological 'signatures' for both fishing and fish trade are also well established. In some cases, where cultivable land was plentiful, fishing was of minor importance, while in others, where good land was scarce, fishing was the mainstay of the economy. Fish formed a staple of the Icelandic diet, together with the milk of cattle and sheep. Soon after the union with Norway in 1262, fish replaced woollens as the island's main export. For centuries dried fish was the most important monetary standard. In modern Icelandic, fish is still used metaphorically to express value standards: a useless object or idea is said not to 'amount to many fish' (*vera ekki uppá marga fiska*). The importance of fish for foreign powers as well as Icelanders themselves can be seen from the fact that ten 'cod wars' have been fought on the fishing grounds around Iceland, the first one starting in 1415 when the Norwegian king charged English fishermen with 'illegal' trading with Icelanders.

To illustrate the context of household production at the local level we may look at one particular hamlet (*hverfi*) on the south-west coast of Iceland, Sandgerði, about which I shall have more to say in the next chapter. The earliest systematic data available on household production are those given in the 1703 census.[2] A general description (Magnússon 1935–36) of production and society in the county in which the hamlet was situated, written around 1785, is also highly informative. In 1703, there were seven household units in the hamlet. Thirty people belonged to these households, including four labourers. The land (approximately 9 hectares) was owned by the family on the main farm, Sandgerði. The other households, six tenant households, paid their rent in butter, fish and labour. Tenants were obliged to 'lend' their labour power to the landowner. The total number of livestock in the hamlet was 18 cattle and 30 sheep. Most of these belonged to the landowner, but each tenant had at least one milking cow. The value of the land was measured in terms of the number of cows it could support. According to the census, the land was 'barely sufficient' to support the reported number of livestock. While the barren coast offered limited opportunities for subsistence, the sea provided an important source of income. Not only did peasants obtain part of their subsistence requirements by exploiting inshore waters, but fish were also sold for export. There were several open rowing boats in the hamlet, most of which had six oars. Access to inshore waters was controlled by ownership of the local bay, the only place where boats could land or depart. During the winter season, boats from other parts of the country might gain access to nearby fishing grounds by paying 'landing tax' to the landowner.

A 'blind date' with the sea

Given the production system described above, how did Icelanders comprehend the realm of the natural? In general, production strategies were characterised by a preoccupation with natural signs. In fishing, for instance, appearances of particular species of birds were taken as signs of the migration of particular species of fish, and birds in general signified the arrival of fish. Inferences were also made about the movements of fish from the colour and smell of the sea. The fishing grounds were said to be 'lively' (*lífleg*) when fish were expected to be abundant. Decisions about fishing trips were made on the basis of an elaborate folk meteorology. All this knowledge was brought together, organised and memorised by a range of mnemonic devices, sayings, proverbs and rhymes. The 'reading' of natural signs was highly important. The concept of 'attentiveness' (*eftirtekt*) frequently referred to by old fishermen when discussing the past underlines the importance of such signs for the peasant's fishing tactics. Despite this knowledge, however, fishing was regarded as an unpredictable encounter with nature – a 'blind date', to borrow the expression of an old informant.

The hunted animals were credited with pragmatic motives equivalent to those of humans. Seals were said to have 'human figures, natures and qualities all complete, concealed beneath their coats of seal skin' (Davíðsson 1900: 314). According to some stories the seal ensured good catches and delivered valuable items upon the foreshore. Sometimes the seal co-operated with humans by warning of danger. On the other hand, if humans violated the rules of the game, the seal could become quite dangerous. One saga (*Laxdæla saga*) provides an account of a boat that gets destroyed in a storm because the crew attempted to shoot a seal.[3] The seal and the black-backed gull were thought to have formed an agreement for their mutual benefit; the seal supplied the gull with food, such as fish livers, in return for the gull's crying warnings of danger when the seal slept on shore. As Kristjánsson points out, 'to seal hunters this belief in a hidden bond between the seal and the black-backed gull was no superstition but simply a matter of experience' (1980: 449).

Fishing peasants spoke of their prey as a 'gift of God' (*guðsgjöf*). The catch was spoken of as a 'contribution' in fish (*fiskigjöf*). To receive gifts, however, one had to reciprocate. Often peasants spoke of 'creating' (*búa til*) fishing spots and 'providing' for them (*dekra*) by throwing into the sea fish remains regarded as useless to humans. In the eighteenth and nineteenth centuries foremen (*formenn*, those responsible for boats and crews) were obliged in some regions to return the remains of a catch to the spot where the fish had been caught on the preceding trip. While official regulations which demanded such provisions emphasise the usefulness of attracting fish to particular spots, there seems to be a symbolic aspect involved as well. By 'feeding' the fish, humans reciprocate the gift of the fish, thus balancing the exchange with nature as if the act of catching were subject to a formal contract or a mutual agreement. Cod roe was eaten by humans, but often some was thrown into the sea, perhaps symbolically to restore the fertility of fish and reproductive capacity of the sea. Fishing was regarded as an exchange with nature.

According to the mythology of *Snorra Edda*, the oceans and lakes were created out of the blood of a giant (*Ýmir*) and governed by the god of *Njörður* who was in charge of fishing and sailing. In this cosmic order humans were but pawns, subject to alien forces. The fate of the fishermen was believed to be determined by a godly design. In order to prevent failure (bad catches and accidents), prayers were read at the beginning of each season and before each fishing trip. Reciting prayers was referred to as *vani*, which means 'habit' or 'the usual'. To redress the balance between humans and the alien forces ruling their fate and conduct, magic could also be used. According to the sagas, the words of some speakers were charged with a particular power. There are many accounts of magic spells inflicted through the act of speaking: chants, libels, and insulting phrases. The rich vocabulary relating to spells suggests a folk theory of speech acts – 'doing things with words'. Often a spell involved a ritual; in some acts of sorcery speech was dominant, in others not – the 'ratio of words to action' (Tambiah 1968: 175) varied from one case to another. The native term *sjónhverfingar* refers both to sight and sound, meaning 'an ocular delusion by spell'. Particular signs, 'fishing signs' (*fiskistafir*), were engraved in boats and fishing gear to ensure good catches (see Kristjánsson 1986: 341–44). Other signs were believed to protect fishermen against whales, storms, and seasickness.

The ritual and magic associated with fishing did not imply, though, that people thought they had much control over nature, rather it ensured that one did not lose what one already had – for instance the ability to fish. Notions of 'fishiness' (*fiskni, fiskiheill*) – the ability to get fish – underlined the natural order of the household economy in that fishiness was considered to be differentially distributed among fishermen independent of their actions. There are many stories of successful fishermen who are mysteriously provided access to fish while others, who are less fortunate, receive nothing despite the fact that they fish in the same spot with the same kind of gear. Fishiness was a quality given to a person once and for all. Boat foremen arranged the seating of their men according to their fishiness. Those who possessed fishiness jigged with handlines while others were seated at the oars to keep the boat in position (see Jónsson 1945: 347). Those who had some but little fishiness (*heldur ófisknir*) had particular seats in the boat, and so did those who lacked entirely the ability to fish (*ófisknir*). Some people were especially unfortunate in that they scared fish away. They were called 'fish-deterrents' (*fiskifælur*). Somehow, then, fishiness was predetermined. According to old proverbs, 'no one catches another man's fish' and 'a poor fisherman gets poor fish'.

Even though fishiness was considered an individual quality, it was part of a grand design over which humans had no control. This was underlined by the concept of 'fate' (see Durrenberger 1984b). In the view of early Icelanders, humans were passive recipients, observers of a mysterious system of rationing. In mythology these relations were sometimes reversed. According to some medieval accounts, it was in Paradise, where presumably the constraints of earthly existence did not apply, that exploited species obeyed human authority: one saga says that 'If a man asks the water for fish, it will provide various kinds at his feet' (*Matheus saga postola*).[4]

Most often the landowner owned the boat, but from time to time tenants rowed in their own boats. The foreman, often the landowner, oversaw several crewmen, usually tenants who partly gained access to land by rowing in the landowner's boat. Foremen did not necessarily possess fishiness and they were not held responsible for fishing success or failure. Expert knowledge was publicly shared and not restricted to the foreman. Often foremen were accompanied by acknowledged advisers (*bitamenn*). The advisers were usually older and more experienced than the foreman and to some extent they shared responsibility for major decisions concerning the timing and location of fishing. Being a foreman, however, was an honourable position. Records of fishing seasons and individual careers, 'trip registers' (*róðratöl*) as they were called, emphasised fishing effort rather than catch. The criterion for assessment was the number of trips made rather than the amount of fish landed. The major qualities attributed to a good foreman were diligence, bravery, seamanship, and the ability to command the crew. These were frequently mentioned in foremen's biographies and obituaries.

Boat-handling terms from the distant past have come into general use in Icelandic. To 'safely take a ship to land' (*sigla heilu skipi í höfn*), for instance, is an expression which may be applied to any risky activity which demands cleverness. When foremen were ranked, it was according to their bravery in difficult weather conditions, their cleverness in directing boat and crew, and the number of trips they made. Good foremen were spoken of as 'sea-goers' (*sjósóknarar*) or 'sea vikings' (*sjóvíkingar*). One of the greatest sea-goers on the south coast in the nineteenth century is said to have made fifty trips in a single winter season of one hundred days (Jónsson 1945: 352).

The reward structure of fishing reflected the idea that the production value of crewmen, including the foreman, was more or less the same. The catch was divided using a share system. According to Magnússon's account from the late eighteenth century (1935–36), boats of two or four oars had the same number of fishermen, one of whom was the foreman, but boats larger than four oars had foremen in addition to fishermen. The foremen received the same as a crewman, one share, but on larger boats they would receive a minor salary, a 'foreman's salary', paid by the boat owner to supplement their share. In a normal winter season, for instance, a foreman on an eight-oar boat, owned by someone else, would receive 11 per cent on top of his one share. If the foreman owned the boat and the gear he or she would receive 33 per cent of the catch, or four shares out of twelve; one for labour, one for gear and two for the boat. The imagery of the boat was often used to underline equity and group responsibility, as witnessed by the expression *að vera á sama báti* (literally 'to be in the same boat') which means 'to be equal'.

While the notion of inequality was often suppressed in relations among crewmen, different species of fish received differential treatment. In a semi-ethnographic novel, which largely deals with the rationality of the herring fishery of the twentieth century, Laxness provides an interesting account of the 'class system of fish' in the peasant society of earlier centuries (1972: Ch. 9). Icelanders, he points out, made a clear distinction between 'herring and fish'. Herring were not considered proper food for ordinary people, except in times of famine, partly due to their bad smell. 'Fish' – that is, cod, haddock, and other 'honest' fish – on the other hand, had a pleasant 'aroma'. The food-preferences of Icelanders were characterised by a respect for aesthetics and orderliness:

... fish with an ugly face were subject to a food-taboo. Cod-fish, especially cod and haddock, seem to have made a positive impression on tastefulness ... because of their pretty faces, calm look, and amicable figure ...

Fish that other people find desirable, Icelanders would throw back into the sea while mumbling some religious formulas . . . Marine invertebrates, such as shellfish and crustaceans . . . , were considered shameful, untouchable beasts (Laxness 1972: 82).

Even though this portrayal may exaggerate and distort, for the purpose of storytelling, no doubt in the consumption discourse of the domestic economy of Icelanders some fish were far more equal than others.

In the peasant economy, fishing was not a separate endeavour with an elaborate role structure of its own but integrated into the subsistence economy. In the model of the peasant economy humans were regarded more as recipients of value than creators, but to ensure a continuation of the metabolism between humans and nature it was necessary to carry out a series of household tasks, all of which, by definition, were useful ones. Whether people specialised in extracting food from the environment or 'domestic' tasks in the narrowest sense made no big difference to their perceived value or the size of their contribution. In this sense women were no less (or more) productive than men. There is no evidence for a cognitive gender barrier similar to those described in many other fishing societies (see, for instance, Cove 1978; Thompson 1985), a barrier which deliberately excluded women from fishing. Nor is there evidence for gender-based notions of purity or cultural taboos in relation to fishing. There is ample evidence indicating that women (*sjókonur* or 'sea-women') participated extensively in fishing, either as crew or foremen (see Pálsson 1987: 146–7). Some eighteenth- and nineteenth-century accounts explicitly state that for women fishing was a natural thing to do and that women's participation in fishing was 'quite common' or 'customary'. Some women were noted for their physical strength, industriousness, and skill in fishing and managing people and boats. The cognitive boundary between male and female may have been an important one, but it did not coincide with the boundaries between the aquatic and terrestrial, nor between nature and culture.

Myth and metaphor

Icelandic beliefs connected with water-beings are more numerous than those connected with other classes of animals. According to some accounts they were thought to be 'more interesting' as well (Stefánsson 1906: 301). Birds were rarely used as metaphors, with the exception of the raven which was cherished by gods and poets. Apparently, birds were less 'good to think', contrary to the thesis of Kleivan and Lévi-Strauss previously mentioned. Ethnographic parallels, one may note, are easy to find. The Tikopia, for instance, show less interest in bird species than marine creatures (Firth 1967: 250). The Icelandic folklorist Davíðsson argued at the turn of the last century that the importance of fish in Icelandic folklore was simply due to their number and availability. He suggests that folklore reflects the lack of land animals in Iceland, and the presence of many species of fish: 'There are few beliefs which relate to land animals, but the inhabitants of the deep ... have for a long time played a great part in the popular fancy, and many a strange idea concerning them has taken hold on the ordinary mind' (Davíðsson 1900: 312). Davíðsson's argument hardly holds, however, because a considerable number of bird species were available to the human mind. Availability, then, does not fully account for the choice of species in the metaphorical language of Icelandic mythology. A functional explanation of the obsession of Icelanders with water-beings does not seem to hold either. Fish were important for the economy, but so were many other animals, some of which were domesticated by humans (sheep, cattle, pigs, goats and horses) and some of which were in the wild (foxes and birds).

The ocean was not only believed to contain species hunted by humans. Various monsters with peculiar characteristics also inhabited the sea. Many anthropologists have argued, Leach (1976) and Douglas (1966) among others, that some animals, because of their anomalous position within a society's categorisation of the natural, are better to think with than others. The anomalous water-beings of Icelandic mythology, however, were not a *selection* from the set of living beings, on the basis of some 'natural' anomaly. The monsters of the sea only existed in the human mind, as food for thought. Anomaly was, therefore, a deliberate construction. As Tapper argues (1988: 51), 'there are always animals about, even if they exist only as *images in the mind*'. Monstrous water-beings were used as models, representing the wild realm of the Other.

The very fact that fish, in their natural habitat, are invisible most of the time, until they are caught, may help to explain why

Icelanders preferred them over terrestrial animals (including birds) as vehicles of metaphorical expression. Perhaps the invisibility of the fish world, their *dissociation* from the world of ordinary humans, made fish more attractive than terrestrial species as vehicles for disembodied thought. The emphasis on invisibility, I suggest, underlined that social power was foreign (Scandinavian), beyond the reach of Icelanders. Just as the roots of power were invisible most of the time, the fish world was to a large extent beyond the empirical knowledge of ordinary Icelanders. Metaphorical statements about nature and society which referred to beastly figures inhabiting the ocean, were particularly appealing because such beings were never brought ashore for careful scrutiny.

The reason why animals were chosen over humans in Icelandic discourse on the Other relates to the relative absence of human Others. Even though otherness is a relative phenomenon in the sense that boundaries between 'insider' and 'outsider' may be variously defined, the number and type of such boundaries will significantly affect the notion of the Other (see Stocking 1982: 184). Despite all the travel accounts of the Vikings, the early Icelandic community appears to have been fairly isolated. Iceland is a small, circumscribed island society and contact with culturally different people was simply not an everyday activity during the medieval period when the bulk of the population lived in scattered households or isolated hamlets. Medieval references to human Others are therefore mostly based on second-hand accounts. One medieval manuscript (*Hauksbók*) provides a particular chapter on 'peoples of various nature'.[5] It describes how, for example, one group of people 'is not affected by the poison of the snake', and others have 'such a large lower lip that they can throw it over their head while they sleep', some have 'no tongue but indicate everything with signs', etc. None of this, of course, is unique to the world-view of Icelanders during the Middle Ages. Similar ideas captured the imagination of other Europeans (see, for instance, Hodgen 1971).

The only Others locally available and invested with 'human' qualities were just as invisible as fish (and powerful foreigners) and their residence remained equally unknown. These were the so-called 'hidden people' (*huldufólk*). Their way of life was similar to that of humans: they maintained themselves through fishing and raising livestock, but they were invisible, living in cliffs, hills and mountains. The hidden people had a reputation for their kindness and exceptional fishing success. Sometimes they co-operated with humans, sometimes not.

The cosmic order, then, was divided into two categories: the realm of the visible, which was directly accessible to the senses of ordinary humans (landed fish, for instance), and the invisible (including uncaught fish, mysterious water-beings and 'hidden people'). Fishiness entailed privileged access to the invisible. The realm of the invisible was not restricted to the spatial and the present; there was a temporal dimension as well, involving events of the past and future. Particular persons, invested with a special divinatory power, provided access to events invisible in time. Some predicted future events (*forspá*), some discovered hidden knowledge from the past (*eftirrýni*, often in relation to thieves and other wrongdoers), and still others did both. One saga tells of a man who 'foresaw the future and was clever in detecting thieves or indeed anything he wanted' (*Eyrbyggja saga*).[6] Diviners were especially consulted when a formal investigation (*rannsókn*), being those procedures specified by law and based on direct evidence, would not work.[7] For most medieval Icelanders, the realm of the hidden was no less real than that of the visible. The distinction between the supernatural and the natural was not a salient one.

The writings of the native-born folklorist Davíðsson were partly motivated by the desire to eradicate such 'erroneous' beliefs in 'supernatural' beings. Davíðsson complained (1900: 313) that his fellow Icelanders were confusing two very different classes of water-beings: 'Those which are altogether supernatural or imaginary . . . and those which really exist but are invested by the popular mind with strange and fanciful properties'. In Davíðsson's view, Icelanders sometimes got things very wrong. His view has received recent support from an unexpected direction, from research based on optics and computer simulations. Lehn and Schroeder argue (1981) that Icelanders may have mistaken an optical phenomenon for monstrous water-beings. Medieval accounts of 'killer-whales' and 'sea-men', they argue, provide accurate descriptions of a rare optical phenomenon occurring in certain atmospheric conditions in Arctic regions.

The major opposition encoded in myth and folk-lore was that between land and sea. One of the ocean-taboos (*sævíti*) implied that if a boat contained some dirt belonging to the land the catches were bound to be poor.[8] A boat had to be cleaned or purified; its terrestrial nature had to be suppressed during fishing. The contrast between land and sea is also underlined in metaphorical language, since anything out of place is referred to as a 'fish on dry land' (*fiskur á þurru landi*). Similar prescriptions regulating contact between the marine and terrestrial have been described for some other coastal societies, for instance the Inuit (Saladin d'Anglure 1984: 498). Icelanders belonged to the land, but their fate was largely shaped by two kinds of uncertainties relating to the sea. On the one hand, there was uncertainty concerning the size of the catch brought ashore for consumption and exchange. On the other hand, expeditions at sea were always potentially dangerous, given the low level of technological development and the stormy conditions of the North Atlantic. Both these uncertainties were said to be interrelated. Unexpected fishing success was thought to be an early sign of the fisherman's death. If a good fisherman caught little, or someone with very limited fishiness fished 'like crazy' he or she would be short-lived.

The anomalous water-beings of Table 4.1 stress the boundary between land and sea. Some beings can move between the two worlds, transforming themselves in the process. One saga (*Völsunga saga*) tells of a man named *Otur* (Otter) who was a great fisherman. He was like an otter during the day when he stayed in the water and caught fish, but during the night he was human and slept ashore.[9]

Table 4.1 *Water-beings in Icelandic mythology*

Habitat	Being
Land and water	Otter (*Ottr*)
	Loki (as salmon)
	Sea-woman (*sækona*)
Water	Jumper (*stökkull*)
	Fin (*öfuguggi*)
	Hairy-trout (*loðsilungur*)
	Horse-whale (*hrosshveli*)
	Mermaid (*margýgur*)
	Sea-dog (*sæhundur*)
	Sea-man (*hafmaður*)
	Water-horse (*vatnanykur*)

Medieval manuscripts describe 'sea-women' who 'have the nature of fish while in the sea but look like humans while ashore'.[10] Sea-women are sexually attractive and sometimes they bear children fathered by sailors. Their children become giants, which are 'not like humans'.

Loki, a giant who often lives with the gods, a trickster figure and one of the major characters in *Snorra Edda*, frequently transforms himself. Once he changes into a woman. On several occasions he changes into salmon to escape the punishment of the gods for mischief for which he is supposed to be responsible among both gods and humans. His transformation into a salmon strongly emphasises the distinction between land and sea. Salmon are not just fish, they are anadromous, ascending rivers from the sea for breeding, living both in fresh water and in the sea. This anomaly is underlined in the myth where Loki faces 'two choices' when escaping from the gods – to head for the sea or to jump inland up the river.

There are many mythological accounts as well of beings which are permanently stationed in the sea. They do not become transformed but they are nevertheless characterised by some anomalous property which highlights the opposition between land and sea. The mermaid (*margýgur*), for instance, has the head and huge breasts of a giant-woman but a whale-like lower part (see Figure 4.1). She sings beautifully but destroys ships and kills people. The 'fin' (*öfuguggi*) is a particular species of fish with reversed fins. When it moves about, it swims backwards. It is poisonous and has red flesh, indicating that it eats the bodies of drowned men. It is non-human and inedible. A particular species of trout, 'hairy-trout' (*loðsilungur*), was said to be covered with hair. It was believed to be created by giants and demons, as a punishment for some human wrongdoing. Sometimes lakes and rivers were filled with fins and hairy trouts, which were considered unfit for consumption.

Several kinds of whales, the so-called 'wicked-whales' (*illhveli*), were said to do damage to ships and men. Wicked-whales know their own name and appear as soon as they hear it mentioned. Fishermen take care not to use their proper name and call them 'big fish' (*stórfiskur*) instead. The 'jumper' (*stökkull*) is one of them. It has flaps of skin hanging down over the eyes and the only way it can lift the flaps and see what is going on is by leaping clear over the water. When in the air it can look out from under the flaps. It

Figure 4.1 *A holy man fights a mermaid* (from a thirteenth-century manuscript, *Flateyjarbók*)

attempts to sink anything that it sees floating. Another wicked-whale is the 'horse-whale'. It was said to resemble a horse, to neigh like a horse, and to have a horse's tail which sent tremendous waves across the ocean and destroyed boats and men. There are similar stories of 'sea-men', 'water-horses', and 'sea-dogs'.

The anomalous position of the above water-beings is not founded on distinctions arbitrarily imposed by alien outsiders. From the point of view of medieval Icelanders, strangeness was a salient property. The term used to refer to anomalous beings, *kynjaverur*, literally means beings with 'astonishing' or unnatural properties. In this peasant society, the world of anomalous water-beings provided a convenient tool for folk analysis, in terms of which Icelanders could account for events and express social realities. The theme is similar in most of the mythical accounts mentioned above. There is constant exchange across the interface between land and sea: in some cases humans are supplied with fish, in other cases inhabitants of the sea are supplied with humans. Bestial and anomalous characteristics usually correlate with danger, while the attribution of quasi-human qualities to water-beings is sometimes associated with good catches (see Pálsson 1990c).

In social exchanges among medieval Icelanders, the rule of reciprocity sometimes applied. Similarly, the ecological relations between humans and animals were presented as the giving and receiving between equal partners. Some water-beings, as we have seen, especially the ones hunted by humans (e.g. seals), were regarded as trade partners, friends or collaborators. On the other hand, anomalous water-beings and humans usually interacted with aggression and hostility. Exchanges with imaginary water-beings rarely obeyed the rule of reciprocity: there was no contract, no fairness or 'civil' order. Anomalous beings posed a threat to humans while at sea, in that they attempted to drag humans into the ocean or destroy their boats. These beings were also used metaphorically in connection with human social relations. Those who were a threat to the social order were spoken of as 'fins': fish which have reversed fins and swim backwards. The same term was used for all kinds of misfits – the eccentric, the outsider and the homosexual. Sometimes too, the 'free-loaders' (the wealthy and powerful) were referred to as 'big fish' (*stórfiskar*) or 'big salmon' (*stórlaxar*). The social world was represented by a natural model.

References to the spatial also suggested a natural state which was a timeless order independent of human action. The fishing grounds were seen to be a closed and stable domain. There were 'shallow waters' (*grunnmið*) and 'deep waters' (*djúpmið*), and beyond that only the mysterious and unknown. Within the realm of the known, there were many fishing locations, each of which was seen to be permanent. Fishing spots were located by visual triangulation. The Icelandic term for spots, *fiskimið*, itself refers to the act of sighting locations. The names of locations, usually associated with some natural feature of the landscape, were obvious and publicly known. There was little secrecy. The 'natural' coding of the fishing grounds by the application of names for landmarks to individual spots reflected the idea that spots were permanent. The peasant's cognitive map of the ocean had an immunity to history; this was a world-view of stasis in which nature was mapped on to society and society on to nature.

I have shown how the peasant's rationality of earlier centuries reflected the constraints of the medieval production system. During most of the medieval period, surpluses were syphoned off through both colonial relations and landlord-tenancy relations. While the ocean was not ownable, landowners controlled access to the sea. There were limited possibilities for agriculture and the fishing technology was simple. Fishing was intimately connected with other aspects of domestic life, and there was a ceiling on production. Accordingly, in the peasant's model humans were seen to be passive recipients of fish. The catch was a 'gift' to humans. The contribution of the ocean was symbolically repaid by throwing residues of fish into the fishing spots that had supplied them. In the folk model, many of the species fished were regarded as collaborators in a network of exchange. While the ability to catch fish – fishiness – was an individual quality, no one was credited or blamed for the size of the catch. The productive value of a foreman was seen to be equivalent to that of an ordinary crewman. When foremen were ranked it was in accordance with their bravery and their relations with the crew rather than the amount of fish landed. During fishing trips, relations on board the boat were usually relaxed and responsibility for major decisions was often shared among foremen and their advisers, sometimes among the entire crew.

In the absence of suitable human Others, the world of animals and 'hidden people' took on the role of representing the Other. The main uncertainty of production related to the danger of fishing trips when humans were subject to forces over which they had little control, and the folk model emphasised this by contrasting the land and water. A particular class of imaginary water-beings, most of which had anomalous characteristics and were hostile to humans, mediated between the ocean and the domain of humans – supplying humans with fish or, more often, fish with humans. The metaphorical language of anomalous water-beings underlined the natural basis of morality and social relations. The transgression of the boundary between land and sea was analogous to a transgression of the dividing line between humanity and animality. Chaos in society was seen to be equivalent to chaos in nature. In domesticating nature, then, Icelanders were domesticating themselves.

5 From nature to society: the market economy

As production systems change so do cultural models. Folk accounts, no less than anthropological theories, differ with respect to their relative emphasis on stasis or change, rules or praxis. As we have seen, the reference to nature in metaphorical language sometimes effectively projects an image of society as a changeless order. Those who, on the other hand, wish to emphasise change and human creativity are likely to use a different kind of language. In this chapter I analyse the production discourse of the Icelandic market economy as an historically-constituted phenomenon. I examine the transformation of the production system during the first half of the twentieth century and the resulting diverse manifestations in present discourse and social interaction. As Icelanders developed new kinds of social relationships, their representations of nature and production were transformed. New conceptions were developed concerning fish and other natural resources. In particular, the relative power of fish and humans was reversed. At the same time, the focus of production discourse was shifted from nature to society. While the folk model of the household producer regarded fishing as a struggle against the elements, the model of the modern skipper holds that the competition with fellow producers – other skippers and their crews – is central. The former model, I shall argue, is an 'egalitarian' one in that it minimises personal differences in productivity while the latter is 'hierarchical', emphasising personal differences.

The account of modern fishing presented in the present chapter and the following one is partly based on fieldwork in Sandgerði, near Keflavík in south-west Iceland, in 1979 and 1981. I refer the reader who may be interested in further ethnographic details to descriptions available elsewhere (Pálsson 1982), but a few words about the fieldwork are in order before going on to the analysis of the modern fishery and its development. Obviously, the fact that I am a native of Iceland affected my fieldwork, my relations with local people, the kinds of questions I addressed, and the answers I

got. While local people found the general topic of my research –
changes in conceptions of fishing and the roles of skippers and
fishermen – a legitimate one, I soon discovered that some of the
questions I asked, especially those concerning success, competition,
and fishing techniques, were seen to be both silly and too personal.
While this is a reaction many fieldworkers are bound to experience
early in their work, it may be somewhat stronger in the case of
a native fieldworker. Why would an academic from the capital
city, I was asked, make an effort to understand this particular
fishing community? Why would an anthropologist talk to fellow
Icelanders, for months and mostly about obvious matters? For
quite some time I felt as if I was not making any progress. I knew
that some important issues were not elaborated upon in my presence and I found it embarrassing to see some of them discussed in
greater detail in newspaper accounts. At one point, however,
during the winter season in 1981, my relations with local people
seemed to undergo a dramatic change. A highly respected local
skipper invited me to join him on one of his fishing trips. 'If you
really want to know what fishing is all about', he said, ' you must
go fishing'. I guess he saw his offer as a test or challenge, knowing
that academics and others who rarely go to sea (*landkrabbar*,
literally 'land-crabs') are prone to seasickness in Icelandic waters,
especially during the often stormy winter season. I accepted his
challenge, and shortly after we left harbour we were in rough seas –
indeed, one of the worst storms of the season. For several hours,
while the skipper and his crew patiently waited for the weather to
improve to be able to draw the nets they had placed in the sea the
day before, I was busy emptying the contents from my stomach. No
doubt my seasickness confirmed the skipper's idea that academics
were hopeless at sea. Then, miraculously, it seemed, the weather
suddenly improved and, fortunately, the feeling of seasickness
vanished. I found the movements of the boat pleasant and relaxing
and for the rest of the trip I plagued the skipper and his crew with a
variety of questions, about boats, gear, skippers, and fishing tactics.
Later on, when ashore, I found out that the attitude towards my
research had changed. My questions seemed to acquire a new
meaning and they were no longer easily avoided or ignored. I had
the feeling of having suddenly become accepted, as a legitimate
participant in local discourse. Apparently, then, the fishing trip was
a rite of passage. I never bothered to ask for an explanation of what

happened, but several people addressed me by reminding me of the fishing trip: 'So, you've been feeding the fish!'.

The social relations and techniques of expansive fishing

During the 'struggle' for independence late in the nineteenth century the leading Icelandic nationalists encouraged peasants to increase production and acquire new technology and knowledge. One of them addressed fishermen in a pamphlet which provided practical information on fishing gear and boat technology. 'It's about time', he said, 'that you use all your power to participate in the progress which the land and the ocean invite' (Sigurðsson 1859: 4–5). Such efforts encouraged innovation which thereby increased productivity of labour; however, further development would not have been possible without structural changes in the colonial economy. With the relaxation of Danish trade monopolies in 1787 local capital accumulation became possible. Icelandic merchants replaced the Danish ones and invested in boats and fishing gear. In the nineteenth century new markets for Icelandic saltfish were developed, especially in Spain and England. Fishing villages grew and there emerged capitalist relations of production. As the labour market developed, the patron-client bond between landowners and landless workers weakened in practice until it was finally abolished in 1894.

At the beginning of this century several attempts were made to establish fishing firms in Iceland. Local merchants often formed shareholding companies by pooling Danish and Icelandic capital. One of these companies rented the harbour at Sandgerði in 1908 and had several motor boats operating from there. Located near the rich fishing grounds found off the south-west coast, Sandgerði attracted several investors. A few years later, two Icelandic merchants became the sole owners of the fishing 'station' at Sandgerði (the harbour and the landing facilities), hiring local labour to work on their boats and process the catch. In subsequent decades they built large fishing firms which employed several hundred people during the winter season. By 1916 they owned approximately ten motor boats, either on their own or together with a local foreman. As the productivity of fishing greatly increased with the introduction of both motor boats and freezing facilities for bait, agriculture became relatively less attractive as a source of subsistence to the local peasantry. With an extended fishing season, which was partly due to technological improvements, fishing became a full-time occupation.

The owners of the fishing stations encouraged fishermen to acquire their own boats. The petty entrepreneurial activity of independent boat owners sustained capitalist fishing in its initial phase of development. Similar observations have been made for other fisheries by Breton (1977: 130) and McCay (1981). If the number of boats declined, the entrepreneurs enlarged their own fleet to ensure a steady source of raw material. Foremen who owned shares in boats together with the entrepreneurs sometimes managed to buy out the merchants' shares and establish full ownership after a few years of fishing. Their sons often became crew members while other household members worked at washing and drying the catch. The catch had to be sold to the entrepreneurs who owned the fishing wharfs. If fishermen sold their catch elsewhere the processors refused to supply them with bait or grant them access to the wharfs.

Löfgren argues, in a comparative article on North Atlantic fishing adaptations (1982), that the transformation of peasant society during the period of 1750–1900 was the result of demographic and social changes whereby the number of landless people continued to grow. For the 'new proletarians' of agrarian capitalism, he argues, fishing became an important alternative. He also suggests (p. 154) that Iceland underwent 'the same process' as coastal regions in Scandinavia but somewhat later. It is true that fishing was an important source of subsistence for landless people in Iceland. But this was the case for quite a long period, at least four centuries. Also, it would be wrong to assume that the real growth in maritime settlements in Iceland was the result of any developments in agriculture. On the contrary, the agrarian system remained virtually unchanged until capitalist production in fishing transformed the political economy of Iceland. The decisive growth in fishing occurred *despite* attempts by the landowners to maintain a labour reserve in farming. As colonial relations with Denmark weakened, traditional household production gave way to different forms of production: those of the skipper-owner or the petty entrepreneur, and the capitalist company. These transitions involved fundamental changes in social relations and means of production.

The relative importance of the petty entrepreneur and the business firm in capitalist fishing has varied since the beginning of this century. It seems that initially (from 1913 to 1916) the merchants owned a substantial part of the Sandgerði fleet (see Pálsson 1982: 67), while there was a gradual increase in fisherman-ownership from 1916 to 1943. From 1943 to 1962 the proportion of fisherman-owned boats declined rapidly, but after that it has remained fairly stable. In 1981 fishermen owned approximately 60 per cent of the local fleet of 46 boats, 45 per cent of the total tonnage.[1] The petty entrepreneur shares the characteristics of the fishing peasant in one important respect. In both cases family members pool their re-sources, capital and labour. The family budget of the entrepreneur is closely tied to that of the boat even though the latter is kept separate on paper to comply with tax laws. Sometimes the whole nuclear family, and some neighbouring kinsfolk as well, are engaged in production related to one boat. The wife of the skipper-owner takes most of the responsibility for running the household while the husband is working irregular hours. She is also responsible for raising their children and keeping regular contacts with neighbours, friends and relatives. Furthermore, she may bait lines, prepare nets, and work in a freezing plant. The wife's earnings may be an important source of additional income, especially if the boat has not been doing well.

By pooling available resources the skipper-owner safeguards himself against the vulnerability of the business. Market conditions fluctuate, the productivity of fishing differs from one season to another, and the need for labour varies with season and fishing gear. One of the barriers to converting a small family business into a company is precisely the difficulty in responding to such fluctua-tions, while at the same time responding to the demands of the labour market. Skippers who own boats do not have to pay salaries every week. However, the absentee-owner must conform to the formal demands of labour unions for immediate payments in order to keep his workers. The extent to which the petty entrepreneur is able to draw upon the labour of his family varies with its composi-tion and stage in the development cycle. The skipper-owners who are the most vulnerable are those who have no sons or whose sons are too young to join them.

If the skipper-owner has one or more sons interested in fishing he may expand his business and buy a larger boat. As his sons grow older they are likely to take over the enterprise. The skipper-owner

then becomes a shore-based 'manager'. If the owner has several
children he may sell the boat when he quits fishing, but more often
the boat remains the property of the family. Sometimes a company
of shareholders is formed at this stage. Later, one or more of the
sons may buy the daughters out. Brothers often pool their resources
but their co-operation is usually limited to a few years. In one case
five brothers who jointly owned a boat split up after several years of
fishing. Three of them bought the two others out, and the latter
in turn bought their own boat. As brothers establish their own
families, their resources and commitments become different and,
consequently, they are likely to have different opinions in matters
of investment and maintenance. Also, during fishing trips the
symmetrical relations between crewmen who are not only brothers
but also co-owners of the boat tend to be incompatible with the
authority relations between skipper and deck-hands.

The modern fleet is composed of vessels of varying sizes, ranging
from 10 to 200 tons. With motors and larger vessels, the technology
of fishing underwent important changes. While handlines, the
typical gear of the peasant economy, are still used, they have largely
been replaced by more complex gear – particularly longlines, gill
nets, and trawl. Some boats use baited longlines (now up to 12
miles long), especially early in the winter season. Fishermen draw
the lines daily, as the bait is only attractive to fish for a limited
period. Later in the season, when the species which cod prey upon
become more plentiful making the bait less attractive, fishermen
begin to use gill nets, stringing together several nets to make a single
barrier. Each boat has a number of such barriers (*trossur*), depending on its size and the number of crew men. The gills of fish
that swim into the net become entangled, and if left for any length
of time the fish die for lack of motion. After a day or two, the
fishermen draw the nets and untangle the fish.

Both longlines and gill nets are stationary gear; they are placed at
particular locations and drawn later on. Trawling, in contrast, is an
active technique in that the gear, a net formed as a sack, is drawn
along particular paths where fishing schools are likely to be,
amassing fish in the process. Trawling requires much engine power
and is, therefore, only practised with larger vessels. The fishing
techniques mentioned so far are restricted to the 'demersal' fishery;
that is, for species, such as cod, saith and haddock, that dwell close
to the ocean floor. Fishing for herring and capelin requires different

techniques. These are 'pelagic' species; that is, normally dwelling close to the ocean surface, and sometimes surfacing. They are much smaller than demersal species and their schooling behaviour is different. Herring and capelin travel in schools that are highly evasive, except when spawning; demersal species are usually more evenly dispersed and more predictable. The ring net is the typical gear in the pelagic fishery. It involves an active technique, some-what like trawling. In this case, a huge net is 'thrown' into the sea and drawn around schools of fish.

Hierarchical models of success

With the emergence of capitalist fishing, production was oriented towards the market and productive targets became indefinite; the previous ceiling on production was removed. As fishing was no longer primarily for subsistence, labour became a marketable com-modity. Motor boats became available and new offshore fishing grounds were opened. With new world-markets, the national econ-omy of Iceland became centred on the extraction, processing and export of fish and derived products. The definition of valuable fish was no longer determined by domestic discourse alone or the criterion of edibility. The aesthetic and somewhat mythological criteria of the peasant economy, which emphasised the smell, behaviour, and looks of fish, became irrelevant; what mattered was market demand, the tastefulness of European and American con-sumers. As a result, Icelanders were fishing several 'ugly' and 'smelly' creatures they would not have considered in the past – including herring, shrimp, and lobster. Gradually, Icelanders re-defined some of them as not only edible but even as delicatessen. Moreover, fish in general were redefined as resources which were 'there for the taking' rather than gifts (from God). The prey is no longer seen to be an offering *to* humans who passively receive what has been allotted to them, rather it is seen to be actively pursued *by* humans and extracted from an indifferent sea. In the folk model, humans have become active, and their labour is said to create value. At the same time, the static world-view has disappeared. The ocean is no longer thought to have some kind of power or force. Its inhabitants are no longer seen to control the fate of humans, except as passive objects of the catch. The peasant's mythology, and its image of the cosmic order, has been replaced by the notion of infinite natural resources. The old metaphors of anomalous water-beings have become obsolete. At the same time, there has developed a new cognitive map of the fishing grounds. Since Icelanders are now exploring and expanding the boundaries of the known, the ocean is seen to have been 'opened up'. There are uncharted spaces to be surveyed and unknown spots to be discovered. Most fishing spots are a matter of secrecy, and each skipper constructs his own personal naming grid. The names are entirely arbitrary, as they do not refer to features of the landscape. The old natural coding of the seascape has been replaced by a system of transient and euphemistic names. The new names are arbitrary, private and unstable. They are *in* history.

The new folk model of fishing not only redefined the notion of production, reversing the roles of fish and humans. The notion of economic productivity also became gender-specific, its application being restricted to the activities of males. The struggle for equal access to productive work, to work *outside* the household, was the central issue of the early women's movement in Iceland (see Kristmundsdóttir 1990). From the beginning of capitalist fishing, women held important economic roles ashore, particularly in the processing sector (first in salt-fish production and later in freezing plants); however, their contributions tended to be regarded as secondary and temporary. Their 'proper' place or permanent location was in the home. To some extent this attitude continues to the present. Women in the fishing sector are sometimes regarded as part-time workers – a 'reserve army' on the labour market, to borrow Gerrard's description (1983) of the situation for northern Norway. They can be sent back into the domestic sphere during lean periods, when there are no raw materials to process, and then called upon in times of plenty, when there is a shortage of labour. Occasionally women do go fishing, but it is not to the same extent as in the peasant economy. Women's participation is regarded as unnatural (see Figure 5.1). The few women who go to sea complain that they are not treated as full-time workers and that fellow male workers regard their presence aboard fishing boats as disrupting, even polluting. And women are never employed as skippers. The modern model of fishing emphasises that fishing is too dangerous for women. This attitude is illustrated by the following remarks, made by two Sandgerði skippers on the inter-boat radio when embarking on a fishing trip in spite of a bad weather forecast:

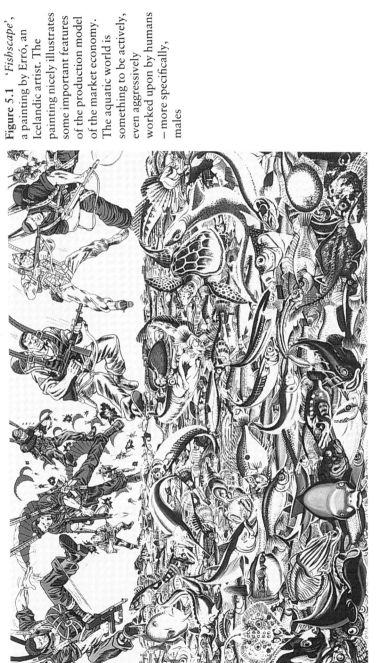

Figure 5.1 '*Fishscape*', a painting by Erró, an Icelandic artist. The painting nicely illustrates some important features of the production model of the market economy. The aquatic world is something to be actively, even aggressively worked upon by humans – more specifically, males

A: Your wife wasn't particularly pleased that you would be going out in this hell.

B: Well, you know how these women are. One would never go out if they were in charge.

A: No, that's for sure!

Such exchanges reinforce the idea that fishing is suitable only for the bravest and physically strongest men.

In the folk model of capitalist fishing, the productivity of labour is not equally distributed among males. The production value of the skipper overshadows that of everyone else. The skipper is said to be critical for fishing success. Catches are said to vary from one boat to another because skippers differ in their ability to locate and catch fish, an innate ability supposedly 'in the blood'. This is the idea of the 'skipper effect' (Pálsson and Durrenberger 1982, 1990). In the present share system the skipper receives twice the share of a deck-hand. This contrasts with the period of peasant production when, though there were different share systems at different times and places, it was usual that the foreman received the same share as an ordinary crewman. The extra share allotted to the skipper is not based on any power of command that he might derive from his ownership of capital (i.e. boat and equipment). Even though the skipper may be the owner of the vessel, a clear distinction is made between the roles of the skipper (*skipstjóri*) and owner (*útgerðarmaður*). An 'absentee-owner', even if he is a former skipper, does not interfere with the technical direction of the skipper. The Icelandic share system recognises the important distinction between expertise and ownership, just as do the Tikopia in the construction and repair of canoes (described by Firth 1965: 130–1).

The skipper is an operator of specialised means of production. The operation of fishing equipment such as electronic gear and modern deck technology demands expertise and institutionalised training. Obviously, too, fishing with modern technology – whether it be longlines, gill nets, or trawl – is very different from the individualistic handline fishery, typical of the past. Modern fishing requires synchronising several operations; during fishing, the crew has to co-operate as a team (see Figure 5.2). Not only, then, must the skipper be a skilful decision-maker and operator of equipment, he also must be in complete control in order to co-ordinate crew activities. But while changes in the nature of the process of extrac-

Figure 5.2 Work on deck on a boat using gill nets (photo: Sigurgeir Jónasson)

tion and the technology of fishing do explain the increase in the share allotted to those in charge during fishing operations, they do not account for the idea that the expertise of the skipper is critical for his success, *relative to that of others*. The reasons must be looked for elsewhere, in the development of capitalist production.

During earlier centuries, of course, someone had to co-ordinate the activities of the crew. This was the foreman. But it was not a particularly honorific role or title. In contrast, the present 'skipper' (*skipstjóri* – literally, ship ruler) is highly respected. The difference between the two roles is acknowledged by a former skipper who says that applying the 'honourable title' of the skipper to the old foremen on their open rowing boats 'sounds strange' to the younger generation (see Árnason 1976: 7). The label 'skipper' was first applied to those who had learned navigation abroad and sailed between Iceland and other countries. The title was thus restricted to those who were in control of large vessels, steamships and trawlers, even though it seems already to have been applied sporadically in some parts of Iceland to those in charge of open rowing boats in the late nineteenth century. As fishing became a full-time occupation, the role of skipper changed. It became a specialised role in an autonomous branch of production. The title of the skipper gradually replaced the title of the 'foreman'. In 1924 the journal of the Icelandic Fisheries Association – a journal which has regularly reported fishing catches from the beginning of the twentieth century – switched from the use of 'foreman' to 'skipper'. These two categories and their labels are sociologically significant; the former is rooted in the 'natural' discourse of household producers during earlier centuries while the latter plays a central role in the 'social' models of success which developed along with the market economy.

With the title of the skipper, a new profession was created with particular legally-enforced rights and obligations. The need for a school for fishermen was already discussed around the middle of the nineteenth century. One of those who argued in favour of formal schooling complained that many foremen 'just rushed out somewhere' looking for fish, and that many of them 'were in no way superior to the deck hands' (quoted in Guðmundsson 1979: 21). With the gradual introduction of sailing smacks, training in navigation was seen to be necessary. In 1891 a Marine Academy was established in the town of Reykjavík.

All participants in fishing benefit from good catches and stand to lose from poor ones. Given these interests, it follows that fishermen construct their own theories to account for differential success, the fact that some boats catch more fish than others. Variations in catch and fishermen's explanations for them are a popular topic of discussion. The different components of the models are weighed and their importance examined in the light of the empirical evidence available to the discussants. Most explanations take the form of what may be called a *stylistic* model. According to the stylistic model the skipper and his personality is the critical factor; he is responsible for the major difference. This is a model on which fishermen draw to organise their long-term experience of fishing seasons and fellow fishermen, and generally it is only tested against selected cases from the past. When fishermen talk about their careers, they often count the number of years they have spent with particular skippers rather than the years they have been on particular boats. After each winter season the names of the 'top' skippers (*aflamenn*; literally, 'catch-men') in the Icelandic fleet are reported in the mass media. In developing accounts for whole seasons as well as careers, people emphasise the personal characteristics and fishing tactics of the skipper. The stylistic model is often elaborated during public occasions (particularly on Fisherman's Day in June) and in the rich literature about successful skippers. It is not, however, simply a matter of nostalgia and stereotyping. For those who participate in fishing it is an accepted truth.

Other explanations of differential success take the form of a *materialistic* model (see Pálsson and Durrenberger 1983). This model emphasises quantifiable differences in equipment and the frequency of their application and is typically applied to everyday reality and short-term differences in catches. When, for instance, comparing the catches of a particular day, fishermen consider the sizes of boats, the size and stability of the crew, the kind and amount of gear (trawl, nets and lines). When accounting for differences over a limited period, a week or a month, they will also consider the number of trips. Fishermen actively discuss all of these factors, most of which are common knowledge, both while ashore and on the radio while engaged in fishing.

One element of the folk explanation for differential success concerns the distinction that is sometimes made between those who fish 'by cleverness' (*af lagni*; literally, with dexterity) and those who fish 'by force' (*af krafti*; literally, with power). This suggests that two skippers may be equally successful, but by different means. Those who fish 'by force' make more trips, use more gear and fuel, and destroy more gear in the process. Those who fish 'by cleverness' or dexterity are said to develop original fishing tactics. The admission of 'force' in the folk model of success may seem to modify the basic claim of the stylistic model that the size of catches is entirely due to the decisions and personal qualities of the skipper. Clearly material factors are also considered. But models of success may differ in their conceptions of technology and in where they draw the boundary between humans and the environment. As Geertz (1973: 9) has shown, a technical construction can be seen either as a feature of the physical landscape within which the individual is set and to which he or she must adapt, or as a cultural 'weapon' in a struggle against a harsh environment. Thus, the boat can be seen either as a part of the fisherman's environment or as an instrumental extension of his person. According to the dominant Icelandic model of success, the boat is a culturally-fashioned tool – an extension of the skipper's personality, analogous to the pen or computer utilised by a writer when creating a story. Even though material factors are considered, these are more a matter of style than of constraint. The distinction between fishing by cleverness and fishing by force probably developed as a response to the rapid capitalisation of the fishing fleet since the beginning of this century. Assuming that larger boats enabled some skippers to catch more than others, due to their larger crew size and amount of gear, fishermen nevertheless insisted that dexterity was quite important.

Prevailing models of fishing are *hierarchical* models in that they emphasise differences among a group of producers, normally within a local fleet. In these models fishing is not only a struggle with fish, it is also a competition *amongst* skippers. The skipper is a 'strong' leader fighting for his place in the hierarchy of prestige. He may use natural signs when deciding upon the timing and location of fishing, just as the foreman of earlier centuries, but as we will see later on, he is also heavily dependent on information about other skippers and their performance, particularly information on the location of their boats. When fishing, the skipper is a noisy commander, shouting directives and commands at his crew. This is unlikely to have been the case with the foremen in the past. As pointed out in one account: 'At sea foremen were usually quiet and taciturn' (see Pálsson 1987: 71). In contrast to the hierarchical

Table 5.1 *Egalitarian and hierarchical models of fishing*

The egalitarian	The hierarchical
Natural focus	Social focus
receiving 'gifts'	creating value
exchange and use value	commodities and prestige
'reading' of natural signs	observing others
personal records of trips	public records of catches
Inclusive participation	Exclusive participation
informal training	formal training
male and female	gender-specific
Co-operation among boats	Competition among boats
minimising differences	underlining differences
agreement in naming grounds	disagreement in naming
sharing information	withholding information
Weak leadership	Strong leadership
the 'foreman'	the 'skipper'
discussions among crew	authoritarian decisions

models of the present, the model of the household economy was an *egalitarian* one in that it minimised differences among producers. Modern fishing records are public documents which compare the catches of *different* skippers or boats for the same season (*aflaskýrslur*; literally, records of catches). The records of the past were personal or private ones, comparing the number of trips of a particular foreman or boat over several *seasons* (*róðratöl*; literally, records of trips). Table 5.1 presents a comparison of the two kinds of models.

According to the hierarchical model of fishing, some skippers catch more fish than others due to their cleverness, being particularly perceptive (*glöggir*) and able to memorise minute details, and because they follow other procedures when making decisions about the locations of prey. A famous skipper, nicknamed 'Binni' (see Figure 5.3), is reported to have said to a less successful skipper: 'You know why you don't catch fish? It's because you don't think like cod!' No doubt it was a sarcastic joke, but it underlined the importance of understanding fish migrations and their causes, of taking the role of fish. The skipper himself, however, is not supposed to elaborate on his knowledge, decisions, and fishing 'tricks', and skippers who have been at the top of the hierarchy of success for several seasons are particularly reluctant to comment upon their own performance. One of Binni's former crewmen remarked in an interview with the author that only after having worked on his boat for several seasons did he begin to detect a pattern in the skipper's fishing tactics. If skippers comment upon their own performance, they usually modestly create the impression that their success is due to the co-operation of the crew or sheer luck. When explaining exceptional catches during single fishing trips, they often refer to intuition and hunches, peculiar experience beyond their understanding and control. Several skippers have described how a dilemma regarding fishing locations was solved by a strange message or intuition, some kind of 'whisper'.

Many successful skippers are said to get into a particular 'fishing mood' (*fiskistuð*). The famous skipper just mentioned, Binni, explains the phenomenon of fishing mood as follows:

There is this mood, as it is called, which no one understands. It's like being possessed. It doesn't matter where you throw the gear, there is always plenty of fish. You come up with various ideas, which you may regard as ridiculous, but if you take them seriously you are bound to fish better than ever (Ási í Bæ 1963: 57).

Some skippers are known to have induced fishing moods by drinking alcohol, but the practice seems to be grossly exaggerated in some folk accounts. Sometimes dreams are said to provide information on a desirable course of action, and the timing or location of fishing. Information is thought to be given by a dead person or to be indicated by particular names or symbols in the dream. Some skippers are known to be dreamers and their accounts have been widely published. One local skipper explains:

I remember my dreams, and I must say it makes life a lot easier to know that one may expect a good catch. I recall a case where a dream told me exactly where to go . . . I dreamt the direction on the compass, east-north-east of Garðskagi. We fished like crazy (*Faxi* 1976: 9).

In his study of Alaska skippers, Gatewood (1983) distinguishes between rational and reasonable decisions. For him, a 'rational' decision involves both a conscious consideration of the alternatives open to the skipper and adherence to specific procedures for calculating or selecting among them. A 'reasonable' decision, in

Figure 5.3 *Binni, a famous skipper from the Vestman Islands*
(photo: Sigurgeir Jónasson)

contrast, lacks the latter procedural criterion; 'the manner by which the final synthesis is accomplished cannot be specified by the decider in advance of the decision itself – the decider does not adhere to a set procedure' (Gatewood 1983: 348–9). The choice of terms is somewhat unfortunate as Gatewood himself implies, emphasising that a reasonable decision is not necessarily 'irrational'. The extent to which a particular decision is rational or not is a rather tricky issue, for if 'rational' refers to what is socially optimal it will always depend on social context. But this need not concern us here; the distinction itself is a useful one. What matters is the expectation of the folk model regarding the procedures of the skipper when deciding upon fishing. In Alaska, Gatewood argues, skippers try to maintain an image of rationality, even though in practice they frequently resort to reasonable decisions. In Iceland, the contrary is the case. A successful skipper may try to maintain the image of someone who follows intuitive or 'reasonable' procedures even when he makes a calculated rational decision.

There is no reason to doubt that Icelandic skippers sometimes follow hunches and dreams as the folk model suggests. Much available evidence indicates that skippers often make 'reasonable' decisions. Statistical analysis shows that even though objective variables (such as boat size, number of boats fishing, and relative catches at different locations) do account for some of the variance in what skippers do, a large portion is left unexplained (see Durrenberger and Pálsson 1986). Hunches and dreams, or any 'reasonable' decisions, may be the result of decision-dilemmas where information is scant and the alternatives open to the skipper are equally attractive (Gatewood 1983). In his account of Icelandic herring fishing Thorlindsson points out (1988: 210) that a skipper has to 'make an inferential leap which is hard to account for in a rational conscious manner'. Orbach observes, one may note, in his ethnography of tuna fishing in California (1978: 79) that hunches can be expected 'after a long time in the search and more especially after a search without fish'. The logic of such procedures is an established topic in anthropological discussion. Some students of cognition argue that dreams generally serve the purpose of solving immediate problems of decision-making. Evans and Newman suggest (1973: 372) that dreams function as a 'memory filter' in that they allow the dreamer to examine the vast amount of information collected in the course of the day and to reject 'redundant or inapposite memories or responses'. Moore suggests that some magical practices may well be efficacious as techniques. He argues that the Naskapi technique of shoulder-blade divination, involving the interpretation of cracks in burned animal scapulae, can be seen as an attempt to randomise behaviour and 'avoid unwitting regularities . . . which can be utilised by adversaries' (1957: 73). Moore's perspective may apply to *some* magical practices, but hardly to fishing if the prey is seen as the 'adversary', simply because of the difficulty fish have in using evasive strategies. It may nevertheless be argued that for a group of skippers it is helpful to randomise the search for schools of fish. McGoodwin shows that shark fishermen in Pacific Mexico deploy their lines in a 'sunburst pattern' when catches are down (1989: 151). Such a random pattern, he claims, helps to maximise catches (see also White 1989).

What is the rationale, then, of accounts of hunches and dreams? All people dream, and dreams may well function at times as an unconscious decision device or memory filter, but a psychological explanation of dreaming in general does not explain why some groups of people are more likely than others to *claim* to use them in order to guide their actions. The importance of hunches and dreams in the folk model does not, therefore, seem to lie primarily in any problem-solving capacity directly related to the reality of extraction. Indeed, the accounts of Icelandic skippers suggest that what is being 'filtered' it not necessarily *their* memory or subconscious. Skippers often claim to use the dreams of others, their wife or a friend, some of whom have never been to sea. In such instances the skipper's own psychological processes are not at issue, except in the sense that he 'reads' the message of the dream. Dreams are interpreted similar to astrological signs. Accounts of hunches and dreams, I suggest, reduce the burden of responsibility on the leader of fishing operations. The idea that individual differences between skippers explain differential success places a high degree of responsibility on Icelandic skippers, and to minimise personal responsibility for success or failure an additional mechanism is used. The skipper's decisions are said to be the result of forces over which he has little or no control. Thus the skipper is sometimes presented as a powerless agent controlled by unconscious thoughts, mysterious powers or psychological states. Even though the qualities of the individual skipper are said to be crucial for his success, the skipper does not really determine his own fate. Such an explanation is

similar to that of Henriksen who argues (1973: 49) that in critical
decision-making situations divination techniques may function to
externalise decisions of where to go and look for prey. Good
Naskapi hunters can safeguard themselves by blaming the technique for occasional failures.[2] Secondly, following Moore's suggestion mentioned above, accounts of hunches and dreams can be seen
as attempts to randomise fishing operations in competitive situations. Skippers may give the *impression* that they avoid a fixed or
explicit pattern of operations, not because of the evasive capabilities
of the prey but rather to confound the observations of other
skippers with whom they share the notion of fishing as a zero-sum
game.

The rationality of the notion of hunches and dreams, then, is
largely located within the realm of social relations. Claims about
the importance of hunches and dreams underline the idea that the
knowledge and decisions of the skipper determine the size of his
catch; they provide one type of answer to the question which
became central to competitive fishing, namely 'how is one skipper
different from others?' Conceptions associated with hunches and
dreams are one element of the stylistic model of differential success
which developed in response to capitalist fishing. Given the role and
the economic place of the skipper as a manager of specialised means
of production, the most important criterion for his success was the
size of his catch relative to that of other skippers.

Information, competition and social honour

Skippers use a wealth of detailed knowledge to decide both when
and where to fish. They must choose times and places to fish on the
basis of their knowledge of currents, the behaviour of different
kinds of fish, bottom features, and past seasons, their ideas about
fish breeding and feeding patterns, and their interpretations of
weather reports. The concentration of fish depends partly on the
availability of food and the temperature of the sea. Spawning
migrations of cod are attributed to such factors and skippers
frequently measure the temperature of the sea and estimate the
extent to which it is mixed or layered in different temperature
strata. They compare their observations and theories of stock
movements and concentrations on the inter-boat radio and in
discussions between fishing trips. By memorising past observations

and keeping diaries, each skipper stores relevant information and uses it to make predictions. In an interview one skipper said:

It's strange. I can remember where I fished 10 or 15 years ago and whether the catch was good or not. I may remember what boats were in the neighbourhood. But I have difficulties in remembering the birthdays of my children!

When going out, the skipper pays attention to his fish-finding equipment as well as observing natural signs and relying on his knowledge of natural features and past experience. The electronic technology is very complex. Some instruments display bottom features while others show schools of fish in all directions (Asdic) or straight below the ship (fish finder). Skippers using active gear (trawls or seines) rely heavily on Asdic while those who use passive gear (nets or lines) rely more on the soundings of the fish finder. Modern fish finders display different soundings using different colours, which sometimes enables the skipper to distinguish between species of fish.

While the decision as to which location to visit is affected by a number of 'natural' variables, especially weather, bottom features, and available information on the movements of fish, guessing where the fish are likely to be is only part of the skipper's decision. Of no less importance is estimating where other skippers will be and how much they will catch. A radio exchange between two line skippers illustrates the kind of information that one may receive during a fishing trip:

A: Are you there? We are pretty close to shore drawing the line. I wanted to get some news from you. Aren't you on the Edge somewhere (a popular fishing area)?

B: I don't know if anyone has tried that. I have only got a few beasts (fish). The fishing is bad. Have you heard anything from X? He got a lot on the line over there yesterday.

There are some benefits in sharing information in this manner with other skippers. Skippers seem to co-operate especially after a long break in fishing. Sharing information on the state of the major areas saves time and fuel and each skipper gains information that he could not possibly acquire on his own. But because skippers compete among themselves for locations and fish, they also use various kinds of deception to mislead others. Thus, a net skipper who expects to get a good catch in some of his *trossur* may discharge the rest of his gear somewhere else only to mislead others. Often skippers attempt to avoid others in order to prevent disputes about territory and to avoid sharing information with them. One skipper commented:

Too much co-operation during fishing can be a disadvantage. Two guys often share information. But sometimes others get the news. It is better to have a chat between fishing trips than to use the radio. If you are telling some mystery you can also use less amplification (of the radio).

Early in the twentieth century, catches were compared according to the volume of fish liver each boat sold to the processors. The processors used records of liver volume as a measure of catch. And so did skippers. Those people responsible for keeping the liver statistics were plagued with questions from skippers about the catches of other boats. They were 'forced' to make a list for each day and record the figures as soon as a boat had landed. The list had to be publicly available, given the demand for the information it provided. Later on (in the 1950s) this demand was met by a local office, the 'Harbour Office', which is run by the communal authorities. Adding the public information provided by the catch records of the Harbour Office to his private knowledge of the location of boats during previous trips (which is often quite detailed) gives the skipper a rough measure of the relative productivity of different fishing spots at that time.

The local catch statistics are an important source of information for every skipper, but their daily use varies with fishing gear. In the case of net fishing, a location may be occupied for an extensive period, since nets are left in the sea between fishing trips and revisited a day or two later, depending on the weather. Lines, in contrast, must be drawn daily and taken ashore to be rebaited. Line skippers cannot, therefore, effectively occupy the same spot for more than a day. On the other hand, line skippers can respond to the information of the Harbour Office more quickly than net skippers can, since nets may be transferred only after they have been revisited.

The significance of the public catch records was particularly evident in Sandgerði during the 1930s when a great number of line boats were fishing locally. The lines of each boat could stretch several miles, and when different boats left the harbour at different

times, competing for locations that had proved to be highly productive on the day before or the previous days, lines often got
chopped and intermingled, especially when currents were strong.
Skippers sometimes tore the gear of their competitors apart, claim-
ing that they had been the first to visit the location in question.
After years of arguments and rivalry, local skippers agreed that in
order to prevent a 'chaos of lines' (*lóðaþvarg*) on the fishing
grounds it was necessary to bring competition under control. The
agreements which followed were meant to regulate the conduct of
fishing by specifying both the point or line of departure and the
timing of trips (*róðratími*, or 'rowing time'), synchronising de-
partures. The rules concerning the rowing time still apply in the line
fishery. Skippers study the catch records between fishing trips and
when they are waiting for a signal to leave again, they carefully
observe the actions of each other in order, as they say, 'not to get
behind'. Decision-making in competitive fishing, then, is intimately
related to the behaviour of other actors. Rather than assume that
skippers are collectively playing a game against the whims of
nature, as some anthropologists have done (Davenport 1960),
skippers should be seen to be playing a game against each other.

The skipper's position or 'seat' in the local competitive hierarchy
is extremely important. Being at the bottom of the daily catch
records is a particularly humiliating position. Skippers who know
that they have done exceptionally badly fear the comments of
others when they reach harbour. Some years ago an 'average'
skipper 'happened to' get a very good landing; his catch turned out
to be greater than that of any other local skipper on that day. When
he landed his catch another fisherman commented sarcastically, 'I
suppose the others must be getting quite something now'. Even
though years have passed since this happened, the skipper admits
that the recollection of these words still arouses a feeling of shame.
Being on top of the fleet for the season, on the other hand – being
aflakóngur (literally, 'catch-king') – brings a high degree of honour
and prestige.

Sometimes the amount of tension and anxiety associated with
the struggle for prestige is out of all proportion, considering the
negligible financial gains directly involved. Only a few kilos of fish
may decide who occupies the top 'seat', and bears the title of 'king'.
Despite his high income, the one who comes second may regard
himself as a loser. On one occasion in the Vestman Islands, in

1932, two skippers who turned out to have caught the same amount of fish at the end of the season, decided while drinking with their crews that the issue of who was entitled to the top seat had to be settled by some means (see Pálsson 1987: 46–7). The skippers summoned their crews while angrily accusing each other of trying to steal the title by cheating and counting 'useless' fish as proper catch. In the fights that ensued few got injured, but the event itself shows how far fishermen were willing to go to settle the issue. Clearly it was necessary to have a king.

Competition among skippers relates first of all to boats and fishing space, and other factors of obvious relevance for production and success. While the connection between competition and financial success may not always be apparent, as in the case of the fight over the title of 'king', prestige is not simply a matter of personal satisfaction or of winning in a competitive game. It is, rather, a matter of central economic importance in determining chances for future success. Prestigious skippers tend to have larger boats, more sophisticated equipment and sounder financial backing. If the skipper improves his position, he has a chance of commanding a larger boat, which is an important component in fishing success. If, on the other hand, he has a low position he risks losing his job. One of the Sandgerði skippers with the lowest prestige was fired at mid-season by his company because 'he did not fish enough'. A skipper's reputation also affects the number of fishing trips he can take in a season. The better a skipper's reputation and the greater his prestige, the more stable his crew. Top-ranking skippers can select from among the most experienced crewmen. The demand for experienced crewmen is particularly strong in the case of the net fishery. A skipper low in the prestige hierarchy admitted when interviewed that he did not 'believe' he was able to recruit the necessary number of crewmen due to his lack of prestige and that, as a result, he was forced to fish with the less labour-intensive and less productive longlines. When competition is tough, only a small difference in prestige and reputation can make all the difference.

While the hierarchy of skippers tends to be reproduced in a similar form one winter season after another, and fishing success (the size of the catch) is the most important avenue to prestige, the hierarchy is the result of a complex process which takes place in a context of flux and movement of boats, skippers and crewmen. A skipper's trust and prestige is not given once and for all from the moment he begins to fish, as, for instance, Barth implies (1966: 10) in his account of Norwegian herring fishing in which he speaks of the 'self-confirming pattern' whereby 'good' skippers get stable crews, fish independently and land high catches.[3] Rather, it is negotiated and maintained in the context of social discourse. The negotiation and maintenance of skippers' reputation and prestige takes place at three interrelated levels: between skipper and crewmen, within the local fleet, and among the general public.

Crew members usually refer to their skipper as 'the man' (*kallinn*) which signifies an attitude of submission and respect. Even though the skipper's role varies according to the kind of production unit involved, size of boat and number of crewmen, the skipper is always solely responsible for decisions relating to fishing and the fate of his vessel. During fishing trips, he demands and receives the unquestioning obedience of his crew. Between trips, however, relationships between crewmen and skippers are quite different. The status hierarchy is de-emphasised and joking is prevalent. The crew may go out with the skipper for entertainment. During such encounters skippers and crew negotiate each others' trust and prestige. Because crew members take current ranking of skippers to be a good indication of future success, they compete for places on the boats of high-ranking skippers. For the crew, however, the reputation of the skipper is not only a matter of financial gains. A skipper's prestige, as Gatewood remarks for Alaska (1983: 356), enhances the social identity of crewmen, a useful asset in many social contexts. When high-ranking skippers change boats, often 'their' crews go with them.

In interaction with his colleagues, the skipper emphasises his independence. His role tends to be that of a man who is careful not to ask others for advice because that would show his dependence on them, and not to be pushed around by other skippers in the competition for space because that would reflect negatively on his prestige. Communication between skippers on the inter-boat radio is an important part of the process of prestige negotiation and impression management. While to the outsider inter-boat communication may sound like a classic example of what Malinowski called 'phatic communion' (1923) – the lengthy and repetitive exchanges between skippers, and the gossip, teasing and joking they contain often seem to be simply an end in themselves – one should not underestimate its social and discursive significance. What skippers say is interpreted on the basis of an extensive prior knowledge of catch records and fellow fishermen. Skippers know, for instance, that some of their colleagues are more prone to lie than others and that different meanings may be attributed to statements made on the radio, or the lack of statements, depending on the personalities involved. During radio exchanges at sea as well as in private discussions between fishing trips, skippers maintain their relationships with other skippers, constructing each other's image and reputation in the process.

The arena of prestige negotiation is not restricted to the sea, for often it extends into the larger sphere of local relations. For instance, many of those involved in the fishing industry ashore – particularly boat owners and operators of fishing plants – regularly listen to the inter-boat radio, a device fishermen call 'the spy', waiting for 'fishing news'. Local people often compare the performance of skippers, discussing the successful and unsuccessful, the old-timers in relation to the young, and in the process evaluating the relative potential and prestige of individual skippers. Some skippers 'really do fish', while others are 'fish deterrents'. When ashore the skipper has to built up his reputation in a highly subtle manner, since modesty is regarded as a virtue and public staging of self is not tolerated. Typically, skippers' accounts of dangers at sea contain few references to emotional states. Their style is often strangely objective, given the nature of the events described. One skipper whose ship had been caught twice by life-threatening breaking seas during the same fishing trip commented during a chat the next day with fellow fishermen ashore that everything on deck which could possibly get damaged had been smashed, adding laconically that one could 'take it like snuff'. People sometimes make fun of unsuccessful skippers, but not, it seems, in terms of their extreme lack of success which is regarded more as tragic. Rather they are ridiculed for not following the rules of the game, such as overstating their manliness and bravery.

The notion of the 'skipper effect' is the cumulative result of such complex negotiations about individual performance in competitive fishing (see Pálsson and Durrenberger 1982, 1983). The idea that skippers differ greatly in their catching potential entered the rhetoric of fishermen, allowing skippers to enhance the demand for their expertise as a unique commodity on the labour market. Among skipper-owners there was competition for the financial support of merchants and processors. Other skippers competed for access to boats. As boat technology developed, the demand for skilled crewmen increased. Labour was no longer guaranteed by law and skippers had to recruit followers. The social relations of capitalist fishing encouraged the idea that skippers are critical for fishing success.

This chapter has analysed transformations in the social relations of Icelanders and their representations of nature and production. During the period of household production, mythology emphasised the distinction between land and sea. A series of anomalous waterbeings mediated between the two domains, thereby determining the fate of humans. Humans were passive recipients of what was allotted to them. With the development of capitalist fishing the ocean and its habitants were redefined. Fish were no longer seen to be superior to humans, rather they were seen to be subject to human control. The earlier mythology of water-beings became redundant. With the development of the market economy, human labour was seen to create value. But some workers were seen to be more productive than others. Conceptually, the labour process became gender-specific. Only the non-domestic work of men was regarded as productive.

Even though according to the early model of the Icelandic market economy the attribute of economic productivity was restricted to males, it was not seen to be equally distributed among them. Skippers were credited with a particular power, fishiness, and some of them were said to be far more productive than others. Even though the new concept was based upon an earlier indigenous notion which also explained differential success in individual terms, the two concepts were not identical. The new conceptual model is more secular than the earlier one. In the previous model, no probability could be assigned to uncertain outcomes of natural events. The present model is much more attuned to the idea that the workings of nature contain an essentially random element, i.e. to the idea of (calculable) risk. With the market economy, the notions of 'luck' and 'chance' were added to the vocabulary of fishing.

In evaluating the risks of production the skipper may use intuitive procedures, 'reasonable' ones in Gatewood's sense (1983). Ecological relations may explain why fishermen often *use* such procedures for decision-making, but they do not explain why particular groups of fishermen account for differential success in such terms while others do not. As we have seen, some groups of fishermen operating within a similar set of ecological relations may reject such accounts. Accounts of hunches and dreams, I have argued, have their own rationale independent of ecological constraints and the uncertainties of fishing. Such accounts reflect the need to externalise decisions and reduce the burden of responsibility in highly competitive situations.

A distinction similar to the one presented above between 'egalitarian' and 'hierarchical' models has been made in research on sport fishing. Hummel and Foster distinguish (1986) between 'elitist' and 'democratic' versions of fishing in terms of technology and conceptions of fair play. Their distinction, however, is not quite the same. Their 'elitist' model agrees with our 'egalitarian' model, not the 'hierarchical', in suggesting that the essence of fishing is in the contest between humans and fish. In such a model, technology is immaterial. For elitist sportsmen, the difficulties in the pursuit of fish may even be self-imposed; what matters is a particular code of fair play and the application of certain skills against a highly mobile prey. In this model, angling is an exclusive high art – fishing by 'cleverness', in the vocabulary of professional fishermen in modern Iceland. The rewards are personal or internal, self-satisfaction. The chief goal is to catch fish under well-defined conditions. The fish tend to be anthropomorphised and depicted as particularly cunning creatures. Such a conception of fishing is quite different from that of the 'democratic' model, the model Hummel and Foster associate with many modern tournaments or recreational fisheries in which case the competitors fight *each other* with ever more complex gadgets. For those who subscribe to the 'democratic' model, the sport exists among human competitors – just as the focus of our 'hierarchical' model of fishing is on the competition between skippers. As Oregon anglers put it, the competitors 'pit their skills against those of others' (Smith 1980: 276). Each sportsman tries to get the biggest catch possible – fishing 'by force' as Icelandic fishermen would say. In this case the rewards are external, determined by public esteem.

The explanatory models which emerged along with the Icelandic market economy – the hierarchical model of the 'skipper effect' and the stylistic model of success – were constructed in order to make sense of the realities of competitive fishing, the fact that some boats caught more fish than others. Differences in fishing success had to be explained. To fully understand the folk model of the skipper effect it is not enough, however, to pay attention to the meaning or information value of the utterances associated with it. We must also attend to what the utterances do – their 'force' or 'performative' aspects, to borrow the language of speech act theorists (Austin 1962). The concept of the skipper effect was the result of a complex and subtle discourse which involved skippers, crewmen and boat owners in acts of negotiation over reputation, trust and prestige. The relations of skippers with crew men, highly important for the production process, became a central concern of production discourse. In order to appropriate fish, skippers had to become fishers of men.

6 The domination of nature: the modern state

Some of the major problems of fisheries policy concern the relationship between the local level and the national level – between the 'grass roots' and the state. In industrial society, indigenous management methods are often replaced by, or combined with, public policies – regional, national or even international ones. People opt for public solutions partly because of the complexity of industrial fishing systems and the need for striking a balance amongst different political factions and interest groups. But while public policies, by definition, remove decision-making from the local community, they must somehow ensure minimal communications between the two levels of government to be effectively constructed and implemented. Even though major decisions are taken by regional or national agencies, it is nevertheless possible to incorporate informal, indigenous management techniques in the planning process. The history of Icelandic fishing provides several examples of democratic solutions to problems of resource management. The co-ordination of the 'rowing time' in line fishing, discussed in the previous chapter, is a case in point. In that episode, we see recognition of a common problem and a collective but informal solution that later attained the status of law. It shows the ability of fishermen to translate common interest into common rules sanctioned and enforced by the state. The national economy of Iceland is heavily dependent on fishing and this means that government policy must be responsive to grass roots politics and the 'needs' of the fishing industry.

But while government policy in Iceland generally respects local demands, it is not necessarily equally responsive to the demands of different sectors of the industry and different kinds of production units. In the case of the new quota system in cod fishing, I argue, an apparently neutral and technical solution to the problem of management has resulted in a massive transfer of power and capital. This chapter discusses the period of state intervention and consolidated capitalism in Icelandic fishing. With the threat of overexploitation of fishing stocks in the 1960s, and the increasing social authority of marine biological research, a 'scientific' discourse on production and resource-use began to develop, and with it emerged a new rationality which assumes that humans are collectively responsible for the maintenance of fish. Not only does the present quota system in demersal fishing put a new ceiling on the total allowable catch during a fishing season, it also specifies the catch to which each boat is entitled. The prevailing rationality of skippers persists, but its credibility diminishes as it loses its social significance. The local discourse of skippers, fishermen, and fish-workers is increasingly being silenced by the more public discourse of marine biologists, politicians, and state bureaucrats. One of the main issues of public discourse is who 'owns' the fish and how access to resources should be allocated. The contracting for tenure or property rights is at the centre of a fiery, national discourse on various issues; fishiness, the environment, gender, and equity – the distribution of wealth and income.

Consolidated capitalism

The roots of the present system of consolidated capitalism can be traced to ecological and economic changes at the time of the Second World War. During the war foreign fishing in Icelandic waters decreased and fish stocks were able to recover, thus ensuring good catches for Icelandic fishermen for some years into the future. There were good prices for fish on foreign markets during the war and immediate post-war period, and fishing success was thereby translated into income. Also, the British and American forces which occupied Iceland in order to prevent German control of the North Atlantic provided many jobs and opportunities for Icelandic entrepreneurs. But perhaps the most significant development was the gaining of full independence from Denmark in 1944 and the formation of a coalition government which lasted until 1947. The first independent government of Iceland was committed to a policy of economic development and concentrated on the fishing industry as a means to that end. Parties of the left and right were united in the common cause of modernisation – involving development of the fishing fleet, improvement of harbours and construction of processing plants. This government was known as the Modernisation Government (*Nýsköpunarstjórn*). In the late 1950s and the early 1960s boat technology underwent further changes largely as a result of changes in herring behaviour.

The state occupied a central role in the making of the modern fishing industry. Governmental support was essential for the capitalisation of boats, ports and fishing plants. Labour was attracted to the fleet by an 'insurance' system which afforded a minimum wage to fishermen. Particular funds were established to encourage private investment and regional development. A complicated 'fund' system was developed to reduce the effects of seasonal fluctuations and to transfer capital among the different sectors of the industry. All this served the national economy by encouraging the extraction of the only marketable resource available. As a result of these developments, decision-making and management were increasingly concentrated in the hands of non-fisherman entrepreneurs, agents of the state and marine biologists.

Since governmental decisions influence all sectors of the industry, those people involved in fishing, processing and export organise to affect policy in their favour. Some of their organisations are formal and permanent associations, such as associations of fishermen and boat owners, the various groups of processors, and the various departments of the semi-governmental Fisheries Association (*Fiskifélag Íslands*), which embraces many of the interest groups involved. All of these groups take part in a complicated political process, the results of which change from one season to another.

Administrative regulations in relation to fishing are made within the framework of a general body of law passed by Parliament in 1976, which regulate fishing within Icelandic waters up to two hundred miles from the coast. These regulations are changed in response to the condition of the stocks, as evaluated by the biologists of the Marine Research Institute, and the demands of various interest groups. Some of these regulations respond only to the demands of local fishermen, others meet the recommendations of the biologists. These regulations are the results of a series of compromises among local and national interest groups.

The size of the most important fishing stock (cod) is subject to some periodic ecological fluctuations which are largely independent of humans, though human exploitation has its effect too. During the first decades of the twentieth century, when full-time fishing was rapidly becoming the livelihood of Icelanders, the fishing effort multiplied as trawlers and motor boats replaced open rowing boats.

Increased effort by both foreign and Icelandic vessels resulted in periodic declines in catches. After the Second World War the Icelandic fleet continued to expand and foreign fleets resumed fishing in waters off Iceland. From 1955 to 1975 the fishing effort doubled, but despite this increase in effort Icelandic catches fell from 306,000 to 266,000 tons. This process led to a classic open-access, common-property tragedy (see Durrenberger and Pálsson 1987a). The opportunistic exploitation of fishing stocks by freely-competing skippers who were trying to get what they could while stocks lasted, led to sharply diminished returns. The 'natural' limit to overexploitation, the 'maximum sustainable yield', had been exceeded. Responding to recognition of this tragedy and the pressures of fishermen, the Icelandic government took the international move of trying to expand its jurisdiction and exclude foreign fishing vessels from waters around Iceland. It drew Great Britain into 'cod wars' that resulted in the exclusion of British trawlers from Icelandic fishing grounds from December 1976 onward. However, the task of restoring depleted stocks and preventing future tragedies remained. An increased use of scientific models and government policies for fisheries management within Iceland's domain has resulted. Iceland's fishermen have had to accept constraints on their activities.

The threat of over-fishing has usually been met with measures that do not discriminate between groups of fishermen. Thus, for some years the government tried to put a ceiling on the total allowable catch of cod by deciding upon the length of the winter season and closing particular popular fishing areas. Such measures affected most fishermen in a similar way. Indeed, there seems to have been general agreement among fishermen that no one should be denied access to the fish. The solutions tended to be ones guaranteeing that the benefits and the costs were spread among all the fishermen rather than concentrated among a few, even though the latter choice might have been simpler to design, administer and enforce as well as ensure a more coherent management policy. Generally, fishermen saw the policy of licensing as a threat that would undermine the previously-held assumptions about equal access. With the introduction of the quota system in cod fishing, this context has been radically changed.

The present system of quota management was introduced late in 1983. By then the total annual cod catch was even less than the amount recommended by fisheries biologists, and the forecast for 1984 was bleak. The government decided to reduce the cod quota for 1984 to 220,000 tons, from an estimated catch of around 290,000 tons. At the annual conference of the Fisheries Association, most interest groups were rather unexpectedly in favour of a boat-quota system that would divide this reduced catch within the industry itself. The precise allocation of catches was debated, until it was agreed that each boat was to be allocated an annual quota on the basis of its average catch over the past three years. This meant that some ships would get higher quotas than the rest of the fleet, a fundamental departure from traditional policy. The individual quota system was recommended by the fishing industry and was to be administered by the Ministry of Fisheries. The maximum catch of each boat is presently decided upon in advance, largely on the basis of its catch in the past. This policy has been re-evaluated every year, but the system remains more or less the same.

By now, there is emerging a rather clear picture of the long-term effects of the quota system on the structure of the industry. The political debate is not so much concerned with the technical details of quota allocation, as with the larger social and political consequences of the system. The most serious criticism of the present system is that it transfers immense resources into the hands of a relatively small group of people, comprised of state officials (the Ministry of Fisheries) and the owners of the biggest boats and the fishing companies. During the cod wars Iceland claimed national ownership of the fishing stocks in coastal waters, a highly valuable resource. The new quota system divides access to this resource among those who happened to be boat owners when the system was introduced. Further, this privileged access is free of charge. Increasingly, this 'gift' from the state is being transferred into capital. On the one hand, boat owners may sell their *boats* and thereby their share of the catch. On the other hand, they may sell their *quota* for any one year, or part thereof, effectively renting the catch to which they are entitled. In both cases an independent market has developed whereby boat owners are able to turn their free licences into profits in accordance with supply and demand. There are reports of vessels being sold at a price which is two or even three times that of their 'real' value. Permanent access to the resource, therefore, is no less valuable in monetary terms than the vessel itself. The temporary transfer of quotas, that is between vessels, is subject to some restrictions and it is difficult to estimate the amount of capital involved in such transactions, but a sizeable part of the annual quota, possibly one quarter, is already changing hands. In 1984 11.6 per cent of the total vessel quota changed hands, 13.5 per cent in 1985. Given the price of a permanent licence, embodied in the excessive value of fishing vessels on the free market, one can assume that temporary tenure is generally being sold at very high prices. The estimated total value of outstanding quotas in 1984 was $24 million USD and $35 million USD in 1985 (Árnason 1986). These figures indicate, Árnason argues, the economic rents produced by the quota system. The tax-authorities have decided, one may note, that quotas are to be reported as 'property' on tax-forms and that the selling of quotas involves a form of 'income'.

These transactions are likely to have profound implications for the distribution of power and income, and indeed the whole structure of Icelandic society. Not only has a permanent right to fish been given to an exclusive group, but this right is increasingly being turned into a marketable commodity. As access has to be bought, and prices of boats and quotas are subject to the mechanism of the market, it becomes increasingly difficult for newcomers to enter the industry. In the past, successful skippers were often able to become boat owners and a relatively large proportion of the fleet is still the property of crewmen and their families. In a few years, one may predict, it will be very hard for skippers to start their own business, since the present system is likely to favour the bigger companies.

It is increasingly difficult for independent skipper-owners to stay in business. Even though kinsmen and friends are prepared to go on working for some time without getting the shares to which they are entitled, such relationships can withstand time-lags in reciprocation for only a limited period. Crew members, whether relatives or not, are unlikely to join a skipper-owner the following season if they have been 'treated badly' during the present one. In recent years several skipper-owners, faced with their commitments to crew members and creditors, the effects of increased prices for extra fish-quotas and the (usual) uncertainties of fishing, have lost their boats, through bankruptcy or forced sales. While this is, no doubt, too much to attribute to the quota system on its own, it is one of the reasons why the independent skipper-owner is having a hard time.

Alternative management schemes are now being discussed by fishermen and the general public. There are demands for a return to the prior system. Such a development, however, is unlikely, given the inadequacies in economic and ecological terms of the previous system. There are also demands for communal quotas where local authorities would be given a certain amount of autonomy as regards the allocation of quotas in their areas, a limited revival of the grass roots politics of earlier decades. Furthermore, some critics of the present system favour public auctions of quotas, in which the state would receive incomes in return for the selling of the right to fish. One of the big issues in the management debate is the extent to which a free-market solution to fisheries problems, in the form of a quota system, can be reconciled with co-management and other ways of delegating responsibility to the local level.

Young (1983) distinguishes between the stated objectives of management schemes, unstated objectives, and unintended side effects. Usually the stated objectives of management proposals are to bring the industry under control, to promote conservation and sustained yield, and to ensure reasonable returns to the average fisherman. The main stated objective of the quota system in demersal fishing in Iceland was to control the total annual catch and to make fishing more economical. While the cost side of the economic equation has been significantly reduced, there has been less success as regards the ecological objective. The proportion of immature cod in the catch has been increasing. It is rather surprising, then, that politicians have been willing to institutionalise such a radical departure from the previous system, given the failure of the new one in securing the reproductive potential of the stocks. The unstated objectives of the new system, perhaps, was to secure the position of the biggest companies and the owners of the largest vessels, thereby favouring some groups of producers over others. Increasingly, fishing becomes the business of large-scale business firms.[1] Apparently neutral and technical management decisions have had important effects on the balance of power and structure of the fishing industry by changing the possibilities and alternatives with respect to access to fish.

No doubt there are some unintended side effects as well. One of them is the tendency of fishermen under the present system to dump low-quality species, immature fish, and excess catch for which they have no quota. Since there is a ceiling on the catch that each boat is entitled to, fishermen are likely to discard parts of their catch. Recent surveys indicate that great quantities of fish are dumped into the sea, and much greater than Icelanders generally like to believe. Illegitimate discarding of fish creates many problems in relation to law enforcement, the policing of the seas. To make sure that all the catch is landed is both expensive and technically difficult (ideally, it would require an inspection officer aboard every fishing vessel). Another problem relates to the reliability of models of recruitment and stock size. If many of the fish that are caught are never landed or reported, estimations of stock size, the whole basis of quota allocations, are obviously rather imprecise.

Changing notions of fishing: the authenticity of the 'skipper effect'

If, as I have argued, models of fishing are motivated by the rationalities of economic systems, we are likely to witness the emergence of a new folk model of fishing in Iceland. The present model of skipperhood and fishing success developed in response to the competition between skippers in the expansive market economy of the first decades of the twentieth century. Now there is a new ceiling on production as catches and quotas are allocated to individual producers. Indeed, fishermen's models seem to be undergoing fundamental changes.

Some of these pertain to spatial conceptions and the perception of fishing space. With national management of fisheries and the installation of a new ceiling on productive targets, the fishing grounds have become a closed and stable domain again. Skippers are no longer frontiersmen, and there is less secrecy among them than before regarding fishing spots. Consequently, there are few 'wild' or unknown domains left in the spatial universe of skippers. This new cognitive map is a relatively static one, much like the system of 'natural' coding by the application of names for landmarks in the peasant society of earlier centuries. The static reference to spatial relations is reinforced by the application of electronic instruments for navigation (the loran technique) and the use of official maps of fishing grounds for the sake of safety, both of which are based on a simple system of numbers and fixed co-ordinates. Icelandic law requires that skippers report their locations on a special radio channel twice a day, to save time and search in the

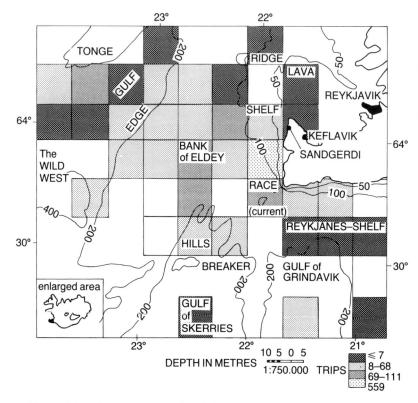

Figure 6.1 *The reporting grid and fishing areas of Sandgerði boats*
(the frequency of fishing refers to the winter season of 1981)

case of emergency. The reporting grid used is one of identical squares, each of which is 15 km on a side, or 225 square km. At first the official grid was 'only' a safety device to which skippers referred primarily to comply with rules made ashore. The skippers continued to speak of fishing space in quite different terms, with a vocabulary of transient and personal names, but gradually the official grid has increasingly replaced the previous map of skippers or been accommodated within it. Figure 6.1 shows the reporting grid and fishing areas visited by Sandgerði skippers during the winter season of 1981.

The models of differential success that have been dominant over the last decades are now also subject to change. Indeed, there are some signs of an entirely new discourse among fishermen. A skipper's prestige is still determined by his performance relative to that of others during a fishing season, but with the quota system the *size* or volume of the catch – the main criterion for success in the folk model of previous decades – has largely been removed from the skipper's sphere of influence. As a result, a new criterion is sometimes being applied to skippers' success – the *value* of their catch *relative to effort* or the number of fishing trips. Skippers point out that while they have always worried about not fishing enough, trying to maximise returns as well as their relative prestige in the competitive hierarchy of success, at present the problem is sometimes the reverse. Under the quota system, they say, their mind is often preoccupied with catching too much, since 'excessive' catches, anything that is beyond the quota allocated to the boat, may mean prosecution by the state. Generally, fishermen show much less interest in the catch records than they did a few years ago, during the golden years of skipperhood and the hierarchical model of success.

When the quota system was first applied there were heated debates about what to allocate and to whom. The issues involved illustrate the conflict between the assumptions and rationalities of the discourse of boat owners and fishermen. Boat owners argued for a '*catch*-quota', to be allocated to their boats. Some fishermen, on the other hand, advocated an '*effort*-quota', to be allocated to skippers or crews. In fishing, they argued, value was created through the application of their expertise and labour power and not that of the equipment, the boat and the fishing gear. A boat-quota would be grossly unfair since the 'best' skippers would be assigned the same quota as the 'bad' ones. When allocated the same amount of effort, measured in number of allowable fishing days in a season, the 'good' and the 'bad' skipper would catch different amounts of fish. Under a system of effort-quotas successful skippers would be rewarded for their exceptional contribution to the economy by an extra catch. The authorities partly conceded to such criticism when revising the regulatory framework of the quota system. While catches were allocated to boats and not skippers, as before, boat owners were offered the right to choose between effort and catch. It turned out, however, that few of them were willing to bet on the effort-quota and the skipper.

Fishermen sometimes express the view that the custom of awarding the most successful skipper of the year a particular prize on Fishermen's Day is a little archaic. The hunting element of fishing (*veiðimennska*), they point out, is rapidly disappearing with increasing governmental control of the industry. As fishing is being 'reduced' to business transactions, success becomes less a matter of fishiness than capital and economics. The top skippers are simply privileged 'quota-kings' (*kvótakóngar*). Significantly, after the winter season of 1989 the skipper highest on the national records of catches (the 'catch-king'), one of the most celebrated skippers in the fleet, publicly declared that he would not accept the prize to which he was entitled. The competition, he argued, was 'unjust' since some skippers were barred from the competition due to the small quota assigned to them. The local committee responsible for the awarding of medals and trophies on Fishermen's Day decided to abolish the custom of giving prizes for exceptional fishing success.

In the past, the view that the competitiveness of fishing might go too far was rarely expressed. There were some examples, however, of critical remarks. Laxness, for instance, pointed out that accidents at sea were not only caused by 'natural' reasons. Fishing expeditions, he argued, were a kind of religious sacrifice, where skippers offered their crews to the sea in order to bolster their image as heroic fishermen and courageous seamen: 'An investigation . . . should be carried out to establish which skippers are seaworthy. At the same time, some ethical concepts associated with seafaring might be re-evaluated, including the concept of the hero of the sea . . .' (1985 [1944]: 39). Laxness went on to discuss the case of a skipper who was honoured for a courageous record, but who allegedly had lost several crewmen during his career due to extreme effort and unnecessary excitement. 'What a primeval hero! What a Viking!', Laxness cynically remarked. In the past, such attacks rarely occurred, and if they did they were quickly rejected as absurd, even a kind of heresy. Nowadays, similar voices are not only frequent but the critics come from the ranks of fishermen themselves. The brave skipper who risks his men for an extra catch is no longer a fisherman's hero. And, indeed, to take such a risk would be quite bizarre, considering the production constraints posed by the quota system.

Fishermen, including skippers, sometimes argue nowadays that successful skippers receive too much attention; the 'worship of the catch-kings' (*aflakóngadekur*), they suggest, is becoming irrelevant. Increasingly fishermen are willing to entertain the idea that differential fishing success has more to do with boats and gear than with skippers and their crews. Some anthropological research does support such a view. Durrenberger and I have argued that in modern Iceland differences in success are statistically explained more by technical and ecological factors than the personal qualities of skippers, contrary to the model of the 'skipper effect' (see Pálsson and Durrenberger 1983, 1990). In order to assess the role of the skipper, we operationalised the notion of skipper effect as the contribution of the skipper to explaining variation in catch among boats – the residual after other variables, effort and boat size, had been taken into account. We could account for all but little (about 15 per cent) of the variance in catch in the demersal cod fishery by a regression model with only two independent variables; boat size and number of fishing trips. The data on catches pertain to the expansive phase prior to the introduction of the quota system, i.e. when there was no ceiling on effort. These results indicated that the skipper effect was much less than one would expect from the folk account. Analyses of fishing tactics, of skipper behaviour, yielded similar results (Durrenberger and Pálsson 1986; Pálsson 1988b). The fishing profiles of successful skippers and unsuccessful ones are not that different. Successful skippers seem to be no more 'independent' than their colleagues in terms of where they fish. They seem to have rather conservative fishing profiles in that they concentrate their effort on relatively few locations. We tested the statistical model we developed to account for differential success in the demersal cod fishery on data for the very different pelagic herring fishery (Durrenberger and Pálsson 1983). While in the latter case boat size and fishing effort accounted for less than half the variance in catch, there was not a high correlation between one year's catch and that of another. The lack of correlation between herring catches from one year to the next, we argued, obviated the explanatory value of the notion of the skipper effect. We account for the high degree of unexplained variance in herring catches with reference to the randomness of herring behaviour, to the fact that herring catches are a kind of lottery, something which is occasionally emphasised in folk accounts. Hilborn and Ledbetter (1985) and Hilborn (1985) come to a similar conclusion about purse seining for salmon off the Pacific coast of Canada.

Statistics rarely provide simple yes or no answers; results must be interpreted in terms of prior expectation or hypotheses.[2] The Icelandic folk model of the skipper effect is misleading in the sense that it assumes that the skipper makes *all* the difference. This is not to say that one should discard all aspects of Icelandic folk models of fishing. As we have seen, the folk models of fishing are quite complex and different aspects are appealed to in different contexts depending on the nature of the discourse. The interesting anthropological question is, when is each model invoked and legitimated as an authoritative, authentic account. In preceding chapters I outlined a historical and sociological explanation for the emphasis on the skipper effect in modern Iceland in terms of the discourse and constraints of competitive fishing.

The issue of differential fishing success sometimes extends far beyond the discourse of fishermen and the academic concerns of social scientists to larger debates about resource management and fishing policy. In some parts of Canada the skipper's contribution and its relevance for quota allocation is a pressing political issue. One programme for reducing the catching power of the fleet is for the government to purchase boats from fishermen in order to take them out of operation. Some programmes recognise differences in boats and offer to purchase them at a price per ton. The argument has been developed, however, that it is not boats that must be removed from the fishery, but the most successful fishermen (Hilborn 1985: 11). Hilborn and Ledbetter point out (1985: 56) that 'if the determinant of catching power is the skipper and not the physical attributes of the vessel he operates, a buy-back of vessels that contribute to production will not reduce catching power'. In a context of power differentials and economic competition between antagonistic interest groups, judgements relating to the nature of skippers' contributions are likely to be informed by political rhetorics.

The established image of the successful skipper may survive for some time, as a romantic or nostalgic reference among the general public to the deeds cherished over the last decades. Occasionally, the modern model of skipperhood, developed in the context of the market economy, is imposed on to the peasants of the distant past. A recent article in a popular magazine boldly claims that 'Icelandic waters have been fished for centuries by a hardy and intrepid breed of men striving to outdo each other for the honour and almost heroic status of catching the most fish' (News from Iceland, 1984

(102): 7). Accounts of skipper effect and fishing mood, however, no longer represent significant moments in a living production discourse as they did in the recent past; they have become curiosities or relics from bygone times, disappearing into folklore just as the accounts of God's gifts and mysterious sea creatures did before them when the discourse of skippers replaced that of foremen.

Competing rationalities: science, equity and power

Ichthyology and marine biology developed relatively late in Iceland as elsewhere. Some marine biological research had already occurred in Iceland at the beginning of the twentieth century, but full-time research started later, in the 1940s. The present Marine Research Institute was established in 1965. Fishermen and the general public regarded the first marine biologists as strange and eccentric people who operated on fish for no obvious reasons, 'spending hours fiddling with all kinds of disgusting little things' (Hagalín 1964: 321). The disrespect seems to have been mutual. One of the pioneers in marine biology was said to 'have quickly realised that various kinds of superstitious beliefs prevented the natural development of this important industry' (Bergsson 1940: 240). In the beginning, the relationship between fishermen and biologists was characterised by shared ignorance. Generally, each group viewed the discourse of the other as entirely irrelevant. Later on, with the progressive development of the forces of production in the fisheries and the increased involvement of the state in the management of the industry, fishermen and biologists confronted each other, armed with their competing theories and rationalities.

As we have seen, capitalist production in fishing has been subject to 'scientific' control and stringent regulations. Marine biology brought with it a new rationality including the notion of homeostatic fisheries, a 'harvesting' orientation which assumes that humans are in total control of the ecological situation.[3] During the cod wars, the fishermen tended to regard internal limitations to access with some scepticism, arguing that if they did not catch the fish, the British and Germans would anyway. But once the common enemy disappeared conflict between fishermen and biologists increased. Each accused the other of following an 'irrational' policy. Often the proposals put forward by the marine biologists were met with distrust and strong emotions from fishermen.

Fishermen, however, are not a homogeneous group. One of the

significant differences in fishing systems concerns the nature of production units. While production in Icelandic fishing is usually geared for the market, the units of production differ in terms of organisation and motives. The capitalist firm is very responsive to changes in the relative profitability of fishing and processing. If the profitability of a particular fishery goes down, the company is likely to transfer some of its capital to another fishery or to processing facilities. For the petty entrepreneur, on the other hand, it is enough to survive the year and hope for better luck next year. Many skipper-owners form shareholding companies, together with family members, in order to prevent total loss of property in case of bankruptcy. Unlike absentee owners, skipper-owners continue to invest when fishing ceases to be profitable, but unlike the peasant fishermen of earlier centuries they do accumulate capital when it is possible to increase returns. Such differences in organisation are likely to correlate with differences in perception of environmental problems. Although the contrast is by no means a stark one, the skipper-owners are more likely than the absentee owners to define environmental conditions as problematic and to take direct collective action to redress the balance.

With the growing importance of biological information for resource management, fishermen in general have become less powerful than before. Power has shifted in favour of the scientists. The researchers at the Marine Research Institute have become an authoritative group while the discourse of fishermen is increasingly being suppressed or silenced. Some of the key elements of the hierarchical model of success discussed in the previous chapter are likely to persist as long as the social constraints of competition and prestige prevail. At the public level of fisheries management, however, the skipper's rationality is being replaced by the more 'plausible' rationality of the scientists. Fishermen complain that all initiative is being taken from them and that 'everything is being banned'. Usually the biologists are the target of their criticism since all major decisions are based on their models and forecasts. Sometimes fishermen question the basic assumptions of biologists and managers. One skipper has argued, for instance, that 'knowledge of fish migrations and the size of different stocks is still infinitely small' and that 'those who have come to know the fishing grounds around Iceland, during a lifelong career in fishing, must become mute when the wise men (*spekingar*) announce their precise measurements of the stocks, to the ton' (Hermannsson 1984). It is understandable that skippers, aware of the discrepancy between reality and the 'pessimistic' forecasts of the past, fail to be impressed with the rhetoric of the scientists. Fishermen, then, have become increasingly dominated by techno-scientific knowledge and the agencies of the state. Confronted with the details of scientific research, fishermen have become powerless, in their words 'mute' (*klumsa*). From their point of view, management has become increasingly the business of wise men who speak a 'strange' language.

Since the introduction of the quota system, politicians and biologists have co-operated closely. The government and the politicians need the scientific arguments and therefore encourage research. One observer notes that political decision-makers have built 'effective constraints in the actual operation design of the research institute, which allows it to be easily influenced by political (and social) considerations' (Hoonaard n.d.: 258). Research is subject to immense political pressures. But while they are dependent on scientific information, the politicians have often regarded biological measurements and analyses with suspicion. Former Ministers of Fisheries have argued that if the scientists had been right in their estimates and predictions, the fisheries would have collapsed. Contrary to the 'Black Report' predictions of 1975 (a report of the Marine Research Institute that was influential in the cod wars), the cod stock remained fairly stable until a sharp decline in catches in 1982. One former Minister has referred to the 'religion of the biologists'. Another former Minister of Fisheries points out that 'in the biologists' own calculations, the size of the 1976 year class of cod keeps increasing' (see *Sjávarfréttir* 1980: 17).

Not only have recent changes in the production system of the fishery brought with them a 'scientific' rationality of fishing. National discourse on the distribution of wealth has begun to change too. Earlier I mentioned the high economic rents produced by the quota system, appropriated by boat owners in the form of increased market value of boats. Now, fishworkers have called for a redefinition of the prevailing notion of 'interest group', partly as a result of recent developments in marketing and processing (see Figure 6.2). Over the last years a part of the cod catch has been sold directly to foreign markets without being processed in Iceland, approximately 8 per cent in 1985 and 12 per cent in 1986. This development, which was largely a response to the demands of

Figure 6.2 *Fishworkers in a freezing plant* (photo: Sigurgeir Jónasson)

European consumers for fresh fish, meant that employment was being reduced domestically. Some people, therefore, questioned the privileged access of either fishermen or boat owners, the 'lords of the sea' as the latter are sometimes called, to the most valuable national resource, arguing that fishing is becoming like third world mining where raw materials are exported with little returns to the national economy. Whether this is a likely development or not, the sheer thought of the possibility has triggered a lively debate on power and production. The 'interest groups' of those involved with fisheries management are no longer unanimously seen to be restricted to owners of fishing plants, boat operators, and fishermen. Processing workers, many of whom are women, are demanding their share of the cake, protesting against unemployment and refusing to be treated as 'outsiders', as economic and political 'invisibles'.

The question of who owns the fish in the sea has become a central issue in Icelandic political debate. Boat owners claim that they alone are entitled to the rents produced by the quota system. The traditional usufruct rights of boat owners, they argue, should be transferred into permanent 'ownership' of the fishing stocks in the form of a fixed share of the catch, a transferable quota. For them, the quota system is only a logical extension of the cod wars and the arguments favoured by the Icelandic government; a 'rational' use of resources, they claim, can only be expected as long as the ones who use them are dependent upon them as owners. Fishermen often insist, on the other hand, that as the 'real' producers of wealth *they* are entitled to quotas. As one skipper put it: 'who has more rights concerning quota-payments . . . , the man who hires crew-men, the one who finds the fish and brings the catch ashore, or the boy who inherits the boat of his father but has never been at sea . . . ?' (Jónsson 1990). The allocation of quotas to skippers on the basis of their fishiness, some skippers have argued, would be economical in the long run; costs and effort might be significantly reduced by making fishing the privilege of the most efficient skippers.

Originally, the quota system was presented as a short-term 'experiment' by the authorities. With the changes in the fisheries legislation which came into effect in January 1991, the experiment had a formal ending. The quota system was extended into the distant future. During debates on the fisheries laws, some members of Parliament raised doubts about the 'legality' of the quota system, arguing that proposed privileges of access might imply permanent, private ownership which contradicted some of the basic tenets of the Icelandic constitution regarding public access to resources. Lawyers concluded that the quota system under discussion was in full agreement with the constitution and that quotas did not represent permanent, private property. The laws which eventually were passed categorically stated that the aim of the authorities was *not* to establish private, government-protected ownership. Many people have argued, however, that boat owners have become *de facto* owners of the fishing stocks.

The most serious challenge to the boat owners in the political arena has come from the academia, in particular from economists favouring the selling of fishing licences. The selling of access in the form of licences on an open market, the economists argued, would not only maximise efficiency, it would also ensure that the rents produced by the quota system were distributed among the public, the real owners of fish and other national resources. This argument, however, has not received much public approval. For one thing, an important counter-argument has been offered by rural politicians who fear that in the future power and economic resources will be increasingly concentrated in the capital city and, possibly, even abroad. A fully free market, they claim, where the right to fish in Icelandic waters would be sold to the highest bidders on international markets, would mean that the trawlers of multinational companies that were expelled during the cod wars would be invited to revisit Icelandic waters. Another reason why the argument of those who favour the selling of fishing licences has not been met with general approval has to do with the rhetorical use of language in debates on management. The opponents of selling licences on a free market – the boat owners, in particular – have emphasised that such licences in effect represent a 'resource-tax' (*auðlindaskattur*), catching on the present dislike of taxes of all kinds. Why should the extraction of fish, they say, traditionally a free enterprise, now be subject to taxation, in an age of bankruptcies and general economic difficulties? For the time being, boat owners have won the battle over 'ownership' and economic rents. Not surprisingly, the idea of the quota system originally came from the union of boat owners.

As the discussion above indicates, debates on fisheries policy often focus on the notion of equity. Generally, Icelanders like to believe that opportunities are equal and that existing differences among them are due to personal rather than structural differences. Because of the value bestowed upon equal opportunities, accounts of real differences in terms of access to capital and resources often have to be formulated *implicitly* in euphemistic language. Explicit accounts are neither acceptable nor convincing. Inequality is reproduced under the cover of an individualistic ideology which suggests that people are very much different but that the differences among them have nothing to do with social structure. The folk theories of differential fishing success discussed in the previous chapter are one example. Icelandic discourse on language is another case in point. Although Icelanders tend to deny the existence of inequality and sociolectic differences, they freely admit that there are non-standard varieties of Icelandic and that those who use them are somehow deficient (see Pálsson 1989).

One issue in the management debate involves the relative importance of emotions and rationality. Marine scientists like to think of themselves as the 'conscience of the nation' – as a sensible force, essential for matching the emotional and irrational impulses of fishermen. As power has shifted in their favour, they have sometimes forgotten that no theory, ecological or economic, can tell what is a 'rational' policy and that theory can only be used to arrive at policy decisions if the goals of policy are specified beforehand. Skippers' strategies of maximising immediate returns are not irrational, though the result is the 'tragedy of the commons'. On the contrary, as McCay paraphrases the theory (1981: 4), it is 'irrational' for the actor who does not own the resource he exploits to limit his efforts, 'because the benefits of his restraint cannot be reserved for himself'. Recent campaigns of environmental and animal welfare organisations against the killing of whales and seals have very much brought the issue of rationality and emotions to the fore, and in this case fishermen and biologists tend to agree (see Einarsson 1990). Several foreign organisations, including Greenpeace International, have effectively opposed the hunting of marine mammals by Icelanders with international campaigns for the boycotting of Icelandic fish products. Whaling and sealing are of minor economic significance for Icelanders, but fishermen and biologists emphasise that the marine mammals in question are not endangered species and that giving in to the pressures of the environmentalists would invite a general, emotional and highly dangerous fisheries policy.

Nowadays, Willis points out, Western culture is 'in a phase that might almost be called neototemistic' (1990: 6). Generally, the discursive pendulum has been swinging from an anthropocentric view of humans as separate from nature, as masters *of* nature, to a more inclusive conception of the relations *among* living beings, including humans. Such conceptions have had some impact in Iceland. While the campaigns of foreign environmentalists have been met with strong domestic reactions (see Brydon 1990), and, generally, Icelanders still regard the meat of whales and seals as economic resources, at least for export, domestic consumers increasingly seem to come to the conclusion that marine mammals are bad food. Foreign tastes have influenced the domestic consumption of marine animals in many respects. Not only have some exotic consumer-icons, including 'fish fingers', enjoyed some local popularity, the whole fish idiom of Icelanders has been changed. To some extent, 'big fish', the species Icelanders invested with great symbolic value in earlier times and classified as tasty but dangerous beasts, have been redefined as inedible non-resources – as friends or fellow mammals. This is not, however, simply a matter of automatically adopting foreign gastronomics; if one wants to understand such changes one has to consider internal social developments as well. The species previously regarded as 'ugly' and 'smelly' – for example, herring and lobster – have assumed a new symbolic role as mediators of social differences and hierarchical relationships. Among middle-class urbanites, the 'simple' food of earlier times, in particular boiled haddock with potatoes, is increasingly defined as cheap and lower-class. Marine food is used to demarcate several other social boundaries, including the ones between the festive and the ordinary, between young and old, and between true and untrue Icelanders.

A number of case studies of the social aspects of scientific fisheries management are now available (see, for instance, Pollnac and Littlefield 1983; Sinclair 1983; Young 1983; Lamson and Hanson 1984). Together they show that even though biological and economic aspects of fisheries often pose major problems for management, its social aspects are no less important. To manage only 'fishing' itself, the narrow process of extraction, is to manage a fraction of the industry. In fact, some of the barriers for the success of management schemes may lie in the management organisations themselves, in the organisational context of fisheries research and policy making. Knowledge about the functioning of innovating organisations and the construction of knowledge in bureaucratic institutions may be just as important as knowledge about fish stocks and the people who exploit them (Parades 1985: 177). The history of the quota system in the Icelandic cod fishery indicates some of the potential political implications of a narrowly technical or 'scientific' approach to the problem of management, even in a relatively democratic system. In the absence of a holistic, contextual analysis of the fishing industry, a discriminatory but seemingly fair and neutral policy was adopted. The fear of environmental disaster has not so much resulted in successful attempts to redress the ecological balance; rather it has instituted a policy which radically alters the balance amongst social groups. In the process, a new model of fishing and skipperhood has begun to emerge.

Different kinds of quota systems and licensing schemes are being introduced in different fishing societies. In the early stages, such schemes only imitate private property rights. Later on, however, true property rights, similar to those found in Western agriculture, may develop. As Scott points out (1989: 33), this evolution 'can be expected to continue until the owner has a share in management decisions regarding the catch; and, further still, until he has an owner's share in management of the biomass and its environment'. The Icelandic fishery is an interesting example of such a development. The appropriative regime of Icelanders is being transformed in a complex, ongoing process of negotiations and lobbying – not only among boat owners, fishermen and fisheries managers, but in Icelandic society generally. The decisive battles over resources, social honour and economic power are no longer fought primarily in face-to-face encounters in the local arena, in the fishing communities, but in a public, national context – in the mass media, in national organisations and interest groups, and Parliament.

In the modern world, reality is increasingly defined by full-time scientific experts who monopolise 'universe-maintenance', to borrow the jargon of Berger and Luckmann (1967). In many fishing societies, including Iceland, marine biologists play a particularly powerful role. In Iceland, marine biologists have been careful not to enter public debates on *how* to divide access to fishing stocks, emphasising that their expertise only allows them to define the upper limits, the total catch. This was important in order to establish the legitimacy of scientific discourse among fishermen. Given the political importance of marine biological knowledge and the close co-operation between the Ministry of Fisheries and the Marine Research Institute, however, a radical distinction between advice and responsibility, between science and politics, is hard to accept. Often, the scientists have defined the terms of discourse. The view which presents the pursuit of environmental knowledge as a relatively straightforward accumulation of 'facts' and radically separates knowledge of nature and the social context in which it is produced has come increasingly under attack in several different fields of scholarship, including anthropology and environmental history. Thus, Durrenberger suggests, in relation to the social use of biological research in the shrimp fishery in the US Gulf of Mexico, that science has become a 'political weapon' in the hands of environmental groups and sport fishermen as against shrimpers: 'Bureaucratic science, by its very nature and conditions, serves the ends of policy . . . and its use is to justify decisions rather than to inform them' (Durrenberger 1990: 70). Knowledge of ecological realities, it is often argued, is a historical construct rooted in social discourse.

While scientific knowledge is often conceived as an 'objective' representation of the external world, in reality the scientific enterprise cannot be fully separated from its social environment. McEvoy claims (1988: 214), for instance, that Hardin's thesis of the tragedy of the commons represents a 'mythology' of resource use, a model 'in narrative form for the genesis and essence of environmental problems'. The claim that access to the ocean is open for everyone in most fishing societies, and that this is the root of all environmental problems, needs to be qualified (for a useful discussion of the ethnographic and empirical evidence regarding resource management, see Acheson 1989). The theory of the tragedy of the commons, then, is an important means for making history, an authoritative claim with a social force of its own, and not simply an attempt to understand the world. Indeed, the argument of the tragedy of the commons has been forcefully used by governments, companies, and individuals when pressing for fishing quotas or for leasehold or freehold rights to be granted to individuals on areas formerly used by the local community. Wilson, a fisheries economist, criticises his colleagues for their 'myopic advocacy of property rights' (1982: 419) in policy matters.

A scholarly model of nature and resource-use like the tragedy of the commons is no more a straightforward or 'factual' representation of reality, independent of the social context in which it is produced, than the 'folk' models of indigenous producers. Paradigmatic, discursive change is not simply a progressive movement from ideology to science, from ignorance to truth, for scientific models are themselves the products of history. Scholarly ideas about ecology are necessarily rooted in their times and scientists cannot easily isolate their perception of nature from social life. 'The history of ecology', Worster points out (1977: 345), 'shows how impossible it has been, even when men have most desired it, to screen out . . . biases. Any attempt to so divorce nature from the rest of the human condition leads to a doctrine of alienation, where the science must occupy one realm and the social and historical consciousness another'. Scientific understanding of the environment is a social construction.

7 Conclusions: beyond the language of nature

I now return to some of the theoretical points raised in the first three chapters of the book, thus moving from the ethnographic details of time and place to more general and comparative issues. The first point concerns anthropological concepts of mode of subsistence. There are good reasons why anthropologists should bother to construct and refine such concepts, including the category of fishing. Some kind of conceptual umbrella is needed to appreciate the different ways in which humans appropriate nature. Kroeber complains that 'anthropologists . . . tend to value personal expertise, technical virtuosity, cleverness in novelty, and do not yet clearly recognise the fundamental value of the humble but indispensable task of classifying – that is, structuring – our body of knowledge . . .' (1963: 169). Obviously, everyday classifications of subsistence strategies need to be examined and refined every now and then, if only 'to reassure their users that they are more than accidental classifications, and are valid rubrics beyond our own language or culture' (Hewes 1948: 238). If anthropology deserves to be called a comparative science, the units of comparison must be established on some logical basis and not just on the grounds that they are traditional. However, the kinds of attributes one adopts as criteria of classification for comparative purposes depend on the theory informing the analysis.

As Steward points out (1955: 50), the units of comparison employed by the early evolutionists were usually defined according to an already established 'idealist' scheme 'derived from an a priori and somewhat philosophical construct, being based more upon the concept of progress than upon empirical data'. In using Morgan's scheme, Engels tried to demonstrate that capitalistic relations of production, private property, exploitation and the state, were not inevitable, but rather the products of certain historical conditions. In his reading of Morgan, Engels was not only fabricating history, along with many contemporary writers, but he also left himself unable to deal with primitive society theoretically (see Bloch 1983: 16–17). The Marxist theory of society emphasised exploitation and class divisions, and if primitive society was undifferentiated and characterised by consensus, harmony and equality, it could hardly be assimilated into a Marxist framework. There are similar theoretical problems with the model of hunter-gatherers which emphasises their unity as nomadic food collectors. If the Marxists failed to account for primitive society employing a model developed to understand its very opposite, the model of the nomadic band is of limited usefulness for the student of sedentary society and evolutionary change. To understand the transformation of the hunter-gatherer way of life we need models of variability, not unity.

The behaviour of hunters and gatherers is often assumed to be particularly adaptive and responsive to ecological relations. The image of hunters and gatherers as 'lay ecologists' has replaced their image as primitives (Bettinger 1987: 123). But to say that behaviour is adaptive and 'grammatical' can mean many different things. To acknowledge that human behaviour is systemic and responsive to natural constraints does not necessarily reduce humans to instruments that mechanistically adapt to the material world as is often assumed by critics of 'materialism'. In fact some of the critics are no less materialist than their targets. As Ellen points out (1982: 4), it is important to distinguish between materialist explanations of particular ethnographic observations and materialism as a paradigm, just as it is necessary to distinguish between empirical data and ideological empiricism. The logical opposite of ideological materialism, the paradigm of *anti*-materialism, needs to be separated as well from particular (anti-materialist) interpretations of empirical observations. The omission of ecological relations in social analysis, the 'suppression of space', may have less to do with empirical details than the anxiety to remove any trace of 'geographical determinism' from ethnographic texts (Giddens 1979: 202).

I have explored some of the reasons why anthropologists tend to account for fishing in terms of a 'natural' model, in materialistic and technical terms. Such a model is rooted in Western discourses on leisure and work, the individual and collective. The organisational, adaptive and cross-cultural aspects of fishing may be interesting topics in their own right. On the other hand, such an emphasis diverts attention from social relations, removing social life from the centre of enquiry. One just cannot speak of the social relations of fishing – a set of relations which unites all fishing societies, as diverse groups as Trobriand argonauts, Japanese shell-divers and Icelandic trawlermen, and sets them apart form the rest of humanity – as one could possibly speak, for example, of the social relations of band society. The search for a common denominator is bound to draw attention to technical acts and ecological context, the extraction of fish from their aquatic habitat. In order to unfold the nature of the social relations in which fishing takes place one has to abandon such an approach. The natural model of fishing is inadequate in that it fails to appreciate the ways in which production systems are differentiated with respect to their social relations. An alternative approach is needed which emphasises that the act of fishing, or any extractive activity, is inevitably embedded in social relations. Alternative, social approaches are being developed in the growing literature on fishing. McCay (1978), for instance, has called for the incorporation of social relations of production into anthropological analyses of social and ecological change. To explore differences amongst fishing systems, I have suggested a model which distinguishes between four kinds of economies, emphasising differences in access (whether or not the resources are ownable) and production (the contrast between use-value and exchange-value).

I do not claim to exhaust all significant differences among appropriative regimes. I simply want to underline some fundamental differences and contrasts, including the contrasts between 'closure' and 'tenure' and the spatial and the social. The issue of definition of a concept such as 'tenure' or property is not a trivial terminological squabble or a 'primarily semantic issue' (Smith 1988: 247). If one adopts the taken-for-granted definitions of one's own society, one risks imposing alien concepts on to the ethnography, in other words, being ethnocentric. Anthropologists have often warned against the danger of applying incorrect translations of indigenous concepts. In his discussion of the Pintupi of Australia, Myers emphasises that the 'legal language' of property is 'too concrete and specific a notion for the meanings that Pintupi give to "objects"' and that it 'does not make for entirely adequate translation' (1988: 53). The Pintupi concept which we may be tempted to render as 'ownership', he suggests, is best translated as 'identification' or 'shared identity'. Translating concepts of ownership across time, the historian tell us, is no less a tricky business than translating across space or culture. In his analysis of representations of property during the Middle Ages, Gurevich (1977), for instance, cautions against the imposition of modern ideas on the minds of people of earlier times. Were we to do so, he says, the dialogue with people removed from our time would 'threaten to become a dialogue of the deaf' (p. 7). In medieval Europe, Gurevich points out, the relationship of man and nature 'was not that of a subject to an external object, but rather the projection of his own being into the external world' (p. 9). People saw themselves as being in communion with the land. Land ownership, therefore, was not restricted to a relation to an objectified 'thing'. Ownership entailed qualities of the person, notions of heritage and belonging, somewhat like the concept of 'identification' among the Pintupi. Despite the rich variety in definitions of the concept of property, evident from both ethnography and history, Western scholarship has often taken it for granted. 'Academic thinking', as Kiernan remarks, 'has been apt to overlook it' (1976: 362).

The Western folk-concept of property continues to inform a diversity of analyses of different times and contexts. In economic discourse the concept of property is even extended to systems of open access and resources that are not owned at all, under the label of 'common property'. As Ciriacy-Wantrup and Bishop point out (1975: 715), 'to describe unowned resources (*res nullius*) as common property (*res communes*) . . . is a self-contradiction'. The concept of property, it seems, expands metaphorically to include almost any relationship. No doubt there are many reasons for this (Durrenberger and Pálsson 1987b: 518). For people of modern state societies there may simply be few other means available. Marx emphasised that in pre-capitalist societies the notion of private property did not exist. When bypassing the word 'property', however, he referred to the 'appropriation of nature', using the root 'property' from the Latin *proprius* which is probably derived from *pro privo*, the private or personal (Kiernan 1976: 365). Another reason has to do with anthropological practice and ideological commitments, the wish to confer legitimacy on native claims to traditional hunting territories under threats of colonialists and administrators (see Scott 1988: 44).

Claims of 'ownership' are not a unified category. The claim of the 'primitive' hunter to the animals killed and the claim of the 'modern' Icelandic whaler are not identical acts of possession. They may be equally forceful claims or speech acts, but there are fundamental differences in social relations. The hunter is making a claim to prestige and parts of his kill are likely to be shared with relatives; the whaler, in contrast, is primarily concerned with access to the resource, withholding the rewards for himself. The hunter's notion of property presupposes social obligations, sharing and reciprocity, the right to give, while the whaler's concept denies social obligations, emphasising the right to have or retain. There are basic differences as well in concepts of human-environmental relations. While in both cases a claim to possession seems to be based on the rule of capture, the hunter and the whaler do not hold identical views of what 'capture' is all about. In the hunter's case to kill an animal is to engage in a dialogue within nature, with an inhabitant of the same world. The whaler, in contrast, 'appropriates' his prey in the sense of removing it *from* the natural domain, a world separated from that of humans. No doubt, the whaler's view is repulsive to hunter-gatherers, probably just as repulsive as the idea of whaling is to modern anti-whalers. Environmentalists, some of whom 'adopt' whales as quasi-humans, are terrified at the thought of appropriating fellow mammals – of transforming them into 'fast fish', as Melville would say, and then consuming them as fast food.

Representations of nature and production, I have argued, reflect the system of production to which they belong. Folk models should not be regarded as being independent of the social – as pre-existing models to be 'lived' or 'practised' (Sahlins 1976: 42) by the producers in the course of their everyday life – but rather as *re*-presentations of existing realities. While folk models are situated in time and space and one would not expect to find exact parallels in different temporal and cultural contexts, the radical claim, informed by 'substantivism' and 'historical particularism', that there are as many models as there are societies and contexts allows no comparison whatsoever. In my view, rather than elaborate on the unique and the idiosyncratic, the apparently boundless variety in ethnography, anthropological analysis should strive to establish both the contrasts and the parallels in production discourse and to look for explanations for such contrasts and parallels.

In some production systems there are substantial differences between the actual contributions of different individuals, in others there are small or negligible differences. Whatever the realities of success and failure, however, the producers are not constrained by them when modelling their activities or their economic system.

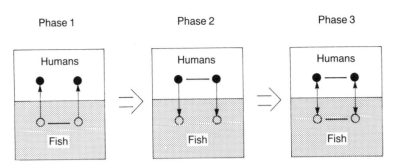

Figure 7.1 *Transformations of production discourse*

Some folk models understate existing differences among producers, often inspired by an egalitarian ethic, while others overstate the facts, exaggerating the realities of personal differences. In either case, the model is rooted in social relations. Cultural models are not constructed simply for their truthfulness or explanatory value, but rather for a multitude of purposes depending on context and the nature of the discourse. Understanding the sources of disagreement between models and reality, relationships of understatement and overstatement, is an intriguing anthropological problem. In some ways, the issue of differential fishing success parallels the larger issue of authenticity and rationality in social theory, the nature and interpretation of folk models.

I have tried to show how Icelandic discourse on production and social honour, their cognitive appropriation of nature and society, reflects the relations Icelanders have entered into at different points in time in the process of appropriating marine resources. In Iceland we can identify three successive phases in the development of social relations of production: the peasant, the expansive, and the consolidated capitalistic. Each had a distinct set of relations of production and a distinct production discourse, characterised by a dominant 'paradigm' or 'episteme' – an underlying framework of understandings and assumptions. Figure 7.1 presents in a schematic form some of the paradigmatic changes involved in the transformation of Icelandic production discourse.

During the peasant phase fishing effort was limited by social as well as technical constraints. In the folk model, fish were allocated to humans according to an unpredictable system of rationing: a divine quota system. Discourse on nature emphasised interactions among water-beings and their various effects on humans, some of which were beneficial and some harmful. With the expansive phase, the ceiling on production was removed and labour was said to create value. The folk model of success emphasised the catches of individual skippers relative to those of others. Attempting to demonstrate their catching potential, skippers watched each other and engaged in deception and secrecy to outwit their rivals. Finally, with consolidated capitalism the resources of the sea have been redefined once again. Production discourse has become centred on *both* ecological and social relations. Humans are not only seen to depend on fish, but fish are seen to depend on humans. The scientific rationality of fishing developed in response to a contradiction between social and ecological relations. Given the competitive nature of expansive fishing, each skipper followed an exponential utility curve. This demanded remedial action, a co-operative implementation of a scientific policy which put a new ceiling on production. In an attempt to fully exploit the reproductive potential of fishing stocks, Icelanders allocate catches among themselves, employing a secular or social quota system.

The changes discussed suggest an inversion in the role of animals as mediators in human relations with the cosmic order. According to the peasants of earlier centuries, fish were responsible for the maintenance of humans. Now, humans are considered collectively responsible for the maintenance of the fishing stocks. Bennett has defined (1976: 3) the 'ecological transition' as the 'progressive incorporation of nature into human frames of purpose and action'. With the new ecological order being founded, the transition of the Icelandic fisheries has come full circle. In the present case, very much like that of subsistence peasants during the medieval era, people are induced to co-operate by the threat of nature; those who violate the new prohibitions are considered guilty of creating disorder in nature. But there is a difference: the fish are no longer a gift from God. If the fish are seen as a 'gift' at all, they are a gift from humans to the new ecological order, which of course serves human ends.

Every society provides some basis for evaluating the social honour of its members and ordering them within a hierarchy of prestige. And systems of distinction and prestige are often important elements of production discourse. The logic and dynamics of such systems are matters of much debate in anthropology. Hatch proposes, following Bourdieu (1984), what he calls a 'self-identity approach' to the topic (Hatch 1989). While systems of prestige, he argues, are sustained by the actors' attempts to achieve a sense of personal accomplishment, their inward-orientation, people cannot pursue their own self-identity in a vacuum, independently of the opinions of others (p. 349). Prevailing values provide us with the model for our actions. The members of society, however, do not meet on an equal basis in the making of the values that come to prevail, nor is their making based on any absolute standards or criteria; on the contrary, such values are arbitrary results of a power struggle. There is always, as Bourdieu points out, 'the imposition of an art of living, that is, the transmutation of an arbitrary way of living into the legitimate way of life which casts every other way of living into arbitrariness' (1984: 57). What counts is access to symbolic resources. The art of fishing, then, the definition of social honour and its distribution among producers, cannot be dissociated from its larger context, the art of living.

Discourse on food production inevitably involves consumption discourse. While I have emphasised the former, I am not suggesting that the latter is unimportant. As Douglas and Isherwood argue (1979: 15), 'tastes' should not be treated as given, as a domain independent of production, since in reality the two domains are part of a circular process whereby each motivates the other. Nor do I wish to suggest that consumption is merely a private issue, a matter of autonomous individuals. If, as I have argued, production is necessarily a social activity, so is consumption. Styles, tastes, and fashions, therefore, are firmly rooted in social discourse. Consumption goods are not only for individual satisfaction; they are important social markers and powerful vehicles of thought. In the subsistence economy of Icelanders, consumption discourse was largely informed by social needs defined in the context of the household. Some species of fish were regarded as edible, others were only used as bait, and still others were discarded on the spot. In general, fish were important as metaphors for talking about local realities. With the market economy, foreign tastes entered the conceptual universe of Icelanders to an increasing extent. 'Anomalous' fish, which formerly were only good to think, now became good to eat. With the development of modern class society, anomalous fish attained a new symbolic significance as mediators of social differences and hierarchical relations.

Notions of gender did not remain immune to the transformation of the Icelandic production system. While peasant society made no fundamental distinction between the economic contributions of men and women, the folk model of the expansive phase defined domestic roles as economically *un*productive, thereby making a new distinction between work and production. About the same time as the idea of the super-productive labour of the male skipper emerged, the related idea of women's labour being unproductive entered the conceptual universe of Icelanders. Just as some early social theories used the durability of the end product of the labour process to identify productive activities and to separate them from unproductive ones – the 'menial tasks and services [which] generally perish in the instant of their performance and seldom leave any trace or value behind them', as Adam Smith put it (citation in Arendt 1958: 89) – so the folk theory of the Icelandic market economy degraded strictly domestic roles as 'passive', apparently on the grounds that they were not embodied in lasting commodities. The change from subsistence economy to capitalist production involved a change from dependence on nature to dependence on commodities. Women were confined to the domestic sphere and, therefore, regarded as unproductive. Men, on the other hand, were regarded as the sole 'providers'.

Some anthropologists have attempted to account for gender-specific notions of production and agency arguing that women, being closer (or generally seen to be closer) to nature than men, tend to be socially invisible (see Ortner 1974). While such a generalisation may have some merit, it hardly applies to the peasant economy of Icelanders. If anything, women were closer to the *cultural* end of Ortner's continuum than the natural one. As Hastrup points out (1985b), in Icelandic peasant society female muteness did not exist in the sense that women no less than men participated in the cultural discourse of the 'inside', the realm of culture as opposed to nature. But while women were insiders in the peasant economy in Hastrup's sense, they were not excluded from fishing in the realm of the 'outside'. Both men and women participated in fishing. Even though women's roles and responsibilities within the household – particularly in relation to pregnancy, breastfeeding and caring for young children – often ensured that they stayed home while the men went fishing, there were no cognitive barriers preventing them from joining fishing crews on their expeditions into the wild. With the growth of capitalist fishing and urban centres, however, women *did* become muted.

The binary concepts of culture and nature, the tame and the wild, the public and the domestic, are problematic constructs. As Strathern has forcefully argued (1988), they need not be equally salient categories for different groups of people. And where they *are* meaningful categories their definition may vary from one period to another. Icelandic household producers defined membership in the category of the 'inside' in terms of both the territory of the farmstead and the social relations of the domestic economy. With the decline of the domestic economy, the inside lost its spatial connotation; the spatial inside and the social one no longer coincided. Women remained insiders in the sense that they still belonged to the domestic unit, but according to the new cultural model they became social outsiders, devoid of power and economic productivity. Social membership, belonging to the inside, became independent of space and redefined in social terms alone, in terms of the emerging relations of the market economy.

In market economies the 'domestic' labour of women tends to be presented as private labour on the grounds that it takes place internal to the household, and that its consumption products are 'perishable' use values, requiring immediate use. Conversely, only the non-domestic work of men is regarded as socialised since it alone involves co-operation between households, the production of exchange values and durable commodities. This view of labour, shared by many professional theorists – both classical economists and Marxist critics – is reminiscent of the Durkheimian dualism discussed in Chapter 1. Domestic labourers are presented as natural beings outside the social life of the market economy – much like the Arctic hunters, if we are to believe Mauss (1979), dispersing and withdrawing from the Inuit collectivity during the summer. But while in Mauss' interpretation of the work process found in hunter-gatherer economies the natural is represented by the extractive activities of autonomous individuals in the 'outside' world, it is in dualistic theories of capitalist economies that the natural is located within the sphere of the domestic, in the privatised but often crowded home. In the capitalist economy women only become social or visible insiders to the extent that they engage in non-domestic production, outside the sphere of reproduction. Clearly, one may speak of the shifting place of the natural and the outside in dualistic thought.

While the devaluation of women's work is not restricted to market economies, the change from a subsistence economy to markets often has important implications for the social construction of gender. With the development of market economies gender often becomes a particularly salient social category. Models of production are usually gender-specific, treating women's domestic contributions as 'private', 'unproductive', and secondary to those of men. Just as extraction is a social activity whether or not it takes place in a group or by isolated individuals, labour is necessarily a social activity whether or not it takes place in a domestic or non-domestic context. As Mackintosh argues (1988), the household is not a private place devoid of social content but a social institution constituted by a particular set of relations – the 'social relations of domestic production' involved in the creation of use values, particularly cooking and child care. Strangely enough, economic theory, which originally defined economic space in terms of the household (*Oikos*), restricts its definition of productive labour to that taking place outside the domestic sphere. Formerly the universe of economic theory, the household is reduced to an empty space.

I have emphasised that to consider production as the activity of autonomous, natural individuals, is to ignore the social relations in which humans are necessarily embedded. An anthropology inspired by the notions of the superorganic suggested by Durkheim and Boas implies a reductionist model of human action. The producer becomes a technical expert operating outside society. The procurement of food becomes an ecological process, the transferring of energy between trophic levels. Similarly, speaking is reduced to acoustics or generative phonology. Not only does the natural model of human action reduce speaking and production to technical transactions in a social void, it also projects a particular view of mind. The mind becomes not an agent, a locus of purpose and intentionality, but an instrument of rules or a container filled with cultural symbols. Attempts by social theorists to bestow life upon the individual are bound to fail as long as they follow the Durkheimian lead, assuming, as Douglas does, that in order to carry out such a project it is necessary to 'ignore what is peculiar to individuals and attend to what is publicly shared...' (1978: 6).

While rejecting the theoretical priority given to rules over action, anthropologists should not endow the actor with an idealised, absolute freedom. As Ortner points out (1984: 151), some praxis theorists in anthropology go too far in their critique of models of enactment and execution in that they portray the producer as an energetic, self-interested, aggressive every-man-for-himself, thereby assuming 'too much active-ness'. Such a romantic individualism not only overlooks the import of the constraints of social life, more importantly it distorts the nature of such constraints. For the advocates of situational analysis and game theory, for instance, the actor is a rational being motivated by intrinsic values or psychological dispositions *independent* of social structure. Praxis theorists which idealise the freedom of the self-contained individual thus remain confined within the very approach they are trying to replace (see Bourdieu 1977a: 26). While social structure is regarded as the outcome of a series of individual decisions, it is reified as an external force: a 'stationary rainbow' to paraphrase Volosinov (1973). The realm of the social becomes analogous to the 'hidden hand' envisioned by some theorists of the market. It is a statistical aggregate, or an accidental authority. The actors are only accorded the ability to *select* among alternative choices visible in the short term, as consumers in a market beyond human control.

As we have seen, the natural model of the individual colonises the speaker and the producer. The households of both language and nature become oppressive, alien orders: residences where the housekeepers – the speaker and the producer – are assigned the status of inmates. The task of developing a social theory which reintroduces purpose and agency into human life remains. Marx proposed a social or constitutive model of the individual. The human being, Marx argued, is 'in the most literal sense... an animal which can individuate itself only in the midst of society' (1973: 84). Such a conception of the individual entails a notion of human action as consciously motivated activities, i.e. as modes of creative praxis – not as implementations of structures laid out in advance. Genuine freedom and creativity are not those of autonomous beings who accidentally erect social structures over their head, but those of socially constituted persons engaged in purposeful activity.

Notes

Chapter 1: Social theory and human ecology

1 Due to the impact of Darwinian theory, however, linguists have discarded the organismic view of language, at least for the time being. For if the principles of natural selection applied to languages no less than organisms their chances of survival had to depend on their internal properties, and linguists reasoned this was not the case. Perhaps the idea that a dead but 'classic' language like Latin was just a maladaptive dinosaur was simply too much to take.

2 Some scholars have attempted to read into Morgan a theory of materialist determination of culture. Maconachie argues (1987: 101–2), for instance, that Morgan 'outlined a history of the family that was, in its intention, materialist' and that he tried to provide an 'exact fit' between changes in the form of the family and changes in subsistence relations. Engels is largely responsible for such a reading. He stated (1942) that Morgan 'in his own way had discovered afresh in America the materialistic conception of history, discovered by Marx forty years ago'. Others have denounced such claims on the grounds that Morgan only *identified* 'epochs of human progress' with successive 'arts of subsistence' (Ingold 1986: 62).

3 Later, Frake seems to have adopted a very different view of language (1980: 334): 'The ethnographer in the field, unlike the linguist in his office, cannot escape the fact that people do not just string words together in an idle game of solitaire. People mean things, intend things, and do things with words. And they accomplish these deeds in concert with other people in social situations'.

4 While Volosinov is critical of Durkheim, at times he seems to subscribe to the Durkheimian notion of the natural individual. He argues, for instance, that the 'organizing center of any utterance, of any experience, is not within but outside – in the social milieu *surrounding* the individual being' (1973: 93, emphasis added).

Chapter 2: Anthropological discussions of fishing economies

1 Some scholars, indeed, continue to take Hardy seriously. Morgan's

'aquatic' theory (1982) of human evolution is inspired by Hardy's work.

2 In support of his theory, Dart inferred from a particular frequency of bones that *Australopithecus* hunted for their subsistence and brought parts of their kill back to their camps for consumption and tool-making, but critics later pointed out that the bones might just as well have been accumulated by hyenas (see Binford 1983: 37).

3 In the *Atlas*, data on hunter-gatherer settlement pattern are coded as follows: (1) *fully migratory* or nomadic bands; (2) *seminomadic* communities, when a migratory band occupies a fixed settlement for a season; (3) *semisedentary* communities, when a community shifts regularly from one to another fixed settlement or occupies permanently a single settlement from which a substantial portion of the population departs seasonally; and (4) compact and *relatively permanent settlements*. In the *Atlas*, one should also note, subsistence economy is scaled according to relative dependence of the society (0–5 per cent, 6–15 per cent, etc.) on gathering, hunting, fishing, animal husbandry and agriculture. A 'mode of subsistence' is the particular combination of values for the subsistence variables.

4 Many of the examples of restrictive access to fishing that are referred to in the ethnography of North American Indians pertain to river fishing. Sometimes ocean fishing was no less significant a part of subsistence than river fishing, but here restrictions of access seem to have been less important (see McEvoy 1986: Ch. 2). The beaches, however, were often considered a considerable asset and in many cases 'beach rights' were clearly recognised, for instance among the Yurok and Pomo.

5 One of the problems associated with assigning 'possession' prior to the kill, following Locke, is that 'we need a principle to tell us when to assign it. Shall we assign it when the hunt begins?' (Rose 1985: 76). A further problem with Locke's argument is that it makes the dubious assumption that one owns one's body and labour. Do not slaves, by his argument, own their products and not the slave owners? Barnard and Woodburn (1988: 24) raise similar questions with respect to the rights that parents have over their children.

6 For Ingold, 'territorial' behaviour is a mode of communication 'serving to convey information about the location of individuals dispersed in space' (1987: 133) while 'tenure' is a mode of social appropriation 'by which persons exert claims over resources dispersed in space'. Sahlins (1972: 92–3), one may note, following Engels, makes a distinction between 'two systems' of 'property' – the 'chiefly' (where a right to things is realised through a hold on persons) and the 'bourgeois' (where a hold on persons is realised through a hold on things). A similar distinction is made by Godelier (1986: Ch. 2).

Chapter 3: Systems of production and social discourse

1 This ambiguity is not peculiar to Icelandic. Jernudd and Thuan (1984) argue that generally there is a lack of correspondence between three fish-naming systems: the scientific, the common, and the folk naming systems.

2 In some respects, however, the Nunu model of success and inequality emphasised the importance of hard work, individual achievement, and initiative. Evident inequalities among free people, Harms argues (1987: 126), were explained in terms that 'sound almost like social Darwinism'. The picture that Harms portrays is a highly complex one. There are important differences in folk models between swamp and river fishing as well as over time.

3 Gudeman provides an interesting account (1986) of the folk models of Panamian peasants which is relevant for the present discussion. In Panama subsistence peasants thought of work primarily as something which only transported value from one item to another. With the development of the wage economy, on the other hand, the folk model accommodated the idea that work got 'mixed' with the land, thereby increasing its value. Labour became a quantifiable and marketable commodity with a force of its own. The producers were credited with a creative force.

4 Acheson suggests (1977) that skills are important in determining catch, since no less than 39 per cent of the variance in income is left unexplained in his regression models. There are some problems, however, with Acheson's study. First, the dependent variable in his regression models, *expected* gross income, is not a precise measure of catch or success. Also, the fishermen in his sample are operating from three different harbours, not a single community. Had Acheson been able to use a more reliable measure of success and control for any differences there may be between localities the residuals might have been much lower. Furthermore, Acheson's argument that the technical skills involved in trap placement are critical for success is supported by rather weak evidences. The analysis is restricted to 33 skippers and one month's fishing and we have limited information on the operationalisation and measurement of the trap-placement variable – the distinction between 'pinpoint trap placement' and 'unpatterned trap placement'. Acheson says in a footnote (1977: 135) that 8 men 'placed their traps carefully', 11 'clearly did not', and the remaining 14 'did not clearly fall into either category'. The 33 men, he adds, were placed in one of these categories 'on the basis of observation of techniques, and other men's assessment of them'. In a later work Acheson qualifies his earlier conclusions regarding skills and success, emphasising that they 'need to be taken with more than a grain of salt' (1988: 105).

Chapter 4: The domestication of nature

1 Chapter 2, p. 2322; see *Íslendinga sögur og þættir* 1987.
2 See *Manntal á Íslandi* 1703, *Jarðabók Árna Magnússonar og Páls Vídalíns* 1923–24.
3 Chapter 18, p. 1556; see *Íslendinga sögur og þættir* 1987.
4 In *Postula sögur* 1874: 828.
5 *Hauksbók* 1892–96: 165–7.
6 Chapter 18, p. 550; see *Íslendinga sögur og þættir* 1987.
7 See *Grágás* 1852, section 230. The consulting of diviners, one may note, had important social functions (see Pálsson 1990a). The mere fact that persons who considered themselves as victims consulted a diviner might force the wrongdoer to come out into the open. The diviner's statements might elicit responses from the community in general and direct the flow of gossip and discourse, making the community collectively responsible for an implicit accusation. Consulting a diviner, then, was a way of spreading the risk of an accusation, reducing the responsibility of the accuser, an important safety valve in case the accusation turned out to be false.
8 *Íslenskar þjóðsögur og sagnir* IV: 311.
9 *Völsunga saga* 1906–1908: 34.
10 *Flóres saga konungs og sona hans* 1927: 167.

Chapter 5: From nature to society

1 Durrenberger and I have argued (Durrenberger and Pálsson 1985) that changes in fleet composition and the relative importance of different kinds of production units are largely the results of changes in the balance between capital and labour. These changes in turn were responses to changing conditions in the summer fishing for herring during the 1940s and 1950s.
2 Tanner argues (1979: 124), on the other hand, that this cannot explain scapulimancy entirely since the Mistassini Cree use the same technique when there is no risk involved. These studies indicate that divinatory techniques may serve different purposes in different contexts. Rather than assuming there is a single problem-solving or decision-making purpose behind them, anthropologists should carefully examine each case separately and the context of the practices themselves.
3 The static picture offered by Barth, who assumes that good herring skippers must start as good and poor ones are doomed to remain at the bottom of the ranks throughout their careers, contradicts both Norwegian and Icelandic ethnography (see Durrenberger and Pálsson 1983). The hierarchy is more stable in the cod fishery than in the case of herring, but it still has to be maintained.

Chapter 6: The domination of nature

1 Young describes (1983) a similar case in Alaska, where the operation of
a market in fishing permits has resulted in windfall profits associated
with entry permits and significant changes in the composition of the
group of permit holders.

2 The conclusions of the statistical study of the skipper effect in Iceland
have not remained unchallenged. Gatewood (1984) and McNabb
(1985) argue that the conclusion regarding the skipper effect is not
warranted, since boat size and skipper effect are confounded variables.
While this argument might apply to the cod fishery it cannot apply to
the herring fishery. Durrenberger and I have shown (1983) that the
skipper effect cannot be disguised by the boat-size variable, since
(unlike in cod fishing) boat size does not statistically explain differences
in herring catches. Thorlindsson would agree with the latter argument,
but he maintains (1988) that the high value of the residual for herring
fishing is an indication of a strong skipper effect, not a weak one. The
main thrust of his argument relates to the consistency in catches from
one season to another. His analysis does indeed show that several
herring skippers are consistently on top of the hierarchy of success over
a period of several seasons. But while consistency in skippers' catches
from one season to another does suggest that the folk notion of skipper
effect may have *some* empirical basis it does not indicate that there is a
strong effect as Thorlindsson argues (see Pálsson and Durrenberger
1990). The consistency observed may be due to other effects, including
the stability of fishing crews, the reputation of skippers, differential
access to landing places, shared information, and fishing technology.
While some of these effects are likely to be related to the skipper effect,
they may have some impact on their own. The problem is that we have
no way of knowing which of the explanations is most important since
we have no way independently to operationalise a measure of fishing
skills. This point is aptly made by Acheson in his analysis of lobster
fishing in Maine (1977). He emphasises that the statistical exercise
'certainly proves nothing conclusive beyond the fact that the output of
lobsters cannot be predicted merely by knowing the physical inputs'
(p. 115).

3 Even though Icelandic discourse generally presents nature, at least the
coastal ecosystem, as a predictable, domesticated domain, as being
under control, the contrary voice is also raised at times. Knowledge of
the ecosystem, it is argued, especially by fishermen, is too imperfect for
making forecasts. Some people even go further, arguing that multispecies fisheries are chaotic systems with too many uncertainties for any
kind of governmental control. Such arguments have been developed in
the scholarly literature on fisheries management by Wilson (1982) and
some others.

Bibliography

Acheson, J. M. 1977. Technical skills and fishing success in the Maine lobster industry. *Human Ecology* 3 (3): 183–207.

——— 1981. Anthropology of fishing. *Annual Reviews of Anthropology* 10: 275–316.

——— 1988. *The lobster gangs of Maine*. Hanover and London: University Press of New England.

——— 1989. Management of common-property resources. In *Economic anthropology* (ed.) S. Plattner. Stanford: Stanford University Press; pp. 351–78.

Alexander, P. 1977. Sea tenure in southern Sri Lanka. *Ethnology* 16 (3): 231–51.

——— 1982. *Sri Lanka fishermen: rural capitalism and peasant society*. Canberra: Australia National University.

Andersen, R. and C. Wadel (eds) 1972. *North Atlantic fishermen: anthropological essays on modern fishing*. Newfoundland social and economic papers no. 5. Toronto: University of Toronto Press.

Anderson, E. N. 1969. Sacred fish. *Man* 4: 443–9.

Arendt, H. 1958. *The human condition*. New York: Doubleday.

Asad, T. 1979. Anthropology and the analysis of ideology. *Man* 14: 607–27.

Austin, J. L. 1962. *How to do things with words*. Cambridge, Mass.: Harvard University Press.

Árnason, I. (ed.) 1976. *Faðir minn skipstjórinn*. Reykjavík: Skuggsjá.

Árnason, R. 1986. Management of the Icelandic demersal fisheries. In *Fisheries access control programs worldwide* (ed.) N. Mollett. Proceedings of the workshop on management options for the North Pacific longline fisheries, Fairbanks; pp. 83–101.

Ási í Bæ (Ástgeir Ólafsson) 1963. Binni í gröf. In *Aflamenn* (ed.) J. Árnason. Reykjavík: Heimskringla; pp. 7–60.

Bailey, G. N. 1983. Problems of site formation and the interpretation of spatial and temporal discontinuities in the distribution of coastal middens. In *Quaternary coastlines and marine archaeology* (eds) P. M. Masters and N. C. Flemming. London: Academic Press; pp. 559–82.

Baks, C. and E. Postel-Coster 1977. Fishing communities on the Scottish east coast: traditions in a modern setting. In *Those who live from the sea* (ed.) M. E. Smith. St Paul: West Publishing Company; pp. 23–40.

Barnard, A. 1983. Contemporary hunter-gatherers: current theoretical issues in ecology and social organization. *Annual Review of Anthropology* 12: 193–214.

Barnard, A. and J. Woodburn 1988. Property, power and ideology in hunter-gathering societies: an introduction. In *Hunters and gatherers: property, power and ideology* (eds) T. Ingold, D. Riches and J. Woodburn. Oxford: Berg Publishers; pp. 4–31.

Barnes, J. A. 1954. Class and committee in a Norwegian island parish. *Human relations* 7: 39–58.

Barth, F. 1966. *Models of social organization*. Occasional paper no. 23. London: Royal Anthropological Institute of Great Britain and Ireland.

Bender, B. 1978. Gatherer-hunter to farmer: a social perspective. *World Archaeology* 10: 204–23.

Bennett, J. W. 1976. *The ecological transition: cultural anthropology and human adaptation*. New York: Pergamon Press Inc.

Berger, P. and T. Luckman 1967. *The social construction of reality: a treatise in the sociology of knowledge*. New York: Doubleday and Company.

Bergsson, K. 1940. Dr. Bjarni Sæmundsson og fiskimennirnir. *Ægir* 11.

Berkes, F. (ed.) 1989. *Common property resources: ecology and community-based sustainable development*. London: Belhaven Press.

Bettinger, R. L. 1987. Archaeological approaches to hunter-gatherers. *Annual Review of Anthropology* 16: 121–42.

Binford, L. R. 1980. Willow smoke and dog's tale: hunter-gatherer settlement systems and archaeological site formation. *American Antiquity* 45 (1): 4–20.

——— 1983. *In pursuit of the past: decoding the archaeological record*. New York: Thames and Hudson.

Bird, E. A. R. 1987. The social construction of nature: theoretical approaches to the history of environmental problems. *Environmental Review* 11: 255–64.

Bird-David, N. 1990. The giving environment: another perspective on the economic system of gatherer-hunters. *Current Anthropology* 31 (2): 189–96.

Bloch, M. 1977. The past and the present in the present. *Man* (NS) 12: 278–92.

——— 1983. *Marxism and anthropology*. Oxford: Oxford University Press.

Bourdieu, P. 1977a. *Outline of a theory of practice*. Translated by R. Nice. Cambridge: Cambridge University Press.

——— 1977b. The economics of linguistic exchanges. *Social Science Information* 16 (6): 645–68.

——— 1984. *Distinction: a social critique of the judgement of taste*. Translated by R. Nice. Chicago: University of Chicago Press.

Bowles, F. P. and M. C. Bowles 1989. Holding the line: property rights in the lobster and herring fisheries of Matinicus Island, Maine. In *A sea of small boats* (ed.) J. Cordell. Cambridge, Mass.: Cultural Survival Inc; pp. 228–57.

Brandt, V. S. R. 1971. *A Korean village between farm and sea*. Cambridge, Mass.: Harvard University Press.

Breton, Y. D. 1973. A comparative study of work groups in an Eastern Canadian peasant fishing community: bilateral kinship and adaptive processes. *Ethnology* 12: 393–418.

—— 1977. The influence of modernization on the modes of production in coastal fishing: an example from Venezuela. In *Those who live from the sea* (ed.) M. E. Smith. St Paul: West Publishing Company; pp. 125–37.

Brown, C. H. 1984. *Language and living things: uniformities in folk classification and naming*. Brunswick: Rutgers University Press.

Bruner, J. 1986. *Actual minds, possible worlds*. Cambridge, Mass.: Harvard University Press.

Brydon, A. 1990. Icelandic nationalism and the whaling issue. *North Atlantic Studies* 1–2: 185–91.

Byron, R. 1980. Skippers and strategies: leadership and innovation in Shetland fishing crews. *Human Organization* 39 (3): 227–32.

—— 1986. *Sea change*. St John's: Memorial University of Newfoundland.

Carrier, J. A. and A. H. Carrier 1989. Marine tenure and economic reward on Ponam Island, Manus Province. In *A sea of small boats* (ed.) J. Cordell. Cambridge, Mass.: Cultural Survival Inc; pp. 94–120.

Carter, A. 1989. *The philosophical foundations of property rights*. New York: Harvester Wheatsheaf.

Cashdan, E. 1983. Territoriality among human foragers: ecological models and an application to four Bushman groups. *Current Anthropology* 24: 47–66.

Caws, P. 1974. Operational, representational and explanatory models. *American Anthropologist* 76: 1–10.

Chapman, M. D. 1987. Women's fishing in Oceania. *Human Ecology* 15 (3): 267–88.

Childe, V. G. 1944. Archaeological ages or technological stages. *Journal of the Royal Anthropological Institute* 74: 1–19.

—— 1951. *Social evolution*. New York: Meridan Books.

—— 1965 [1936]. *Man makes himself*. London: Collins.

Chomsky, N. 1980. *Rules and representations*. Oxford: Blackwell.

—— 1986. *Knowledge of language: its nature, origin, and use*. New York: Praeger.

Ciriacy-Wantrup, S. V. and R. C. Bishop 1975. 'Common property' as a concept in natural resources policy. *Natural Resource Journal* 15 (4): 713–27.

Cohen, M. N. 1977. *The food crisis in prehistory.* New Haven: Yale University Press.

—— 1985. Prehistoric hunter-gatherers: the meaning of social complexity. In *Hunter-gatherers: the emergence of cultural complexity* (eds) T. D. Price and J. A. Brown. Orlando: Academic Press; pp. 99–119.

Cole, S. 1988. The sexual division of labor and social change in a Portuguese fishery. In *To work and to weep: women in fishing economies* (eds) J. Nadel-Klein and D. Lee Davis. St John's: Institute of Social and Economic Research, Memorial University of Newfoundland; pp. 169–89.

Cook, S. 1973. Production, ecology and economic anthropology: notes toward an integrated frame of reference. *Social Science Information* 12 (1): 25–52.

Cordell, J. (ed.) 1989. *A sea of small boats.* Cambridge, Mass.: Cultural Survival Inc.

Cove, J. J. 1978. Ecology, structuralism and fishing taboos. In *Adaptation and symbolism: essays on social organization* (eds) K. A. Watson-Gegeo and S. L. Seaton. Honolulu: University Press of Hawaii; pp. 143–54.

Dart, R. A. 1960. The recency of man's aquatic past. *The New Scientist* 7: 1668–70.

Darwin, C. 1871. *Journal of researches into the natural history and geology of the countries visited during the voyage of H.M.S. Beagle round the world.* New York: Harper.

—— 1952 [1874]. *The descent of man and selection in relation to sex.* Chicago: Encyclopædia Britannica Inc.

Davenport, W. C. 1960. *Jamaican fishing: a game theory analysis.* New Haven: Yale University Press.

Davis, S. 1989. Aboriginal tenure of the sea in Arnhem Land, Northern Australia. In *A sea of small boats* (ed.) J. Cordell. Cambridge, Mass.: Cultural Survival; pp. 37–59.

Davíðsson, Ó. 1900. Folklore of Icelandic fishes. *The Scottish Review* 72: 312–32.

Douglas, M. 1966. *Purity and danger: an analysis of the concepts of pollution and taboo.* London: Routledge and Kegan Paul.

—— 1978. *Cultural bias.* Occasional paper no. 34. London: Royal Anthropological Institute.

Douglas, M. and Baron Isherwood 1979. *The world of goods.* New York: Basic Books.

Dumézil, G. 1958. *L'idéologie tri-partite.* Brussels: Latomus.

Durkheim, E. 1965. *The elementary forms of religious life.* New York: The Free Press.

—— 1966 [1895]. *The rules of sociological method.* Translated by S. A. Solovay and J. H. Mueller. New York: The Free Press.

—— 1972. *Emile Durkheim: selected writings*. Edited, translated, and with an introduction by A. Giddens. Cambridge: Cambridge University Press.

Durkheim, E. and M. Mauss 1963 (1903). *Primitive classification*. Translated, edited and with an introduction by R. Needham. London: Cohen & West.

Durrenberger, E. P. (ed.) 1984a. *Chayanov, peasants, and economic anthropology*. Orlando: Academic Press.

—— 1984b. Icelandic saga heroes: the anthropology of natural existentialists. *Anthropology and Humanism Quarterly* 9: 3–8.

—— 1989. Anthropological perspectives on the commonwealth period. In *The anthropology of Iceland* (eds) E. P. Durrenberger and G. Pálsson. Iowa City: University of Iowa Press; pp. 228–46.

—— 1990. Policy, power and science: the implementation of turtle excluder device regulations in the U.S. Gulf of Mexico shrimp fishery. *Maritime Anthropological Studies* 3 (1): 69–86.

Durrenberger, E. P. and G. Pálsson 1983. Riddles of herring and rhetorics of success. *Journal of Anthropological Research* 39: 323–35.

—— 1985. Peasants, entrepreneurs and companies: the evolution of Icelandic fishing. *Ethnos* 1–2: 103–22.

—— 1986. Finding fish: the tactics of Icelandic fishermen. *American Ethnologist* 13: 213–29.

—— 1987a. The grass roots and the state: resource management in Icelandic fishing. In *The question of the commons: the cultural ecology of communal resources* (eds) B. M. McCay and J. M. Acheson. Tucson: University of Arizona Press; pp. 370–92.

—— 1987b. Ownership at sea: fishing territories and access to sea resources. *American Ethnologist* 14 (3): 508–22.

Eder, J. F. 1984. The impact of subsistence change on mobility and settlement pattern in a tropical forest foraging economy: some implications for archaeology. *American Anthropologist* 86 (4): 837–53.

Einarsson, N. 1990. Of seals and souls: changes in the position of seals in the world-view of Icelandic small-scale fishermen. *Maritime Anthropological Studies* 3 (2): 35–48.

Ellen, R. 1982. *Environment, subsistence and system*. Cambridge: Cambridge University Press.

Endicott, K. and K. L. Endicott 1986. The question of hunter-gatherer territoriality: the case of the Batek of Malaysia. In *The past and future of !Kung ethnography: critical reflections and symbolic perspectives. Essays in honour of Lorna Marshall* (eds) M. Biesele, R. Gordon and R. Lee. Hamburg: Helmut Buske Verlag; pp. 137–62.

Engels, F. 1942 (1884). *The origin of the family, private property and the state*. New York: International Publishers.

Evans, C. R. and E. H. Newman 1973. Dreaming: an analogy from computers. In *Dreams and dreaming* (eds) S. G. M. Lee and A. R. Mayes. Middlesex: Penguin; pp. 371–7.

Evans-Pritchard, E. E. 1965. *Theories of primitive religion.* London: Oxford University Press.

Faris, J. C. 1975. Social evolution, population, and production. In *Population, ecology, and social evolution* (ed.) S. Polgar. The Hague and Paris: Mouton; pp. 235–71.

—— 1977. Primitive accumulation in small-scale fishing communities. In *Those who live from the sea* (ed.) M. E. Smith. St Paul: West Publishing Company; pp. 235–49.

Faxi 1976 (5). Ég er sjómaður – ekkert annað. Keflavík.

Firth, R. 1946. *Malay fishermen: their peasant economy.* London: Routledge and Kegan Paul.

—— 1965. *Primitive Polynesian economy.* London: Routledge and Kegan Paul.

—— 1967. *Tikopia ritual and belief.* Boston: Beacon Press.

—— 1981. Figuration and symbolism in Tikopia fishing and fish use. *Journal de la Société des Oceanistes* 72–3: 219–26.

Flóres saga konungs og sona hans 1927. Hallea/S: Ake Lagerholm (14th century).

Foucault, M. 1972. *The archaeology of knowledge and the discourse on language.* New York: Pantheon.

—— 1980. *Power/knowledge.* Ed by C. Gordon. Brighton: Harvester Press.

Frake, C. O. 1980. *Language and cultural description.* Essays selected and introduced by A. S. Dil. Stanford: Stanford University Press.

Gatewood, J. B. 1983. Deciding where to fish: the skippers' dilemma in Southeast Alaskan salmon seining. *Coastal Zone Management Journal* 10 (4): 347–67.

—— 1984. Is the 'skipper effect' really a false ideology? *American Ethnologist* 11: 378–9.

Geertz, C. 1973. *The interpretation of cultures.* London: Hutchinson.

Gellner, E. 1970. Concepts and society. In *Rationality* (ed.) B. Wilson. Oxford: Basil Blackwell; pp. 18–49.

Gerrard, S. 1983. Kvinder i fiskeridistrikter: fiskerinæringas 'bakkemannskap'. In *Kan fiskerinæringa styres?* (ed.) B. Hersoug. Oslo: Novus; pp. 217–41.

Giddens, A. 1979. *Central problems in social theory: action, structure and contradiction in social analysis.* London: The Macmillan Press.

Gladwin T. 1970. *East is a big bird.* Cambridge, Mass.: Harvard University Press.

Godelier, M. 1986. *The mental and the material.* London: Verso.

Goodlad, C. A. 1972. Old and trusted, new and unknown: technological confrontation in the Shetland herring fishery. In *North Atlantic fishermen: anthropological essays on modern fishing* (eds) R. Andersen and C. Wadel. Toronto: University of Toronto Press; pp. 61–81.

Goodwin, B. 1988. Organisms and minds: the dialectics of the animal-human interface. In *What is an animal?* (ed.) T. Ingold. London: Unwin Hyman.

Goody, J. 1987. *The interface between the written and the oral.* Cambridge: Cambridge University Press.

Grágás 1852. Islendingernes lovbog i fristatens tid, udgivet efter det Kongelige Biblioteks Haandskrift. Copenhagen: Brödrene Berlings Bogtrykeri.

Gudeman, S. 1986. *Economics as culture: models and metaphors of livelihood.* London: Routledge and Kegan Paul.

Guðmundsson, Gils 1979. Sjómannafræðsla á Íslandi. In *Skipstjóra- og stýrimannatal, I.* Reykjavík: Ægisútgáfan; pp. 11–39.

Gurevich, A. 1977. Representations of property during the high Middle Ages. *Economy and Society* 6 (1): 1–30.

Hagalín, G. G. 1964. *Í fararbroddi: ævisaga Haralds Böðvarssonar.* Hafnarfjörður: Skuggsjá.

Hardin, G. 1968. The tragedy of the commons. *Science* 162: 1243–8.

Hardy, A. 1960. Was man more aquatic in the past? *The New Scientist* (March): 642–5.

Harms, R. 1987. *Games against nature: an eco-cultural history of the Nunu of equatorial Africa.* New York: Cambridge University Press.

Harris, M. 1980. *Cultural materialism: the struggle for a science of culture.* New York: Vintage Books.

Harris, R. 1980. *The language-makers.* London: Duckworth.

——— 1988. *Language, Saussure and Wittgenstein.* London: Routledge.

Hastrup, K. 1985a. *Culture and history in medieval Iceland: an anthropological analysis of structure and change.* Oxford: Oxford University Press.

——— 1985b. Male and female in Icelandic culture. *Folk* 27: 49–64.

Hatch, E. 1973. The growth of economic, subsistence, and ecological studies in American anthropology. *Journal of Anthropological Research* 29 (4): 221–43.

——— 1989. Theories of social honor. *American Anthropologist* 91 (2): 341–52.

Haugen, E. 1972. *The ecology of language.* Edited by A. S. Dil. Stanford: Stanford University Press.

Hauksbók 1892–96. Copenhagen: Det kongelige Nordiske oldskrift-selskab.

Henriksen, G. 1973. *Hunters in the barrens: the Naskapi on the edge of the white man's world*. Newfoundland social and economic studies no. 12. St John's: Institute of Social and Economic Research, Memorial University of Newfoundland.

Hermannsson, H. 1984. Svipull er sjávarafli. *Morgunblaðið* 17 March. Reykjavík.

Hewes, G. W. 1948. The rubric 'fishing and fisheries'. *American Anthropologist* 50: 238–46.

Hilborn, R. 1985. Fleet dynamics and individual variation: why some people catch more fish than others. *Canadian Journal of Fisheries and Aquatic Sciences* 42: 2–13.

Hilborn, R. and M. Ledbetter 1985. Determinants of catching power in the British Columbia salmon purse seine fleet. *Canadian Journal of Fisheries and Aquatic Sciences* 42: 51–6.

Hitchcock, R. K. 1982. Patterns of sedentism among the Basarwa of eastern Botswana. In *Politics and history in band societies* (eds) E. Leacock and R. Lee. Cambridge: Cambridge University Press; pp. 223–67.

Hodgen, M. T. 1971. *Early anthropology in the sixteenth and seventeenth centuries*. Philadelphia: University of Pennsylvania Press.

Holy, L. (ed.) 1987. *Comparative anthropology*. Oxford: Basil Blackwell.

Holy, L. and M. Stuchlik (eds) 1981. *The structure of folk models*. London: Academic Press.

Hoonaard, W. C. van den n.d. *Fishing for identity: the shrimp fishermen of Iceland* (unpublished manuscript).

Hornell, J. 1950. *Fishing in many waters*. Cambridge: Cambridge University Press.

Hummel, R. L. and G. S. Foster 1986. A sporting chance: relationships between technological change and concepts of fair play in fishing. *Journal of Leisure Research* 18 (1): 40–52.

Hunn, E. 1982. The utilitarian factor in folk biological classification. *American Anthropologist* 84 (4): 830–47.

Hymes, D. 1974. *Foundations in sociolinguistics: an ethnographic approach*. London: Tavistock.

Ingold, T. 1986. *Evolution and social life*. Cambridge: Cambridge University Press.

—— 1987. *The appropriation of nature: essays on human ecology and social relations*. Iowa City: University of Iowa Press.

—— 1988 Notes on the foraging mode of production. In *Hunters and gatherers: history, evolution and social change* (eds) T. Ingold, D. Riches, and J. Woodburn. Oxford: Berg Publishers; pp. 269–85.

Íslendinga sögur og þættir I–III, 1987. Reykjavík: Svart á hvítu.

Íslenskar þjóðsögur og sagnir IV 1982. Collected by Sigfús Sigfússon. Reykjavík: þjóðsaga.

Jameson, F. 1972. *The prison-house of language: a critical account of structuralism and Russian formalism*. Princeton: Princeton University Press.

Jarðabók Árna Magnússonar og Páls Vídalíns 3 1923–24. Copenhagen: Hið Íslenska fræðafélag.

Jentoft, S. 1989. Fisheries co-management. *Marine Policy* April: 137–54.

Jernudd, B. H. and E. Thuan 1984. Naming fish: a problem exploration. *Language in society* 13 (2): 235–44.

Jolly, A. 1972. *The evolution of primate behavior*. New York: Macmillan.

Jonquil, B. 1988. *Izaak Walton's The compleat angler: the art of recreation*. Brighton: Harvester Press.

Jorion, P. 1976. To be a good fisherman you do not need any fish. *Cambridge Anthropology* 1: 1–12.

―――― 1984. Chayanov should be right: testing Chayanov's rule in a French fishing community. In *Chayanov, peasants, and economic anthropology* (ed.) E. P. Durrenberger. Orlando: Academic Press; pp. 71–95.

Jónsson, Finnur 1945. *Þjóðhættir og ævisögur frá 19. öld*. Akureyri: Bókaútg. P. H. Jónssonar.

Jónsson, Ó. Ö. 1990. Fiskveiðistefnan og framtíðin. *Morgunblaðið* 4 May.

Kalland, A. 1988. *Fishing villages in Togukawa Japan: the case of the Fukuoka domain*. Doctoral dissertation, Department of East Asian Studies, University of Oslo.

―――― 1990. Sea tenure and the Japanese experience: resource management in coastal fisheries. In *Unwrapping Japan* (eds) E. Ben-Ari, B. Moeran and J. Valentine. Manchester: Manchester University Press; pp. 188–204.

Keesing, R. M. 1987. Models, 'folk' and 'cultural': paradigms regained? In *Cultural models in language and thought* (eds) D. Holland and N. Quinn. Cambridge: Cambridge University Press; pp. 369–93.

Kelly, R. L. 1983. Hunter-gatherer mobility strategies. *Journal of Anthropological Research* 39 (3): 277–306.

Kiernan, V. G. 1976. Private property in history. In *Family and inheritance: rural society in Western Europe, 1200–1800* (eds) J. Goody, J. Thirsk and E.P. Thompson. Cambridge: Cambridge University Press; pp. 361–98.

Kirch, P. V. and T. S. Dye 1979. Ethno-archaeology and the development of Polynesian fishing strategies. *Journal of the Polynesian Society* 88 (1): 53–76.

Kleivan, I. 1984. The fish world as a metaphorical Eskimo society. In *The fishing culture of the world: studies in ethnology, cultural ecology and folklore*, vols I & II (ed.) B. Gunda. Budapest: Akadémiae Kiadó; pp. 887–91.

Knipe, E. 1984. *Gamrie: an exploration in cultural ecology: a study of maritime adaptation in a Scottish fishing village.* New York: University Press of North America.

Kottak, C. P. 1966. *The structure of equality in a Brazilian fishing community.* Doctoral dissertation, Columbia University.

Krause, A. 1956 [1885]. *The Tlingit Indians: results of a trip to the north-west coast of America and the Bering Straits.* Seattle: University of Washington Press.

Kripke, S. 1982. *Wittgenstein on rules and private language.* Cambridge, Mass.: Harvard University Press.

Kristjánsson, L. 1980. *Íslenskir sjávarhættir, 1.* Reykjavík: Menningarsjóður.

—— 1986. *Íslenskir sjávarhættir, 5.* Reykjavík: Menningarsjóður.

Kristmundsdóttir, S. D. 1990. *Doing and becoming: women's movements and women's personhood in Iceland 1870–1990.* Doctoral dissertation, Department of Anthropology, University of Rochester.

Kroeber, A. L. 1932. The Patwin and their neighbors. *University of California Publications in American Archaeology and Ethnology* 29: 253–424.

—— 1963. *An anthropologist looks at history.* Berkeley: University of California Press.

Kuper, A. 1988. *The invention of primitive society: transformations of an illusion.* London: Routledge.

Laguna, G. A. de 1963 [1927]. *Speech: its function and development.* Bloomington: Indiana University Press.

Lakoff, G. 1972. Linguistics and natural logic. In *Semantics of natural language* (eds) D. Davidson and G. Hartman. Dordrecht: D. Reidel Publishing Company; pp. 545–665.

Lamson, C. and A. J. Hanson (eds) 1984. *Atlantic fisheries and local communities: fisheries decision making case studies.* Halifax: Dalhousie Ocean Studies Programme.

Laxness, H. 1968. *Christianity at glacier.* Translated from the Icelandic by Magnus Magnusson. Reykjavík: Helgafell.

—— 1972. *Guðsgjafarþula.* Reykjavík: Helgafell.

—— 1985 [1944]. Háheilög mannblót. *Sjómannablaðið víkingur* 11–12: 37–9.

Leach, E. 1964 *Political systems of highland Burma: a study of Kachin social structure.* London: The Atholl Press.

—— 1976. *Culture and communication: the logic by which symbols are connected.* Cambridge: Cambridge University Press.

Leap, W. L. 1977. Maritime subsistence in anthropological perspective: a statement of priorities. In *Those who live from the sea* (ed.) M. E. Smith. St Paul: West Publishing Company; pp. 251–63.

Lee, R. B. 1968. What hunters do for a living, or, how to make out on scarce resources. In *Man the hunter* (eds) R. B. Lee and I. DeVore. Chicago: Aldine Publishing Company; pp. 30–48.

—— 1984. *The Dobe !Kung*. New York: Holt, Rinehart and Winston.

—— 1988. Reflections on primitive communism. In *Hunters and gatherers: history, evolution and social change* (eds) T. Ingold, D. Riches and J. Woodburn. Oxford: Berg; pp. 252–68.

Lee, R. B. and I. DeVore (eds.) 1968 *Man the hunter*. Chicago: Aldine Publishing Company.

Le Goff, J. 1988. *The medieval imagination*. Chicago: The University of Chicago Press.

Lehn, W. H. and I. Schroeder 1981. The Norse merman as an optical phenomenon. *Nature* 289, 29 January: 362–6.

Levieil, D. P. and B. Orlove 1990. Local control of aquatic resources: community and ecology in Lake Titicaca, Preu. *American Anthropologist* 92 (2): 362–82.

Levine, H. B. 1984. Controlling access: forms of 'territoriality' in three New Zealand crayfishing villages. *Ethnology* 23 (2): 89–100.

—— 1989. Maori fishing rights: ideological developments and practical impacts. *Maritime Anthropological Studies* 2 (1): 21–33.

Lévi-Strauss, C. 1963. *Structural anthropology*. Middlesex: Penguin Books.

—— 1972. *The savage mind*. London: Weidenfeld and Nicolson.

—— 1985. *The view from afar*. Oxford: Basil Blackwell.

Libecap, G. D. 1989. *Contracting for property rights*. Cambridge: Cambridge University Press.

Lourandos, H. 1988. Palaeopolitics: resource intensification in Aboriginal Australia and Papua New Guinea. In *Hunters and gatherers: history, evolution and social change* (eds) T. Ingold, D. Riches, and J. Woodburn. Oxford: Berg Publishers; pp. 148–60.

Lubbock, J. 1913 [1869]. *Prehistoric times as illustrated by ancient remains and the manners and customs of modern savages*. New York: Henry Holt and Co.

Löfgren, O. 1982. From peasant fishing to industrial trawling: a comparative discussion of modernization processes in some North Atlantic regions. In *Modernization and marine fisheries policy* (eds) J. R. Maiolo and M. K. Orbach. Ann Arbor: Ann Arbor Science; pp. 151–76.

McCay, B. J. 1978. Systems ecology, people ecology, and the anthropology of fishing communities. *Human Ecology* 6 (4): 397–422.

—— 1981. Development issues in fisheries as agrarian systems. *Culture and Agriculture* 11: 1–8.

—— 1984. The pirates of piscary: ethnohistory of illegal fishing in New Jersey. *Ethnohistory* 31 (1): 17–37.

—— 1987. The culture of the commoners: historical observations on Old and New World fisheries. In *The question of the commons: the culture and ecology of communal resources* (eds) B. J. McCay and J. M. Acheson. Tucson: The University of Arizona Press; pp. 195–216.

McCay, B. J. and J. M. Acheson (eds) 1987. *The question of the commons: the culture and ecology of communal resources.* Tucson: The University of Arizona Press.

McEvoy, A. F. 1986. *The fisherman's problem: ecology and law in the California fisheries 1850–1980.* Cambridge: Cambridge University Press.

—— 1988. Toward an interactive theory of nature and culture: ecology, production, and cognition in the California fishing industry. In *The ends of the earth: perspectives on modern environmental history* (ed.) D. Worster. Cambridge: Cambridge University Press.

McGoodwin, J. R. 1989. Do randomizing devices aid marine hunters? *Maritime Anthropological Studies* 2 (2): 134–53.

McGovern, T. H., G. Bigelow, and D. Russell 1988. Northern islands, human error, and environmental degradation: a view of social and ecological change in the Medieval North Atlantic. *Human Ecology* 16: 225–70.

Mackintosh, M. M. 1988. Domestic labour and the household. In *On work: historical, comparative and theoretical approaches* (ed.) R. E. Pahl. Oxford: Basil Blackwell; pp. 392–406.

McNabb, S. L. 1985. A final comment on the measurement of the 'skipper effect'. *American Ethnologist* 12: 543–4.

Maconachie, M. 1987. Engels, sexual divisions, and the family. In *Engels revisited* (eds) J. Sayers, M. Evans and N. Redclift. London: Tavistock;

Magnússon, S. 1935–36 [1785]. Lýsing Gullbringu- og kjósarsýslu. In *Landnám Ingólfs.* Reykjavík: Ingólfur; pp. 1–196.

Malinowski, B. 1923. The problem of meaning in primitive languages. In *The meaning of meaning* (eds) C. K. Ogden and I. A. Richards. London: Kegan Paul, Trench, Trubner & Co; pp. 451–510.

Manntal á Íslandi [1703]. Reykjavík: Gutenberg.

Marquardt, W. H. 1986. The development of cultural complexity in southwest Florida: elements of a critique. *Southeastern Archaeology* 5: 63–70.

—— 1988. Politics and production among the Calusa of south Florida. In *Hunters and gatherers: history, evolution and social change* (eds) T. Ingold, D. Riches, and J. Woodburn. Oxford: Berg Publishers; pp. 161–88.

Marx, K. 1961 [1844]. *Economic and philosophical manuscripts of 1844.* Moscow: Foreign Language Publishing House.

—— 1964. *Pre-capitalist economic formations.* Edited and with an Introduction by E. J. Hobsbawm. London: Lawrence and Wishart.

—— 1973 [1857–8]. *Grundrisse*. Translated by Martin Nicolaus. Harmondsworth: Penguin Books.

Marx, K. and F. Engels 1970. *The German ideology*. Edited with an introduction by C. J. Arthur. New York: International Publishers.

Mauss, M. (in collaboration with H. Beuchat) 1979 [1906]. *Seasonal variations of the Eskimo: a study in social morphology*. Translated with a foreword by J. J. Fox. London: Routledge and Kegan Paul.

—— 1970 [1925]. *The gift: forms and functions of exchange in archaic societies*. London: Cohen and West.

Meehan, B. 1982. *Shell bed to shell midden*. Canberra: Australian Institute of Aboriginal Studies.

Melville, H. 1962 [1851]. *Moby Dick*. New York: Macmillan Company.

Miedema, J. 1986. *Pre-capitalism and cosmology: description and analysis of the Meybrat fishery and Kain Timur complex*. Dordrecht: Foris.

Miller, M. L. and J. van Maanen 1979. 'Boats don't fish, people do': some ethnographic notes on the federal management of fisheries in Gloucester. *Human Organization* 38 (4): 377–85.

Moore, O. K. 1957. Divination: a new perspective. *American Anthropologist* 59: 69–74.

Morgan, E. 1982. *The aquatic ape: a theory of human evolution*. London: Souvenir Press.

Morgan, L. H. 1928 [1877]. *Ancient society*. Chicago: Charles H. Kerr.

Morrill, W. T. 1967. Ethnoichthyology of the Cha-Cha. *Ethnology* 6: 409–16.

Murdock, G. P. 1967. Ethnographic atlas: a summary. *Ethnology* 6: 109–236.

—— 1969. Correlations of exploitative and settlement patterns. In *Contributions to anthropology: ecological essays* (ed.) D. Damas. Bulletin no. 230. Ottawa: National Museum of Canada; pp. 129–46.

Myers, F. 1988. Burning the truck and holding the country: property, time and the negotiation of identity among the Pintupi Aborigines. In *Hunters and gatherers: property, power and ideology* (eds) T. Ingold, D. Riches, and J. Woodburn. Oxford: Berg Publishers; pp. 52–74.

Nadel-Klein, J. and D. L. Davis (eds) 1988. *To work and to weep: women in fishing economies*. St John's: Institute of Social and Economic Research, Memorial University of Newfoundland.

Newmeyer, F. J. 1986. *The politics of linguistics*. Chicago: University of Chicago Press.

News from Iceland 1984, July. Reykjavík.

Nietschmann, B. 1972. Hunting and fishing focus among the Miskito Indians, Eastern Nicaraqua. *Human Ecology* 1 (1): 41–67.

Norr, J. L. and K. F. Norr 1978. Work organization in modern fishing. *Human Organization* 37: 163–71.

Orbach, M. K. 1978. *Hunters, seamen, and entrepreneurs: the tuna seinermen of San Diego*. Berkeley University of California Press.

Ortner, S. B. 1974. Is female to male as nature is to culture? In *Woman, culture and society* (eds) M. Z. Rosaldo and L. Lampere. Stanford: Stanford University Press; pp. 67–87.

—— 1984. Theory in anthropology since the sixties. *Comparative Studies in Society and History* 1: 126–66.

Osborn, A. J. 1977. Strandloopers, mermaids and other fairy tales: ecological determinants of marine resource utilization. In *For theory building in archaeology* (ed.) L. R. Binford. New York: Academic Press; pp. 157–205.

Oswalt, W. E. 1973. *Habitat and technology: the evolution of hunting*. New York: Holt, Rinehart and Winston.

Overbey, M. M. 1989. Self-regulation among fishermen of the Gulf of Mexico. In *Marine resource utilization: a conference on social science issues* (eds) S. J. Thomas, L. Maril and E. P. Durrenberger. Mobile: University of South Alabama College of Arts and Sciences Publication, vol. 1; pp. 165–72.

Pálsson, G. 1982. *Representations and reality: cognitive models and social relations among the fishermen of Sandgerði, Iceland*. Doctoral dissertation, University of Manchester.

—— 1987. *Sambúð manns og sjávar*. Reykjavík: Svart á hvítu.

—— 1988a. Hunters and gatherers of the sea. In *Hunters and gatherers: history, evolution and social change* (eds) T. Ingold, D. Riches, and J. Woodburn. Oxford: Berg Publishers; pp. 189–204.

—— 1988b. Models for fishing and models of success. *Maritime Anthropological Studies* 1 (1): 15–28.

—— 1989. Language and society: the ethnolinguistics of Icelanders. In *The Anthropology of Iceland* (eds) E. P. Durrenberger and G. Pálsson. Iowa City: University of Iowa Press; pp. 121–39.

—— 1990a. The name of the witch: sagas, sorcery and social context. In *Oromo Studies and Other Essays in Honor of Paul Baxter* (ed.) D. Brokensha. Syracuse, New York: Maxwell School of Citizenship and Public Affairs (African Series of Foreign and Comparative Program) (in press).

—— 1990b. Cultural models in Cape Verdean fishing. In *From water to world-making: African models and arid lands* (ed.) G. Pálsson. Uppsala: Scandinavian Institute of African Studies (in press).

—— 1990c. The idea of fish: land and sea in the Icelandic world-view. In *Signifying animals: human meaning in the natural world* (ed.) R. Willis. London: Unwin Hyman; pp. 119–33.

Pálsson, G. and E. P. Durrenberger 1982. To dream of fish: the causes of Icelandic skippers' fishing success. *Journal of Anthropological Research* 38 (2): 227–42.

—— 1983. Icelandic foremen and skippers: the structure and evolution of a folk model. *American Ethnologist* 10 (3): 511–28.

—— 1990. Systems of production and social discourse: the skipper effect revisited. *American Anthropologist* 92: 130–41.

Parades, J. A. 1985. 'Any comments on the sociology section, Tony?': committee work as applied anthropology. *Human Organization* 44 (2): 177–82.

Pastner, S. 1978. Baluchi fishermen in Pakistan. *Asian Affairs* 9: 161–7.

—— 1980. Desert and coast: population flux between pastoral and maritime adaptations in the Old World arid zone. *Nomadic Peoples* 6: 13–22. Bulletin of the Commission on Nomadic Peoples, International Union of Anthropological and Ethnological Sciences.

Perlman, S. 1980. An optimum diet model, coastal variability, and hunter-gatherer behavior. In *Recent advances in archaeological method and theory*, 3 (ed.) M. L. Schiffer. New York: Academic Press; pp. 257–310.

Pernetta, J. and L. Hill 1983. A review of marine resource use in coastal Papua. *Journal de la Société des Oceanistes* 37: 175–91.

Pinkerton, E. (ed.) 1989. *Co-operative management of local fisheries: new directions for improved management & community development.* Vancouver: University of British Columbia Press.

Plath, D. W. and J. Hill 1987. The reefs of rivalry: expertness and competition among Japanese shellfish divers. *Ethnology* 26: 151–63.

Pollnac, R. B. and S. J. Littlefield 1983. Sociocultural aspects of fisheries management. *Ocean Development and International Law Journal* 12 (3–4): 209–46.

Postula sögur 1874. Christiania: C. R. Unger (13th century).

Renouf, M. A. P. 1984. Northern coastal hunter-fishers: an archaeological model. *World Archaeology* 16 (1): 18–27.

Rosaldo, M. Z. 1982. The things we do with words: Ilongot speech acts and speech act theory in philosophy. *Language in Society* 11: 203–37.

Rose, C. M. 1985. Possession as the origin of property. *The University of Chicago Law Review* 52: 73–88.

Rossi-Landi, F. 1983. *Language as work and trade: a semiotic homology for linguistics and economics.* South Hadley: Bergin and Carvey.

Ruddle, K. and T. Akimichi (eds) 1984. *Maritime institutions in the Western Pacific.* Osaka: National Museum of Ethnology.

Ruddle, K. and R. E. Johannes (eds) 1985. *The traditional knowledge and management of coastal systems in Asia and the Pacific.* Jakarta: UNESCO.

Sack, R. D. 1986. *Human territoriality: its theory and history.* Cambridge: Cambridge University Press.

Sahlins, M. 1972. *Stone age economics.* London: Tavistock Publications.

—— 1976. *Culture and practical reason*. Chicago: The University of Chicago Press.

Saladin d'Anglure, B. 1984. Arctic Quebec Inuit. In *Handbook of American Indians*, 5 (ed.) D. Damas; pp. 476–507.

Sapir, E. 1929. The status of linguistics as a science. *Language* 5: 207–14.

Sauer, C. O. 1962. Seashore – primitive home of man? In *Land and life: a selection from the writings of Carl Ortwig Sauer* (ed.) J. Leighly. Berkeley: University of California Press; pp. 300–12.

Saussure, F. de 1959 (1916). *Course in general linguistics*. New York: McGraw-Hill.

Schalk, R. F. 1979. Land use and organizational complexity among foragers of northwestern North America. In *Affluent foragers: Pacific coast east and west* (eds) S. Koyawa and D. H. Thomas. Osaka: National Museum of Ethnology; pp. 53–75.

Schmidt, A. 1971. *The concept of nature in Marx*. London: New Left Books.

Scott, A. D. 1989. Conceptual origins of rights based fishing. In *Rights based fishing* (eds) P. A. Neher, R. Arnason and N. Mollett. Dordrecht: Kluwer Academic Publishers; pp. 11–38.

Scott, C. 1988. Property, practice and aboriginal rights among Quebec Cree hunters. In *Hunters and gatherers: property, power and ideology* (eds) T. Ingold, D. Riches and J. Woodburn. Oxford: Berg Publishers; pp. 35–51.

Searle, J. R. 1969. *Speech acts: an essay in the philosophy of language*. Cambridge: Cambridge University Press.

Sharp, H. S. 1981. The null case: the Chipewyan. In *Woman the gatherer* (ed.) F. Dahlberg. New Haven: Yale University Press; pp. 221–44.

—— 1988. Dry meat and gender: the absence of Chipewyan ritual for the regulation of hunting and animal numbers. In *Hunters and gatherers: property, power and ideology* (eds) T. Ingold, D. Riches and J. Woodburn. Oxford: Berg; pp. 183–91.

Sherzer, J. 1987. A discourse-centered approach to language and culture. *American Anthropologist* 89 (2): 295–309.

Sigurðsson, J. 1859. *Lítil fiskibók*. Copenhagen.

Sinclair, P. R. 1983. Fishermen divided: the impact of limited entry licensing in Northwest Newfoundland. *Human Organization* 42 (4): 307–13.

Sjávarfréttir 1980 (12). Stjórnun fiskveiða. Reykjavík.

Smith, C. L. 1974. Fishing success in a regulated commons. *Ocean Development and International Law Journal* 1: 369–81.

—— 1980. Attitudes about the value of steelhead and salmon angling. *Transactions of the American Fisheries Society* 109: 207–81.

Smith, E. A. 1988. Risk and uncertainty in the 'original affluent society':

evolutionary ecology of resource-sharing and land tenure. In *Hunters and gatherers: history, evolution and social change* (eds) T. Ingold, D. Riches and J. Woodburn. Oxford: Berg Publishers; pp. 222–51.

Snorra Edda 1975. Reykjavík: Iðunn (early 14th century).

Sopher, D. E. 1965. *The sea nomads: a study based on the literature of the maritime boat people of southeast Asia.* Singapore: Memoirs of the National Museum no. 5.

Spencer, J. 1989. Anthropology as a kind of writing. *Man* 24 (1): 145–64.

Stefánsson, V. 1906. Icelandic beast and bird lore. *Journal of American Folklore* 19: 300–8.

Steward, J. H. 1955. *Theory of culture change.* Urbana: University of Illinois Press.

Stiles, R. G. 1972. Fishermen, wives, and radios: aspects of communication in a Newfoundland fishing community. In *North Atlantic Fishermen: anthropological essays on modern fishing* (eds) R. Andersen and C. Wadel. Toronto: University of Toronto Press; pp. 35–60.

Stocking, G. W. 1982. Afterword: a view from the center. *Ethnos* 1–2: 172–86.

Strathern, M. 1988. *The gender and the gift: problems with women and problems with society in Melanesia.* Berkeley: University of California Press.

Sudo, K. 1984. Social organization and types of sea-tenure in Micronesia. In *Maritime institutions in the Western Pacific* (eds) K. Ruddle and T. Akimichi. Osaka: National Museum of Ethnology; pp. 203–30.

Suttles, W. 1968. Coping with abundance: subsistence on the Northwest Coast. In *Man the hunter* (eds) R. B. Lee and I. DeVore. Chicago: Aldine; pp. 56–68.

Tacon, P. S. C. 1989. Art and the essence of being: symbolic and economic aspects of fish among the peoples of western Arnhem Land, Australia. In *Animals into art* (ed.) H. Morphy. London: Unwin Hyman; pp. 236–50.

Tambiah, S. J. 1968. The magical power of words. *Man* 3: 175–208.

Tanner, A. 1979. *Bringing home animals: religious ideology and mode of production of the Mistassini Cree hunters.* London: C. Hurst & Company.

Tanner, N. M. 1981. *On becoming human.* Cambridge: Cambridge University Press.

Tapper, R. L. 1988. Animality, humanity, morality, society. In *What is an animal?* (ed.) T. Ingold. London: Unwin Hyman; pp. 47–62.

Testart, A. 1982. The significance of food storage among hunter-gatherers: residence patterns, population densities, and social inequalities. *Current Anthropology* 23 (5): 523–37.

Thompson, E. P. 1977 Folklore, anthropology, and social history. *The Indian Historical Review* 3: 247–66.

Thompson, P. 1985. Women in the fishing: the roots of power between the sexes. *Comparative Studies in Society and History* 27 (1): 3–32.

Thorlindsson, T. 1988. The skipper effect in the Icelandic herring fishery. *Human Organization* 47 (3): 199–212.

Torrence, R. 1983. Time budgeting and hunter-gatherer technology. In *Hunter-gatherer economy in prehistory: a European perspective* (ed.) G. Bailey. Cambridge: Cambridge University Press; pp. 11–22.

Tuan, Y.-F. 1984. *Dominance and affection: the making of pets*. New Haven: Yale University Press.

Tyler, S. A. 1986. Post-modern ethnography: from document of the occult to occult document. In *Writing culture* (eds) J. Clifford and G. E. Marcus. Berkeley: University of California Press; pp. 122–40.

Tylor, E. B. 1916 (1875). *Anthropology*. New York and London: Appleton.

Uhle, M. 1907. The Emeryville shellmound: final report. *University of California Publications in American Anthropology and Ethnology* 7: i–84.

Volosinov, V. N. 1973 (1929). *Marxism and the philosophy of language*. Translated by L. Matejka and I. R. Titunik. Cambridge, Mass.: Harvard University Press.

Völsunga saga 1906–08. Copenhagen: Samfund til udgivelse av gammel nordisk literatur (13th century).

Wadel, C. 1972. Capitalization and ownership: the persistence of fishermen-ownership in the Norwegian herring fishery. In *North Atlantic fishermen: anthropological essays on modern fishing* (eds) R. Andersen and C. Wadel. Toronto: University of Toronto Press; pp. 104–19.

Walton, I. n.d. [1653]. *The compleat angler*. With an Introduction by A. Lang. London: J. M. Dent and Co.

Washburn, S. L. and C. S. Lancaster 1968. The evolution of hunting. In *Man the hunter* (eds) R. B. Lee and I. DeVore. Chicago: Aldine; pp. 293–303.

Waterman, T. T. 1920. Yurok geography. *University of California Publications in American Archaeology and Ethnology* 16: 177–314.

Watson, O. M. 1970. *Proxemic behavior: a cross-cultural study*. The Hague: Mouton.

Weddle, R. S. 1985. *Spanish sea: the Gulf of Mexico in North American discovery, 1500–1685*. College Station, Texas: Texas A&M University Press.

White, D. R. M. 1989. Knocking 'em dead: Alabama shrimp boats and the 'fleet effect'. In *Marine resource utilization: a conference on social science issues* (eds) J. S. Thomas, L. Maril, and E. P. Durrenberger. Mobile: University of South Alabama College of Arts and Sciences Publication vol. 1 and the Missisippi-Alabama Sea Grant Consortium; pp. 25–37.

Willis, R. 1990. Introduction. In *Signifying animals: human meaning in the natural world* (ed.) R. Willis. London: Unwin Hyman Ltd; pp. 1–24.

Wilson, J. A. 1982. The economical management of multispecies fisheries. *Land Economics* 58 (4): 417–34.

Wolf, E. 1982. *Europe and the people without history*. Berkeley: University of California Press.

Woodburn, J. 1972. Ecology, nomadic movement and the composition of the local group among hunters and gatherers: an East African example. In *Man, settlement and urbanism* (eds) P. J. Ucko, R. Tringham and G. W. Dimbleby. London: Duckworth; pp. 193–206.

—— 1980. Hunters and gatherers today and reconstruction of the past. In *Soviet and Western anthropology* (ed.) E. Gellner. New York: Columbia University Press; pp. 95–117.

Worster, D. 1977. *Nature's economy: a history of ecological ideas*. Cambridge: Cambridge University Press.

Wright, A. 1985. Marine resource use in Papua New Guinea: can traditional concepts and contemporary development be integrated? In *The traditional knowledge and management of coastal systems in Asia and the Pacific* (eds) K. Ruddle and R. E. Johannes. Jakarta Pusat: UNESCO; pp. 79–100.

Yesner, D. R. 1980. Maritime hunter-gatherers. *Ecology and Prehistory* 21, 725–50.

—— 1987. Life in the 'Garden of Eden': causes and consequences of the adoption of marine diets by human societies. In *Food and evolution: toward a theory of human food* (eds) M. Harris and E. B. Ross. Philadelphia: Temple University Press; pp. 285–310.

Young, O. R. 1983. Fishing by permit: restricted common property in practice. *Ocean Development and International Law Journal* 13 (2): 121–70.

Index

absentee-ownership, of boats, 76, 107, 112, 146
access to resources, 23, 44–53, 69–70, 73–8, 158
see also tenure; closure
Acheson, James M., 16, 38–9, 44, 48, 51, 68, 77–80, 154, 170 n. 4
advicers (bitamenn), 91
agency, notions of
in folk models, 66–80, 161–2
in social theory, 4, 13–20, 60, 164–7
Akimichi, Tomoya, 44
Alaska, 120, 127
Alexander, Paul, 41, 73, 74
Andersen, Raoul, 41
Anderson, E. N., 63
animals, see human animal relations
anomalous beings (kynjaverur), 94–101, 129, 163–4
concept of, 99
appropriation, 18, 47–50, 153
concept of, 159–60
of space, 47–50
see also closure; ownership; possession; property; tenure
aquatic v. terrestrial, 23, 35, 39, 45, 61, 64, 70, 94–5, 97
and social organisation, 29–34
see also land v. water
Arendt, Hannah, 164
Arnhem Land, 62
Asad, Talal, 81
Asdic, 123
attentiveness (eftirtekt), 89
Austin, J. L., 18, 131

Árnason, Ingólfur, 114
Árnason, Ragnar, 137
Ási í Bæ (Ástgeir Ólafsson), 118

Bailey, G. N., 28, 29
Baks, Chris, 75
Baluch, 72
Barnard, Alan, 30, 43, 46
Barnes, John A., 75
Barth, Fredrik, 68, 127
base-superstructure models, 14, 58–9
Batek, 50
Bender, Barbara, 34
Bennett, John W., 2, 162
Berger, Peter, 153
Bergsson, K., 145
Berkes, Fikret, 44
Bettinger, Robert L., 157
big fish (stórfiskar), 100, 152
Binford, Lewis R., 27, 30–3
Binni (Benóný Friðriksson), 117–19
Bird, Elizabeth Ann R., 2
Bird-David, Nurit, 80
Bishop, R. C., 159
'Black Report', 147
Bloch, Maurice, 13
Boas, F., 4, 6–7, 14–19, 60, 166
boat owners, 71, 76, 91, 107, 134, 141, 146, 149–50, 153
boats, representations of, 71
Bobb, Franz, 4
Bourdieu, Pierre, 5, 163, 167
Bowles, F. P., 51
Bowles, M. C., 51
Brandt, V. S. R., 67
Brazil, 79

Breton, Yvan D., 38–9, 106
Brown, C. H., 62
Bruner, Jerome, 82
Brydon, Anne, 152
Byron, Reginald, 68, 75–6

Calusa, 33
Cape Verde Islands, 71
  town, 76
  village, 71–2
Carrier, A. H., 49
Carrier, J. A., 49
Carter, A., 19
Cashdan, Elizabeth, 47
catch-king (*aflakóngur*), title of,
  125
Caws, Peter, 82
Chapman, Margaret D., 66
Chayanov's theory, 43–4
chieftains (*goðar*), 84–5
Childe, V. G., 29, 33, 39
Chipewyans, 64, 71
Chomsky, Noam, 4, 5, 10, 11, 17,
  20
circulation, modes of, 24, 43–4,
  51, 69
Ciriacy-Wantrup, S. V., 159
civilisation, development of, 27, 33
classification
  of animals, 13, 62
  of modes of subsistence, 13, 23,
    34–8, 52–3, 64, 156–8
closure, *v.* tenure, 48–53, 158
'co-adventure', 41
co-managing, of resources, 44
cod wars, 87, 135, 145, 159
Cohen, M. N., 28, 32
Cole, Sally, 77
collecting, *see* hunting and
  gathering
collective, *v.* individual, 5–22
  quantitative *v.* qualitative
    notions of, 11–12

commons, 15, 44, 53, 159
  almenningar, 86–7
Commonwealth Period, 84–5
competition, among fishermen,
  116, 122–31, 139
consolidated capitalism, 77, 81,
  133–8
constitutive model, 20, 46–7, 59,
  166–7
  see also individual *v.* collective
consumption discourse, 93, 109,
  152, 162–3, 165
contracting, for property, 51
Cook, Scott, 8
Cordell, John, 44, 53
Cornwall, 64
Cove, J. J., 64, 93
Cratylus, 56, 80
crew organisation, 38–9, 71
cultural comparison, 30, 81, 160
cultural determinism, 14–19, 59
cultural ecology, 8, 38
cultural materialism, 8
cultural models, 52, 54–5, 61–7,
  80–1, 103, 155, 160–1
  authenticity of, 80–1, 139–45,
    161
culture
  concept of, 7, 14, 16, 59, 60
  v. nature, 165–6
  as text, 19, 55

Danish colonialism, 85–6, 105–6,
  133
Dart, Raymond A., 27, 29
Darwin, Charles, 5, 25–6, 64
Davenport, William C., 125
Davis, Dona L., 66, 77
Davis, S., 51
Davíðsson, Ólafur, 88, 94, 96
delayed return, systems of, 70
demersal fishery, *v.* pelagic,
  108–9, 143, 172, n. 2

democratic *v.* élitist fishing, 130
determinism, 4, 20, 21, 57
   see also cultural determinism
DeVore, Irvin, 29
discourse, concept of, 2–3, 54, 144
divination, 85, 96, 171 n. 7
Dobe! Kung, 70
domestic labour, 164–6
domestic mode, 43, 69–75, 83–8,
   106, 129, 161–2, 165
Douglas, M., 94, 163, 166
dreams, function of, 120–2
   see also fishing mood; hunches
Dumézil, Georges, 36
Durkheim, Emile, 4–15, 18–21,
   57–8, 165–6
Durrenberger, E. Paul, 44, 68, 84,
   91, 112, 115, 120, 128, 135,
   143, 154, 159
Dye, T. S., 64

ecological anthropology, 1–3
ecological determinism, 20, 58, 157
   see also cultural materialism
ecology, 1–3, 6–7, 32, 39, 41, 48,
   50, 58, 68, 80, 129, 134–5,
   145, 155, 157, 159, 172 n. 3
economics, 8, 58, 165–6
Eder, J. F., 30, 34
effective temperature (ET), 32
effort-quota (*sóknarkvóti*), 141
egalitarian models, of success, *v.*
   hierarchical, 103, 116–17,
   130
egalitarianism, 70–2, 92, 151
Einarsson, Níels, 151
élitist *v.* democratic fishing, 130
Ellen, Roy F., 2, 6, 35, 157
emotions, *v.* rationality, 151
Endicott, K., 50, 65
Endicott, K. L., 50
Engels, Friedrich, 22, 25
environmental determinism, 1, 157
   see also ecological determinism

environmentalism
   as policy, 3, 151–2, 80, 151,
      153–4
   in social theory, 1–3, 52, 155
Erró (Guðmundur Guðmundsson),
   111
Eskimo, *see* Inuit
'ethnical periods', 24, 65
ethnocentrism, 1, 47–8, 52, 158
Ethnographic Atlas, 32, 36, 45, 66
ethnography, 1, 55, 81, 83, 168
   see also fieldwork
ethnolinguistics, 17
ethnoscience, 14
Evans-Pritchard, E. E., 57–8
evolutionism, 4, 5, 23, 40, 52
exchange, 8–9, 69, 158
   see also circulation

Faris, James, C., 22, 41, 73
fieldwork, 1, 25, 52, 84, 103–5
   in Sandgerði, 103–5
fins (*öfuguggar*), 97, 98, 100
Firth, Raymond, 23, 63, 64, 76, 94,
   112
fish
   classificiation of, 62, 92, 163,
      170 n. 1
   as pets, 61, 63
   prices of, 85
   representations of, 61–4, 110,
      162
   as symbols, 62–4, 93–101,
      163–4
fish-farming, 67
fish finding, 122–4
fish processing, 147, 149
Fisheries Assocation (*Fiskifélag*),
   114, 134, 136
Fisherman's Day, 115
fishiness (*fiskni*), 90–1, 96, 101,
   112–18, 129, 149
   see also success

fishing
 v. agriculture, 23, 35, 41, 67, 73,
  106, 153
 anthropology of, 2
 category of, 23, 34–43, 52, 61,
  152, 156
 among hunter gatherers, 23,
  29–34
 v. hunting and gathering, 23,
  35–43
 licenses, 77, 135, 150, 172 n. 1
 limits (*fiskhelgi*), 87
 in natural models, 23, 39–43,
  53, 157–8
 origin of, 24–9
 v. pastoralism, 23
 representations of, 54, 66–81
 signs (*fiskistafir*), 90
 and social evolution, 24–6,
  33–4
 as sport, 40, 130
 spots, 89, 100, 110, 139
 systems of, 24, 43–55, 67–82
fishing mood (*fiskistuð*), 118
fishworkers, 147–9
folk models, *see* cultural models;
  discourse
foraging, 36
 see also hunting and gathering;
  modes of subsistence
force *v.* cleverness, in fishing,
  115–16, 130
foreman, in fishing, 71–2
 formaður, 89, 91–2, 101, 112,
  114, 116
 salary, 92
'forms of life', 10
Foster, G. S., 130
Foucault, Michel, 3, 60
Frake, Charles O., 14, 17, 168 n. 3
France, 72

Galton's problem, 30
Game Laws, 40

game theory, 167
Gatewood, John B., 118, 120, 127,
  129
gathering, *see* hunting and
  gathering
gear, in fishing, 48, 49, 68, 108–9,
  112, 123
 handlines, 68, 86, 90, 108
 longlines, 108, 124, 126
 nets, 68, 108, 123–4, 126
 ring net, 68, 109
 trawl, 41, 108
Geertz, Clifford, 54, 116
Gellner, Ernest, 81
gender
 and fishing, 53, 64–6, 77,
  110–11, 117, 129, 133, 164
 notions of, 60, 110–11, 164–6
 and observers' bias, 64, 66
 see also women
Gerrard, Siri, 110
Giddens, Anthony, 60, 157
Gidjingali, 36
gift of God (*guðsgjöf*), 89, 101,
  109, 145, 162
gill nets, *see* gear
Gladwin, Thomas, 61
Godelier, Maurice, 33, 58–9
goðar, see chieftains
Goodlad, C. A., 67–8, 75
Goodwin, Brian, 15
Goody, Jack, 15
Grágás, 86
grammatical relations, 4, 15, 57,
  157
 see also language; *langue*
Greenpeace International, 151
Grotius, Hugo de, 52
Grundlage, 58–9
Gudeman, Stephen, 80, 170 n. 3
Gurevich, Aaron, 158–9
Guðmundsson, Gils, 114

habitat *v.* niche, 1, 2

Hadza, 21
Hagalín, Guðmundur G., 145
Hall, Edward, 47
Hanson, Arthur J., 152
Harbour Office, 124
Hardin, Garrett, 15, 16, 154
Hardy, Alister, 27–8
Harms, Robert, 74
Harris, Marvin, 8, 58
Harris, Roy, 10, 15, 56
Hastrup, Kirsten, 84, 164
Hatch, Elvin, 8, 14, 163
Haugen, Einar, 5
Henriksen, Georg, 122
Hermannsson, Halldór, 147
Hewes, Gordon W., 33, 35–7, 61, 156
hidden-people (*huldufólk*), 95–6
hierarchical models, of success, 75, 109, 116–17, 141
   v. egalitarian, 116–17, 130
Hilborn, Ray, 76, 143, 144
Hill, J., 37
historical particularism, 8, 160
Hitchcock, R. K., 34
Hodgen, Margareth T., 95
Holy, Ladislav, 80
Hoonaard, W. C. van den, 147
Hornell, J., 35, 41–3
human ecology, 2–3, 50
human–environmental
   interactions, 1–3, 6, 45, 54, 61, 81, 116, 154
   see also ecology;
   environmentalism; human
   ecology
humans, *v.* animals, 41–3, 47, 54, 56, 61–4, 67, 89, 94, 101–2, 110, 129, 151–2, 161–2
Hummel, R. L., 130
hunches, in fishing, 118–22
Hunn, Eugene, 54
hunting and gathering, 6, 21, 23,

24–39, 48–51, 53, 67, 70, 79, 159, 165
   characteristics of, 29
   transformation of, 33–4, 50–1, 157
   variability of, 29–34, 50–1, 53, 70, 157
Hymes, Dell, 17

idealism, 20, 58
Ilongot, 18
immediate return, system of, 70
individual, *v.* collective, 5–22, 46, 157–8, 165–7
individual differences, in fishing, 71–81, 112–13, 129, 141–5, 160–1
   see also success
Ingold, Tim, 3, 8, 12, 13, 20, 37, 41, 43, 46, 59, 60, 169 n. 6
inside *v.* outside, 95, 149, 164–6
inter-boat radio, 127–8, 139
interest groups, 147–9
interpretive anthropology, 55, 59
Inuit, 6–12, 18–21, 97
Isherwood, Baron, 163

Jameson, Fredric, 20
Japan, 37, 78
Jentoft, Svein, 44
Jernudd, Björn H., 170 n. 1
Johannes, R. E., 44
Jolly, Alison, 47
Jonquil, Bevan, 41
Jorion, Paul, 72
Jónsson, Finnur, 90, 92
Jónsson, Ólafur Ö., 149

Kachins, 87
Kalland, Arne, 53, 69, 78
Keesing, Roger M., 14–15
Kelly, R. L., 30–2

Kiernan, V. G., 159
Kirch, P. V., 64
'kitchen-middens', 26
Kleivan, Inge, 63–4, 94
Knipe, Ed, 63
Korea, 67
Kottak, Conrad P., 79
Krause, Aurel, 31
Kripke, Saul, 10
Kristjánsson, Lúðvík, 89
Kristmundsdóttir, Sigríður D., 110
Kroeber, Alfred L., 45, 156
Kuper, Adam, 52

labour, passive *v.* generative
    notions of, 66–7, 70, 75,
    91, 109, 129, 162, 164–6,
    170 n. 3
  see also agency
Laguna, Grace A. de, 16
Lakoff, George, 81
Lamson, Cynthia, 152
Lancaster, C. S., 28
land *v.* water, 23, 41, 53, 60, 73,
    97, 102
  see also aquatic *v.* terrestrial
language
  codes, 12
  competence, 10, 17
  evolution of, 5, 22, 27–8,
    168 n. 1
  game, 10, 17
  models of, 3–22, 151
  organismic view of, 4, 10,
    168 n. 1
  as praxis, 17, 22
langue, v. parole, 9, 12, 60
Laxness, Halldór, 55, 92–3, 142
Le Goff, Jacques, 83
Leach, Edmund, 87, 94
Leap, W. L., 36
Ledbetter, Max, 76, 143, 144
Lee, Richard B., 29, 37, 70

Lehn, W. H., 96
Lévi-Strauss, Claude, 20–1, 54, 56,
    60, 63, 94
Levieil, Dominique P., 48
Levine, Hal B., 47, 51
Leviticus, 65
Libecap, G. D., 51
Littlefield, S., 152
Locke, John, 19, 20, 45
Loki, 98
longlines, *see* gear
Lourandos, Harry, 34
Lubbock, John, 26, 40, 66
luck, 72, 74, 129
Luckmann, Thomas, 153
Löfgren, Orvar, 106

Maanen, J. van, 78
McCay, B. J., 2, 16, 40, 41, 44, 46,
    53, 106, 151, 158
McEvoy, Arthur F., 16, 45, 154
McGoodwin, James R., 121
McGovern, Thomas H., 84
Mackintosh, Maureen M., 166
McNabb, Stephen L., 172 n. 2
Maconachie, M., 168 n. 2
magic, 74, 90
Magnússon, Skúli, 88, 92
Maine, 51, 68, 76, 78
Malay, 64, 76
male and female, 26, 60, 93, 98,
    117, 164
  see also gender; women
Malinowski, Bronislaw, 16, 17, 22,
    127
man the hunter, hypothesis of, 26,
    40
  v. man the fisher, 26–8
Maori, 51
marine biology
  development of, 133–4, 145
  role of, 146–7, 151, 153–4
marine mammals, 98–9, 151

Marine Research Institute
    (*Hafrannsóknastofnun*), 134,
    145–6, 154
market economy
    changes in, 132–53, 162
    development of, 69, 103–8,
        162–4, 165
Marquardt, William H., 33
Marx, Karl, 4, 12, 20–2, 25, 57,
    58–9, 167
Marxism, 59, 156–7, 165
Massachusetts, 78
materialism, 8, 20, 41, 57–9, 157
Mauss, Marcel, 6–13, 18–21, 53,
    165
Mawken, 31
Meehan, Betty, 25, 36–7, 65
Melville, Herman, 45, 160
Meybrat, 73
Micronesia, 73
Middle Ages, 83–102, 158
    definition of, 83
    in Iceland, 83–102
Miedema, Jelle, 73–4
Miller, M. L., 78
mind, notions of, 166
Miskito Indians, 64
Mistassini Cree, 70
Moalans, 60
mobile gear, *see* gear; technology
mobile *v.* sedentary species, 37–8,
    48, 68
mobility, *see* settlement pattern;
    nomadic movement
models of production, *see* cultural
    models; discourse; fishing;
    production
modernisation, 133–4
modes of access, *see* access to
    resources
modes of subsistence, 23, 35–8, 41,
    156–9, 169 n. 3
Moore, O. K., 121–2

Morgan, Elaine, 168 n. 1
Morgan, Lewis H., 14, 23, 24–6,
    29, 65, 156, 168 n. 2
Morrill, W. T., 61
Murdock, George P., 29, 31, 33,
    36, 45, 66
muteness, 147, 164–5
Myers, Fred, 158
mythology, 20–60, 74, 90–101,
    109, 129, 154

Nadel-Klein, Jane, 66, 77
Naskapi, 122
natural models, in social theory, 3,
    8–22, 39, 166–7
    see also individual *v.* collective
nature
    category of, 4–5, 172 n. 3
    v. culture, 164–5
    knowledge of, 154–5
net-areas (*netlög*), 86
New Zealand, 47, 51
Newfoundland, 66, 67, 72
Nietschmann, B., 64
Niuans, 64
nomadic movement, 21, 29–34
    kinds of, 31
    logistic *v.* residential, 30–1
    v. sedentism, 34, 50–1
    see also settlement pattern
Norr, J. L., 38–9, 44
Norr, K. F., 38–9, 44
North American Indians
    in California, 44–5
    north-west coast, 29, 31–3
Norway, 68, 75, 79, 126
Nunu, 74

Oikos, 1, 5, 59, 166
open access, 48–50, 53
    see also access to resources
Orbach, M. K., 76, 120
Oregon, 75, 130

Orlove, Benjamin, 48
Ortner, Sherry B., 60, 164, 167
Osborn, A. J., 23, 28
Oswalt, W. E., 39
Other, the, 1, 94–5, 101
Overby, M. Margaret, 51
ownership, 44–6, 49–51, 69–70,
  133, 137, 149–50, 154
  concepts of, 45–9, 158–60
  evolution of, 50–1
  v. non-ownership, 49–50,
    69–70, 158
  theories of, 45–7
  see also access to resources;
    property

Pálsson, Gísli, 31–3, 44, 68, 71,
  93, 100, 103, 112, 115, 116,
  120, 126, 128, 135, 143, 151,
  159
Parades, J. Anthony, 153
parole, 9, 12, 60, 79
Pastner, Stephen, 44, 73
patron–client relations
  (*vistarband*), 85, 105
Patwin, 45
pelagic fishery, *v.* demersal, 108–9,
  143
Perlman, S., 29, 31–2
petty entrepreneurs, 106–8, 146
'phatic communion', 17, 127
Pinkerton, E., 44
Pintupi, 158
Plath, D. W., 37
Pollnac, Richard B., 152
Ponam Island, 49
Porter, Marilyn, 66
Portugal, 77
possession, 18, 19, 46, 169, n. 5
  as text, 19
  see also ownership; property
post-modernism, 55
Postel-Coster, E., 75

praxis theory, *see* agency
prestige
  of skippers, 126–9, 131, 141,
    153
  systems of, 160, 162–3
primitive
  communism, 70
  v. Western, 1, 52, 80
private language, 10–13
private models, 10, 20
  definition of, 20
  see also individual *v.* collective
problem of reference, 56–7
production
  discourse on, 54–82, 160–3
  v. execution, 13, 43, 53, 158
  in social theory, 3–5, 8–13,
    15–22, 59, 157–8, 166
  systems of, 22, 43–55, 67–82,
    103, 158, 160–1, 164
  targets, 43, 72, 86, 109, 162
  see also fishing; natural models
property, 18, 25, 33, 44–8, 73–4,
  77–8, 87, 137, 141, 153, 159,
  169 n. 6
  concept of, 159
  theory of, 18–20, 45–6, 159
  see also ownership
proxemics, 47

quota kings (*kvótakóngar*), 142
quotas, in fishing, 48, 77, 132,
  135–55, 144, 154, 162
  catch *v.* effort, 141
  development of, 135–6, 154
  and economic rent, 136–7, 150
  impact of, 137–45
  transfer of, 136–7

rational *v.* reasonable decisions,
  118, 120, 129
rationality, 58, 80, 100, 139,
  145–7, 149, 161

reasonable decisions, 118, 120, 129
reciprocity, 70, 85, 160
Redfield, Robert, 22
Renouf, M. A. P., 29
resource management, 132–8, 172
   n. 3
ring net, *see* gear
Rosaldo, Michelle Z., 18
Rose, Carol M., 18–19, 45–6
Rossi-Landi, Ferruccio, 5
rowing time (*róðratími*), 125, 132
Ruddle, Kenneth, 44
rules, *v.* action, 10, 15, 17
   see also agency

Sack, R. D., 47
saga(s), 83–4, 90
Sahlins, Marshall, 20, 43, 58, 60,
   73, 78, 160
Saladin d'Anglure, Bernard, 97
Sandgerði, 88, 103–9, 110, 124,
   126, 140
   fishing grounds, 140
   fishing 'station', 105
   fleet, 107–9, 171 n. 1
   hamlet of, 87–8
Sapir, Edward, 4
Sauer, Carl O., 26–8
Saussure, Ferdinand de, 9–12,
   16–17, 79
scapulimancy, 121–2, 171 n. 2
Schalk, R. F., 28, 32
Schmidt, Alfred, 22
Schroeder, I., 96
science, 77, 133, 145–55, 162
   see also marine biology
Scotland, 75
Scott, Anthony D., 153
Scott, Colin, 159
'sea-dwellers' (*sæbúar*), 62
'sea gypsies', 31, 37
sea-ranching, 67
sea-viking (*sjóvíkingur*), 92, 142

seals, 88, 151
   see also marine mammals
Searle, J. R., 18
seasonal variations, 6–11
secrecy, in fishing, 48, 49, 110, 123,
   128, 162
settlement pattern, 6, 7, 21, 32–4,
   169 n. 3
   see also nomadic movement
share systems, 92, 112
Sharp, Henry S., 65–71
shells, collecting of, 26, 37, 64, 65
Sherzer, Joel, 3
Shetlands, 67–8, 75–6
Sigurðsson, Jón, 105
Sinclair, Peter R., 152
skills, in fishing, 70–80, 170 n. 4
   see also 'skipper effect'; success
skipper (*skipstjóri*), in fishing
   v. foreman, 103, 112, 114
   image of, 117–18, 127–8, 153
   relations with boat-owners, 112
   relations with crew, 116, 118,
   126–8
   role of, 112, 114, 116, 122, 127
   title of, 114
skipper effect, 112, 128, 130,
   139–44
   statistical analyses of, 120,
   143–4, 172 n. 2
   see also success
Smith, Adam, 164
Smith, Courtland L., 75, 130
Smith, Eric A., 48, 158
social complexity, 29, 32–4
social organisation, *see* social
   relations
social relations
   v. culture, 58–9
   v. ecological relations, 1–3, 41,
   58, 100, 157, 162
   v. social organisation, 8, 23,
   38–43

sociolinguistics, 5
Sopher, D. E., 31, 37
speaking, 3, 15–18, 166
  see also parole
speech acts, theories of, 17–19, 47,
  90, 131, 159
Spencer, Jonathan, 55–6
Sri Lanka, 73–4
stationary gear, *see* gear;
  technology
Stefánsson, Vilhjálmur, 94
Steward, Julian H., 2, 8, 33, 38–9,
  41
Stiles, R. G., 67, 72
Stocking, G. W., 95
storage, 70
Strathern, Marilyn, 165
structuralism, 17, 56, 60
Stuchlik, M., 80
Sturlung Period, 84
stylistic *v.* materialistic models,
  115, 122
subsistence economy, *see* domestic
  mode
substantivism, 160
success
  criteria of, 76–7, 91, 141
  differences in, 71–80, 97,
    112–17, 140–5
  models of, 68–80, 109–22,
    140–5, 160–3
Sudo, K., 73
superorganic, 3, 6–12, 16, 47,
  166–7
Suttles, W., 36
symbolic systems, 19, 58–60,
  62–4, 82
  see also cultural models;
    discourse

taboo, 93, 96–7
Tacon, Paul S. C., 62
Tambiah, S. J., 90

Tanner, Adrian, 71
Tanner, Nancy M., 26, 40
Tapper, R. L., 67, 94
tastes, *see* consumption discourse
technology, 8, 39, 68, 108–9, 116
  passive *v.* active, 68, 123
  see also gear
tenure, 48–53, 158, 169 n. 6
territoriality, 47–50, 159, 169 n. 6
  see also closure
Testart, Alain, 31, 70
Thompson, E. P., 59
Thompson, Paul, 66, 93
Thorlindsson, Thorolfur, 79–80,
  120, 172 n. 2
Thuan, Elizabeth, 170 n. 1
Tierra del Fuego, 25–6
Tikopia, 63, 94, 112
Tithe Law, 85
Tlingit, 31
Torrence, Robin, 39
trade monopoly, 86, 105
'tragedy of the commons', 15, 16,
  77, 135, 151, 154
trawling, *see* gear
Tuan, Yi-Fu, 61
Tyler, S. A., 55
Tylor, E. B., 40, 80

Uhle, M., 26

Vestman Islands, 119, 125–6
visible, *v.* invisible, 61–2, 95, 164
Volosinov, V. N., 17, 167, 168 n. 4

Wadel, Cato, 41, 79
Walton, Izaak, 34, 40
Washburn, S. L., 28
water-beings (*sæbúar*), 94–101
  concept of, 94
Waterman, T. T., 44–5
Watson, O. M., 47
'ways of speaking', 17

whales, 45, 97–9, 151, 159–60
White, David R. M., 121
wild and tame, 46, 53, 67, 139, 165
Willis, Roy, 152
Wilson, James A., 154
Wittgenstein, L., 10–11
Wolf, Eric, 30
woman the gatherer, hypothesis of,
    26
women
  as domestic labourers, 77, 93,
    107, 164–6
  in fishing, 53, 64–6, 93, 107,
    110–11, 117, 149, 164–6
  as *sjókonur*, 93
  as *sækonur*, 97–8
  see also gender
Woodburn, James, 21, 43, 46, 70
Worster, Donald, 155
Wright, A., 23

Yesner, D. R., 28, 29, 34
Yolngu, 51
Young, Oran R., 138
Yurok, 44